# Penal Servitude in Early Modern Spain

# Penal Servitude
# in
# Early Modern Spain

## Ruth Pike

The University of Wisconsin Press

Published 1983

The University of Wisconsin Press
114 North Murray Street
Madison, Wisconsin 53715

The University of Wisconsin Press, Ltd.
1 Gower Street
London WC1E 6HA, England

First printing

Printed in the United States of America

For LC CIP information see the colophon

ISBN 0-299-09260

# Contents

# Illustrations

# Tables

# Preface

Among the growing body of literature focusing on crime and criminal justice in early modern Europe, the practice of punishment has not attracted much interest. There still are few books that treat the changing methods of dealing with criminals. The basic works in this field are Georg Rusche and Otto Kirchheimer, *Punishment and Social Structure* (1939) and Michel Foucault, *Discipline and Punish: The Birth of the Prison* (1979). To these standard accounts can be added the recent works by Michael Ignatieff, *A Just Measure of Pain: The Penitentiary in the Industrial Revolution, 1750–1850* (1978), Nicole Castan, *Justice et répression en Languedoc à l'époque des Lumières* (1980), and Michael Weisser, *Crime and Punishment in Early Modern Europe* (1979). The early history of incarceration has been studied by J. Thorsten Sellin, *Pioneering in Penology: The Amsterdam Houses of Correction in the Sixteenth and Seventeenth Centuries* (Philadelphia, 1944) and William Callahan, "The Problem of Confinement: An Aspect of Poor Relief in Eighteenth-Century Spain" (1971). Also there is the article by U. R. Q. Henriques, "The Rise and Decline of the Separate System of Prison Discipline" (1972).

The galleys as a penal institution are the subject of several accounts. For France, there is the impressive work by Paul Bamford, *Fighting Ships and Prisons: The Mediterranean Galleys of France in the Age of Louis XIV* (1973), as well as an older study by Paul Masson, "Les galères de France" (1937). André Zysberg's article, "La société des galériens au milieu du XVIIIème siècle" (1975) represents another important contribution. As for the Spanish galleys, the principal work remains that of Félix Sevilla y Solanas, *Historia penitenciaria española (la galera), apuntes de archivo* (1917). Additional information can be found in Gregorio Lasala Navarro, *Galeotes y presidiarios al servicio de la Marina de Guerra de España* (1979), and I. A. A. Thompson, "A Map of Crime in Sixteenth-Century Spain" (1968).

Aside from the galleys, penal servitude has remained a relatively unexplored field of investigation with the exception of the work of J. Thorsten Sellin, who has studied it on a comparative basis.[1] In Spain, as in other Mediterranean countries, penal servitude, derived from the *opus publicum* of antiquity, has a long and important history. Throughout the sixteenth and seventeenth centuries, convicted criminals were sentenced to terms at hard labor on the galleys and in the mercury mines of Almadén and the military presidios in North Africa. After the abolition of the galleys in 1748, penal labor in the form of presidio sentences became the most common form of punishment.

Despite its significant place in the evolution of penal institutions in Spain, the history of penal servitude remains to be written. The Spanish penologists Rafael Salillas and Fernando Cadalso included brief accounts of it in their general surveys of Spanish penal history published in 1918 and 1922, respectively, but it has never before been the subject of a book-length study.[2] The purpose of this work is to provide that account by examining the origins and development of penal servitude in early modern Spain with special reference to the changing purposes for which penal labor was intended to serve. Its principal theme, with Foucault's model as a point of reference, is the evolution of punishment in Spain from the harsh capital and corporal penalties of the Middle Ages to penal servitude, one of the most characteristic methods of punishment in the early modern era, and finally, after a series of eighteenth-century reforms, to incarceration and rehabilitation. In this respect, events and developments in Spain were part of a European-wide evolution of penal systems and theories of punishment. This work also emphasizes the fact that Spain's heavy imperial commitments necessitated the extensive use of galley and presidio service. Whereas in other European countries the mobilization and coercion of felons was stimulated by measures to deal with poverty, the motivating factor in Spain was manpower needs generated by war and empire.

The first part of this book covers the sixteenth and seventeenth centuries, when penal servitude was seen primarily as retribution. The second part covers the eighteenth century, when the still predominant punitive and utilitarian aspects of the penalty began to be joined with the aim of rehabilitation. In addition, the book presents quantitative analyses of the crimes for which the prisoners were convicted, the geographical and occupational origins of the prisoners, and statistics on sentences, releases, deaths, and escapes. These data provide important insights into the patterns of crime in early modern Spain and the socioeconomic setting in which the offenders operated. Furthermore, the book takes note of the slaves who worked alongside the convicts on the galleys and in the naval arsenals, where penal servitude and slavery coexisted for centuries. Finally, it describes the transfer of the presidio system to Spanish America and the establishment in the eighteenth century of a network of penal institutions embracing the Spanish empire.

This work is the result of several years of research in the Spanish archives. I am grateful to the staffs of the following archives for their courtesy and assistance: the Archivo General de Simancas, the Archivo Histórico Nacional, the Archivo de Indias, the Museo Naval, and the Archivo de Villa. I also wish to thank the Research Foundation of the City University of New York for funds to complete research for this study.

A portion of chapter 1 appeared in altered form in the *Journal of European Economic History* 1 (1982): 197–217. A portion of chapter 2 appeared in altered form in *Societas — A Review of Social History* 3 (1973). A portion of chapter 8 was published in an earlier version in the *Hispanic American Historical Review* 58 (February, 1978) copyright © 1978, Duke University Press (Durham, N.C.). I am grateful to the editors of the journals for permission to use this material.

# Abbreviations

AGI   Archivo General de Indias, Seville
AGN  Archivo General de la Nación (Mexico)
AGS   Archivo General de Simancas, Valladolid
AHN  Archivo Histórico Nacional, Madrid
AVM  Archivo de Villa, Madrid
MN    Museo Naval, Madrid
NR    *Nueva Recopilación de las leyes de España*

# Currency

cuarto = 4 maravedís
real = 34 maravedís
peseta = 136 maravedís (4 reales)
ducat = 375 maravedís
peso = 450 maravedís
doblón = 2720 maravedís (80 reales)

The maravedí was the smallest unit of account in the Castilian monetary system; its approximate value was one-sixth of a cent.

# Part 1
# The Sixteenth
# and Seventeenth Centuries

canon law from shedding blood) used imprisonment for offenders under its jurisdiction, and life sentences to prisons operated by the monastic orders were employed at times, ostensibly for correction and penance.[3]

The reappearance of penal labor in western Europe at the end of the Middle Ages coincided with the emergence of the national state and an increase in its wealth and power. Along with the extension of royal jurisdiction and the greater degree of centralization characteristic of state-building in the early sixteenth century, there developed the idea that the state could utilize the labor power of prisoners for its own interests. In this period the needs of the Spanish monarchs were overwhelmingly military. Particularly vital was the defense of Spain's southern and southeastern coasts and its shipping through the maintenance of a standing galley fleet in the Mediterranean. Thus, for those guilty of capital crimes, penal servitude at hard labor on the galleys was introduced in the reign of Ferdinand and Isabella as an alternative form of corporal punishment more useful to the state than other existing afflictive penalties.[4]

As the galley squadrons grew in response to the constant warfare between Spain and the Islamic empire in the Mediterranean in the sixteenth century, it became increasingly difficult to man the benches. This situation was closely related to changing economic conditions in the sixteenth century, in particular, the Price Revolution. As prices rose, the cost of maintaining salaried free oarsmen or *buenas boyas* became excessive. In 1538, for example, the salary of a free oarsman was one ducat a month, but by 1571 it had risen to eight ducats per month including a two-ducat clothing allotment. In order to avoid a crushing economic burden there was no alternative but to depend on a servile rowing force. Free oarsmen almost disappeared from the Spanish galleys by the end of the sixteenth century, and in the seventeenth century those rowers who bore that title were convict oarsmen or *forzados* who had completed their sentences and were being retained illegally because of the critical shortage of rowers. They were given the ration and title of *buenas boyas* and were known as *buenas boyas forzados*.[5] Hence, a combination of rising prices and an increase in the scale of warfare led ultimately to the establishment of galley service as the most common form of punishment.

The establishment of galley service for men ultimately affected changes in the punishment of women. Female offenders (with the exception of those belonging to the noble and clerical estates) were subject to the same capital and corporal penalties as men. Since they were not given the death penalty except for particularly heinous crimes and their physical limitations prevented them from being sent to the galleys, they were customarily punished with public shame, flogging, and banishment. Although these penalties were rigorously enforced, the number of women offenders continued to increase in the last quarter of the sixteenth century. Between 1592 and 1598 the Castilian Cortes repeatedly complained about the vagrant and licentious women who filled the streets and public places of towns like Madrid, Seville, Toledo, and Valladolid.[6] By that time it was apparent that the established methods of dealing with women delinquents were ineffective.[7] In 1598 Dr. Cristóbal Pérez de Herrera claimed that instead of reducing crime, they actually contributed to the professionalization of criminals. The continued application of public shame and lashes eventually destroyed their intimidative effect, while banishment merely served to remove culprits from the site of their crimes and transfer them to other areas where they were unknown to authorities.[8]

The success of the galleys as a penal institution for men inspired their adaptation to the punishment of women. In 1608 a nun by the name of Mother Magdalena de San Jerónimo formulated a plan for the establishment of a house of confinement and punishment (*galera*) for delinquent women, which led to the creation of the *galera de mujeres* in Madrid in the early years of the seventeenth century.[9] The *galera* was to be the equivalent of the galleys. In the words of Mother San Jerónimo, "it was to have the same severity and rigor so that the mere mention of its name would suffice to inspire fear."[10] In order to recreate the same conditions as on the galleys, the hair of the inmates was to be shaved with a razor, and their diet was to consist of coarse black bread or biscuit (hardtack) and vegetables. The women were supposed to work continuously, and misdemeanors and infractions of the rules were to be punished by the application of chains, handcuffs, fetters, and other means of coercion so that "the institution would in every way resemble its name."[11]

From the beginning, the *galera* lacked sufficient funding. Its only reliable source of income was the municipality, and it had to depend almost entirely on private charity. According to Galdiano y Croy, its total income in 1676 was a mere 954 ducats, while its operating expenses amounted to 1,936 ducats.[12] Its meager resources severely limited the number of women who could be admitted to a maximum of seventy or eighty. In 1676 there were only fifty-nine women in the *galera,* and they were living in conditions of extreme poverty and want, a situation that continued to characterize this establishment through the eighteenth century.[13]

In contrast to the limited operations of the *galera* for women, the galleys became the principal male penal institution in early modern Spain. Sources for the study of the galleys as a penal establishment are few and incomplete. The galley registers in existence in Cartagena some fifty years ago have long since disappeared, and they seem to have been fragmentary. Whatever remained of them at the beginning of the twentieth century was used by the Spanish penologist Félix Sevilla y Solanas in his *Historia penitenciaria española (la galera)* (Segovia, 1917), still the principal work on this subject. In the absence of the galley registers, contemporary opinion and legislation form the main source of information. Over the course of three centuries a formidable corpus of royal and administrative regulations and decrees was issued for the galleys, and much of this material has been preserved.[14] In addition, there exist numerous references to the galleys in the works of Spanish writers of the period, and some of them, notably Cervantes, Mateo Alemán, and Vélez de Guevara, had a direct acquaintance with the marginal and delinquent types who made up the *chusma* or rowing force of the galleys.

A series of laws beginning in 1530 gradually extended galley service to all kinds of offenders (both major and minor) as well as those whose deviant behavior was defined by the laws of the period as crimes. As early as 1539 all male gypsies between the ages of twenty and fifty years who were without employment and living without a master could be sent to the galleys for six years. In 1552 the penalty for vagabondage was increased to four years on the galleys for the first offense, eight for the second, and life for the third. This legislation defined vagabonds as gypsies, foreign tinkers, and healthy mendicant poor. By the second half of the sixteenth century, bigamists and blasphemers tried by either the Inquisition or the secular courts (both had jurisdiction in these cases) could be sent to galleys, as well as commoners who made, used, or sold playing dice, false witnesses in civil and criminal cases, male procurers, and persons who resisted arrest. In the seventeenth century the list was further extended.[15] Such legislation was made the more effective by constant royal pressure on magistrates to condemn as many men as possible to the galleys; and by the second half of the sixteenth century the normal sentence for convicted male criminals, with the exception of nobles and clergy, was the galleys. Nobles could not be sentenced to any form of degrading punishment such as lashes or the galleys, and except in cases of treason, their sentences usually were commuted to banishment or military service. Likewise, the clergy could be prosecuted only by the ecclesiastical authorities, but if convicted of capital crimes, they were often secularized and sentenced to the galleys.[16]

Indeed, so great was the pressure to make more men available for the oar that it became standard practice to take convicted offenders who were awaiting the outcome of their appeals in jails to serve during the interim (*en depósito*) on the galleys. Although the legality of this practice was questionable, it was deemed necessary in view of the long delays involved in the appeals system. It was not uncommon for prisoners to spend from three to six years waiting for a decision on their appeals, and during that time they often died, escaped, or committed additional crimes. By sending men to the galleys immediately after their initial sentencing, it was possible to avoid the evils of long encarceration and to obtain maximum utilization of convict labor for the state.[17]

Sentences ranged from two years to life, with an average term oscillating between four and six years. Condemnations for less than two years were deemed inappropriate, because men needed at least a year to become fully serviceable at the oar. On the other hand, sentences for more than ten years were rejected on humanitarian and utilitarian grounds (considered excessive and, in the long run, unprofitable). By 1653 sentences had been set at ten years, but frequently prisoners were not released after the completion of their sentences. Until 1663, for example, men could be detained for nonpayment of fines and court fees imposed at the time of their original sentencing. In addition, *forzados* were retained as a result of sentences given for crimes committed on board while serving their terms. Cases of this kind were tried under military law by a special judge known as the *auditor de las galeras*.[18]

Neither old age not youth seems to have constituted disqualification for condemnation to the galleys, even though both groups were entirely useless at the oars. A minimum of seventeen years of age was established in 1566, but it is quite clear that it was not always respected. In 1734 Philip V lowered the age requirement to fifteen years for those found guilty of theft at court.[19] Despite the laws, magistrates, who had wide discretionary powers in this period to increase or decrease penalties, usually were reluctant to send offenders under seventeen years of age to the galleys except in the case of those they considered incorrigibles, e.g., habitual thieves and vagrants. When they did sentence juveniles to the galleys, they often stipulated that they be used as cabin boys or servants of the galley officers. Whether this was stated or not, all served in similar positions, because boys and adolescents were able to perform only a few functions on the galleys.[20]

Like youths, old men were sent to the galleys despite their unserviceability. There was always a sizeable proportion of aged and invalid *forzados* on the galleys, but almost all of them had been reduced to this condition as a result of years of service. How many of them were sentenced to the galleys initially at an advanced age is a question that cannot be readily answered because no legal maximums were ever set, and it is not clear what was the definition of "old" in this period (examples can be found to suggest any age from fifty upwards). Nevertheless, it seems likely that relatively few men over fifty years of age were sentenced to the galleys—not because of any legal or humane considerations, but rather because a large percentage of the crimes in this period were committed by men between the ages of eighteen and thirty-five, precisely the age group considered best for the exercise of the oars.[21]

While *forzados* made up one part of the galley *chusma*, slaves constituted the remainder. There were several kinds of slaves, their classifications reflecting their mode of acquisition, that is, by capture, purchase, private donation, or judicial sentence. Moreover, within these four general categories there were other subdivisions. In the first classification were Moslem prisoners of war captured in the continuous struggles between Spain and the Islamic empire in the Mediterranean and North Africa. The enslavement of prisoners of war was a well-established custom in the Mediterranean world. Christians enslaved Moslems and Moslems retaliated in kind. The majority of the Moslem prisoners of war were North Africans (Moroccans, Algerians, and Tunisians), but there also were Moriscos (converted Spanish Moslems) and renegades.[22] Almost all were captured off North African vessels and were professional seamen and corsairs. Once captured they became *esclavos del rey* (royal slaves), and were sent to serve on the galleys. When military forays and expeditions failed to provide sufficient numbers of prisoners, royal officials purchased slaves, but they had to be Moslems because legally only infidels could be enslaved on the Christian galleys. The standard price for these slaves remained at 100 ducats apiece in the sixteenth and seventeenth centuries, but in the eighteenth century it was somewhat higher, usually around 130 ducats. Most often the money utilized in these purchases came from the sale of old and unserviceable galley slaves who customarily were auctioned off to the highest bidder.[23] This system enabled the king to replace slaves at a minimum cost to the royal treasury.

Not all enslaved Moslem prisoners of war could be disposed of so easily and profitably when no longer serviceable. Within this classification there also was a special category of slaves considered too dangerous and pernicious ever to be alienated from royal possession. They included the *arraeces* or captains of the corsair vessels, renegades, and Moriscos. All three groups were held to be royal slaves in perpetuity, that is, they could never be freed, exchanged (for Christians in Moslem captivity, a common practice), or sold. In contrast to the rest of the Moslem slaves, they could not be used in any occupation on the galleys except at the oars, and like the *forzados* they were kept chained permanently to their benches.[24]

In addition to those who became galley slaves as a result of warfare or purchase, there were others who originally were private domestic slaves. Masters often chose to punish rebellious and troublesome slaves by donating them to the king to be used on the galleys, and in this way they, too, became *esclavos del rey*. For slaveholders this proved to be a convenient method both of punishing disobedient slaves at no cost to themselves and of letting the fate of these troublemakers serve as an object lesson for the rest of their slaves. The only requirement, which was that slaves must be infidels, appears to have been violated frequently (especially in the case of black slaves), as witnessed by repeated royal decrees prohibiting the acceptance of donated slaves who were Christians.[25] These slaves were particularly numerous in the galleys in the last quarter of the sixteenth century, a period in which slavery reached its zenith on the Iberian Peninsula. In 1568 it was found necessary to establish the rule that in the event of escape or death of donated slaves, the king did not bear any financial responsibility for them, and no compensation would be paid to their owners. In the 1580s there were so many of them on the galleys that royal officials were ordered not to accept any more.[26]

In the seventeenth century the situation changed dramatically. Black slaves became less available and more costly as their sources of supply began to contract, especially after the loss of Portugal in the 1640s.[27] In these circumstances slaveholders became less willing to donate slaves, even the most troublesome, since their investment was now more valuable. On the other hand, the fact that private slaves could be utilized by the king in this manner, that is, transferred from private to state control, set a precedent for government actions in the seventeenth century. Several times during that century—for example in 1639 and 1647, when there was an acute shortage of rowers—the king forced individual owners to send their slaves to the galleys to serve "temporarily," a situation that usually lasted several years.[28]

The fourth classification of slaves were those who were on the galleys because of judicial sentences. Slaves, like free persons, could be tried by the courts for delicts and, if convicted, condemned to serve terms on the galleys. In this event, the conditions of slave and *forzado* clearly overlapped. Slaves serving judicial sentences on the galleys remained slaves, but for the duration of their terms they became *forzados* as well.[29] As *forzados* they remained chained to their benches and were prohibited from performing any labor other than pulling the oars. After the completion of their sentences, as slaves, they were subject to the legal limitations and restrictions inherent in that status. They could not be freed like the convict oarsmen, but rather they had to be returned to their owners. If their masters did not reclaim them, they remained on the galleys as slaves, but in this capacity they could be used in other tasks besides rowing. When they became old or unserviceable, they were given their freedom (literally turned out to die) with the proviso that they withdraw from the coastal regions of the country on the penalty of being returned to the galleys as royal slaves in perpetuity.[30]

Loss of the galley registers and lack of other sufficient quantitative data hamper any systematic accounting of slaves and *forzados* making up the *chusma* on the Spanish galleys. Their number and proportion depended on many factors—in particular, the size of the galley fleet and the capacity of its vessels. During the early modern period the size of the Spanish fleet varied considerably depending on time and place, although for most of the sixteenth and seventeenth centuries there were five permanent squadrons. The number of vessels making up these squadrons also fluctuated. In 1612 the squadron of Spain, the largest one in the Spanish fleet, consisted of eleven galleys, but by 1668 there were seven.[31] However, galleys grew larger to accommodate more fighting men and cannon as the scale of warfare intensified between Spain and Islam in the Mediterranean. As galleys increased in size, the rowing forces expanded proportionally. In 1587 the standard galleys of the squadron of Spain were required to have 170 rowers each, but in 1621 the galley ordinances called for 260 oarsmen per galley, with 375 and 280 respectively for the two principal ships of the squadron, the *Capitana* and the *Patrona*.[32] These quotas still were considered standard in the early years of the eighteenth century, but stipulated quotas bore little relation to reality. At all times, the actual number of oarsmen differed from their authorized quotas. In the year 1655 there were 1,882 rowers in the squadron of Spain, some forty-two more than were required, while in 1668 the total of 2,080 oarsmen included 125 extra men (see tables 1.2 and 1.3).

Despite the apparent surplus of *chusma*, these figures are really misleading, because they include men who were unserviceable, that is, either crippled, incurably ill, or too old to be used at the oar. Since these men usually numbered some fifty to 100, the actual number available to work the oars was much smaller. If the propor-

Table 1.1. Oarsmen in the Squadron of Spain, 1612

| Galley* | Forzados | Slaves | Total |
|---|---|---|---|
| Capitana | 303 | 135 | 438 |
| Patrona | 206 | 71 | 277 |
| Santa Bárbara | 164 | 71 | 235 |
| San Pedro | 142 | 44 | 186 |
| San Ramón | 160 | 40 | 200 |
| Santiago | 125 | 69 | 194 |
| Sandovala | 174 | 56 | 230 |
| San Jorge | 136 | 55 | 191 |
| Toledana | 160 | 34 | 194 |
| San Francisco | 130 | 47 | 177 |
| Santa Ana | 139 | 31 | 170 |
| Total | 1,839 | 653 | 2,492 |

*Figures for *buenas boyas forzados* are missing.
Source: MN, Vargas Ponce, tomo 20, doc. 84, Nov. 6, 1612.

Table 1.2. Oarsmen in the Squadron of Spain, 1655

| Galley | Buenas Boyas Forzados | Forzados | Slaves | Total |
|---|---|---|---|---|
| Patrona | 3 | 171 | 112 | 286 |
| San Francisco | 16 | 173 | 87 | 276 |
| Nuestra Señora de Guadalupe | 4 | 174 | 79 | 257 |
| Santa María | 3 | 173 | 83 | 259 |
| San Miguel | 7 | 201 | 65 | 273 |
| San Genaro | 4 | 177 | 90 | 271 |
| Nuestra Señora de la Soledad | 17 | 178 | 65 | 260 |
| Total | 54 | 1,247 | 581 | 1,882 |

Source: MN, Vargas Ponce, tomo 25, doc. 73, Aug. 22, 1655.

tion of aged and incurables is added to those being held illegally (*buenas boyas forzados*), the situation changes substantially.[33] In view of these circumstances, it is easier to comprehend the complaints of the galley officials who claimed that there never was a large enough *chusma*.

A comparison of the figures in tables 1.1 and 1.3 shows an increase in the number of slaves between 1612 and 1668. Galley rules held that for security reasons the proportion of slaves on

Table 1.3 Oarsmen in the Squadron of Spain, 1668

| Galley | Buenas Boyas Forzados | Forzados | Slaves | Total |
|---|---|---|---|---|
| Capitana | 53 | 148 | 178 | 379 |
| Patrona | 23 | 144 | 110 | 277 |
| San Pedro | 21 | 135 | 106 | 262 |
| San Miguel | 33 | 144 | 125 | 302 |
| Soledad | 32 | 137 | 122 | 291 |
| Santa Teresa | 23 | 140 | 94 | 257 |
| Almudena | 32 | 157 | 123 | 312 |
| Total | 217 | 1,005 | 858 | 2,080 |

Source: MN, Vargas Ponce, tomo 27, doc. 58, Sept. 21, 1668.

each vessel should be strictly limited. In the sixteenth century their specific number was left to the discretion of the fleet commanders. In 1607 official quotas were fixed at forty slaves for a standard galley and eighty and fifty for the *Capitana* and *Patrona,* respectively, but this rule seems to have been consistently ignored.[34] As the seventeenth century advanced, their numbers grew steadily. In 1612 they made up 26 percent of the rowing force on the squadron of Spain, while in 1668, 41 percent of the *chusma* were slaves, almost all of whom were Moslems.[35]

Coincidentally with the rise in the proportion of slaves there was a decrease in the *forzado* component of the *chusma.* In 1612, 73 percent of the rowing force consisted of *forzados,* but by 1668 that figure had declined to 48 percent. Notwithstanding an increase in demand as the fleet and the capacity of the vessels grew larger, the contraction in the number of convict oarsmen was closely related to the general demographic decline in seventeenth-century Spain. The epidemics and subsistence crises of this period particularly affected the lower economic groups, the poor and marginal classes from which the galley *chusma* was drawn. At the same time, the military needs of the second half of the seventeenth century absorbed a large part of this group, since the armies were drawn from these same classes. It was also in this period that common criminals sentenced to the galleys began to be sent instead to the expanding network of North African presidios.[36] Thus, the galleys had to compete with the army and the North African presidios for a declining reserve of convict manpower. In this context, repeated legislation ordering the requisitioning of slaves belonging to private individuals and the conscription of gypsies represent desperate acts by the government to fill the galley benches.[37]

As fewer condemned men became available for service at the oar, the number of *buenas boyas forzados* rose dramatically. The illegal retention of prisoners after the completion of their sentences was one of the worst abuses of the galleys, and it continued for three centuries. Men were retained beyond their terms because the king needed their services. Originally, it was reasoned that since it took several years for men to become proficient in handling the oars, the king could not afford to release seasoned oarsmen. At times, men were offered the opportunity to remain voluntarily as free salaried oarsmen, but this system was unsuccessful. As it became more and more difficult to find replacements, illegal retention became common. In an effort to legitimize it, retainees automatically were converted into *buenas boyas forzados* and often remained in that status for years.[38] The proportion of *buenas boyas forzados* more than tripled between 1655 and 1668. (See tables 1.2 and 1.3.) In 1655 they made up 3 percent of the *chusma* in the squadron of Spain, while in 1668 they represented 10 percent. Together with the slaves, they constituted 52 percent of the rowing force in 1668.

Given the circumstances, particularly in the second half of the seventeenth century, legal limitations on sentences were practically meaningless. Regardless of whether they were sentenced for life or a term of years, most men could expect to spend the rest of their lives at the oars, or until age, illness, or death ended their sufferings. Money, of course, could alter the situation, since there was some possibility of obtaining release by supplying a replacement, i.e., a Moslem slave, or the price of a slave. Although this system was well established, little is known about how it actually worked and the extent to which it was practiced. Retainees, especially the ill and disabled, were the most favorable candidates for these exchanges, but at times even able-bodied oarsmen were released. In 1642, for example, several *buenas boyas forzados* who had been held illegally for years after the completion of their sentences successfully obtained their releases from the king after offering slave replacements. Nor was it always necessary to petition the king, since galley captains and *cómitres* at times also accepted slave replacements or payments for releases, especially when the petitioning oarsmen were weak or unfit. Although verification is wanting, there is some indication that these illegal releases were standard practice on the galleys.[39]

While the hardships and privations of life on the galleys were well known and condemnations to them greatly feared, they were an improvement on the death penalty. There always existed the possibility (remote or not) of a return from the galleys, while the gallows were final—*finisbusterrae,* as expressed in the colorful thieves' jargon of the era.[40] Spanish literature of the period is quite revealing in this regard. One of the best examples can be found in Vélez de Guevara's play *El águila del agua,* where the *galeote* Escamilla is reproached by his girlfriend for having preferred the galleys to "dying with honor" on the gallows. Escamilla's reply sums up the criminal's point of view: he states that it was better to be alive and "hitting the waves" than hanging from the gallows. With life there was hope, and everything bad came to an end eventually. Once the noose was avoided, the galleys were mere pastime.[41] The same opinion is encountered in *Don Quijote* when one of the prisoners in the chain of *forzados,* who is sentenced to six years on the galleys, exclaims: "I am young yet; and if I live long enough, everything will come out all right."[42] Similar expressions can be found in the statements of the prisoners whose cases were on appeal before the *Chancillería* of Granada in 1572.

Although the criminal elements were optimistic about their chances for survival on the galleys, there is no way to test their assumptions, because of lack of data to estimate mortality rates. Significantly, there is no mention in extant records or contemporary accounts of prisoners returning from the galleys after the completion of their terms; but this may be more a reflection of the practice of retaining them illegally than of high mortality rates. Even men who were totally unserviceable, i.e., blind or crippled, were retained after the termination of their sentences. Given the loss of records, the question remains unanswerable. It does seem that the prisoners probably were right in their belief that survival was possible on the galleys (some hearty souls lived ten or more years), but more problematic was the possibility of returning home from them.

Prison conditions in this period are another factor to be considered. In the early modern era jails were places of detention for persons awaiting trial or decisions on their appeals, a procedure that usually lasted several years.[43] During that time no provisions were made for their upkeep, and if prisoners could not afford to purchase food and other necessities of life from wardens and jailers, then it was expected that they would be supported by relatives and friends. Failing this, inmates supported themselves by begging and with alms donated by religious and charitable institutions, but the funds collected in this manner were hardly enough to sustain life. Many poor and destitute prisoners died of starvation.[44] In contrast to the lack of rations in the jails, prisoners on the galleys were supported by the king. Though badly prepared and monotonous, the king's ration represented regular meals, and there were also periodic clothing allotments. As Fernand Braudel has noted, the true poor and unfortunate in this period were those who had no official provider, either warlike or charitable.[45] Whether or not the food ration on the galleys was as inadequate as is often assumed is debatable, since the diet of the lower classes in early modern Europe was universally limited, unvaried, and devoid of meat. Many vagrants and unemployed in Spain lived on a soup (*sopa boba*) provided by religious establishments that was not very different from the vegetable stew of the galley rowers. Prisoners eking out their days in the jails sometimes were so desperate that they asked to be sent to the galleys before the termination of their appeals. In December, 1572, for example, the *Corregidor* of La Coruña wrote to the king that a number of convicted criminals who had been in the town jail for three years or more awaiting the outcome of their appeals had petitioned him repeatedly to send them to the galleys where they could "serve the king instead of slowly starving to death."[46]

As for the labor of the galleys, pulling an oar required practice and skill, but once learned it became routine and the oarsmen grew resistant to fatigue. In the Middle Ages the job of rowing the galleys was done by volunteers. The work could be hard and oppressive when the ships were at sea, especially when in flight, under attack, or in a storm, when the *cómitre* lashed the rowers to increase speed. But according to the *pícaro-forzado* Guzmán de Alfarache, when traveling between ports they ordinarily rowed at a leisurely pace, alternating by pairs according to odd and even numbers, almost like a kind of diversion or exercise.[47] Such labor was seasonal, for the galleys were tied up in port some seven or eight months a year. When the fleet was in, the prisoners remained on board, and it was not until the end of the seventeenth century that convict oarsmen were sent ashore to work in ports and arsenals. Criminals were aware of the long "slack period" on the galleys. The *pícaro* Ginés de Pasamonte in *Don Quijote,* for example, felt that he would be able to finish his autobiography while serving his sentence because there was plenty of leisure time on the Spanish galleys.[48] The same opinion is expressed by the protagonist in *El donado hablador* by Dr. Jerónimo Alcalá Yáñez when he says that the *galeotes* have their "winter season" when they rest in the ports and little work is done.[49] A similar view of life on the galleys was held by the prisoners in the mercury mines of Almadén. When they were asked by a royal investigator in 1593 what could be done to improve their conditions, they all answered that they preferred to finish their sentences on the galleys. At Almadén the convicts worked mainly at bailing water out of the mines to prevent flooding. This labor was constant and strenuous even though the risk of mercury poisoning was less than at the furnaces. In sworn depositions the prisoners declared that despite the fact that the food, living conditions, and medical conditions at Almadén were adequate (actually far superior to the galleys), they could not tolerate the continuous toil to which they were being subjected, and for this reason they wanted to be transferred to the galleys.[50]

If the labor on the galleys was not as arduous as it appeared to be, living conditions there, although unsanitary, were not as unbearable as modern historians have concluded. In the early modern era the poor both in countryside and in city lived in deprivation, squalor, and stench. The rest of the crew and any passengers as well also had to put up with conditions that were typical of shipboard life in this period. Contemporary accounts vividly report the inconveniences and hardships of sea voyages for all concerned. What made the galleys so feared in the popular consciousness was the loss of freedom that they represented—particularly the practice of chaining men to their benches and the uncertainty of release. Yet, as the *forzado* Escamilla said, where there is life there is hope, and for these men and others in the period there existed a condition both physically and psychologically more oppressive and hopeless. It is mentioned by the principal character in *El donado hablador*: if rowing on the Spanish galleys is a temporal hell, he says, even *it* is better than being a Christian captive chained to the bench of a North African galley.[51]

Convicted criminals sentenced to the galleys were sent by their local justices to the central prisons (*depósitos de rematados a galeras*) of their respective judicial areas (Toledo, Soria, Valladolid, Seville, Granada). When enough of them were gathered (not less than twelve), they were chained together and manacled and marched overland under heavy guard until they reached the galleys. Oarsmen were taken on at a number of ports along the southern and southeastern coasts, principally at Cartagena, Málaga, and Puerto de Santa María. Generally, prisoners from the *depósitos* of Toledo, Valladolid, and Granada were sent to the Málaga, while those from Seville and Soria went to Puerto de Santa María and Cartagena, respectively.[52] But the destinations of the individual "chains," as the troops of prisoners were called, depended on the immediate needs and locations of the galley squadrons.

In the sixteenth and seventeenth centuries the system of servicing the chains was poorly organized and ineffectively controlled, despite the existence of a special government agency, the *Superintendencia de conducciones, fugas y solturas de galeotes y condenados a presidios y campañas* (established by Philip II in 1566), to oversee its operations. One of the principal defects of the system was the way in which those who conducted the chains were selected and paid. Usually the conductors were constables, or other law enforcement officers, but at times the position was auctioned off to the highest bidder. The conductors were paid a fixed sum for every prisoner they delivered alive at their destination, regardless of physical condition. In the sixteenth century the conductors normally received five ducats a head for each prisoner, but by the end of the seventeenth century the cost had tripled. In 1671 the conductor of a chain from Toledo to Cartagena purchased his commission to take thirty-four convicts to the galleys at fifteen ducats a head. The per capita fee was supposed to cover all the conductor's costs: subsistence for the chain, the necessary carts and mules, salaries for the guards and

CARTOGRAPHIC LABORATORY, UNIVERSITY OF WISCONSIN — MADISON

Central prisons, galley ports, and presidios in Spain

notary.[53] Since everything beyond that was the conductor's remuneration, the system encouraged fraud and corruption on the part of the conductors.

In the eighteenth century the procedure was better organized and more effectively controlled.[54] More vehicles were provided for the weak and sick, and there was a greater readiness to allow all convicts to ride in instances of rough terrain or bad weather. An effort was made to avoid dispatching chains in winter, since cold weather could be disastrous for prisoners on the road. These improvements began to appear in the first half of the eighteenth century, but the system was not reorganized until the second half of the eighteenth century (after the abolition of the galleys in 1748), when the chains were destined for the naval arsenals and overseas presidios.

On the march the convicts wore collars made of bands of iron (*colleras*), which were joined along the length of a long central chain. They walked, and sometimes rode in carts, along routes established early in the sixteenth century and maintained unchanged through the eighteenth century. The journey from Toledo to any one of the galley ports required some three weeks depending on climatic conditions and other circumstances, but conductors often tried to shorten the trip by forcing the chain to cover more than the accustomed distance per day. In this way, particularly if the chain was large, conductors could reduce their expenses and increase their profits. The towns and villages along the route were obliged to provide shelter for the chain, either in local jails or (when jails were unavailable) in barns and stables. Food and all other supplies had to be purchased along the way.[55]

On arrival at their destination prisoners were turned over to the galley officials, who registered each man's name, age, place of origin, crimes, sentences, and other pertinent information in the galley registers. At the same time they were given physical examinations to discover any hidden defects or special physical characteristics. In instances of physical disability, only galley officials on the advice of the galley physicians had the authority to reject men, who would then be returned to the central prisons. In practice, except in cases of obvious incapacity or infectious desease, almost all men regardless of age or infirmities were accepted.[56] On the other hand, prisoners with serious physical disabilities were not sentenced to the galleys in the first place. For major crimes they were given the death penalty, and for lesser offenses some other form of punishment, such as flogging and banishment. In cases where healthy prisoners became disabled after being sentenced to the galleys, they could be disqualified for service by the prison physicians before being placed in the chains. The requirement that all prisoners be examined by the jail doctors before the departure of the chains gave rise to frauds and abuses. Prisoners tried all kinds of expedients to make themselves physically unfit for the galleys. Moreover, doctors in some prisons (Seville was particularly notorious for this) had the reputation of accepting bribes and payments to declare men unserviceable for the galleys.[57]

Slaves (with the exception of those under judicial sentence who were joined to the chains with the convicts) were brought to the galleys in gangs (*gavillas*), and like the *forzados* went through the same procedure of registration and examination.[58] Once aboard the galleys, the differences between slaves and *forzados* were further muted. The newcomers, regardless of status, were assigned their places according to the needs of the individual galleys and each man's estimated strength and capacity for work at the oars. The galley ordinances afforded equal treatment to slaves and *forzados* in all aspects of their life on the galleys, but because of the essential difference in the nature of their conditions, the punishments meted out to them were not always the same. While flogging was the common penalty applied to all oarsmen for minor offenses, in instances of rebellion or attempted escape the penalties differed. *Forzados* customarily were punished for major offenses with additional sentences, or in cases of mutiny (considered the most heinous crime on the galleys) with the death penalty. In contrast, slaves (except for those under judicial sentence) were on the galleys in perpetuity and therefore could not be castigated by extending their terms; and they were far too valuable to be sentenced to death except in extreme circumstances. Instead, they often were subjected to the cutting off of an ear or a nose, which served not only as punishment but as a visual warning to others. Aside from these two penalties, oarsmen in general were protected by the galley ordinances against any crippling injuries, since it was in the interest of the king to preserve the rowers.[59]

All oarsmen received the same food and clothing rations. The standard fare on the galleys per man per day was twenty-six ounces of biscuit or hard tack and a vegetable stew composed of six ounces of rice prepared in water and olive oil. Water was the customary beverage except on special occasions when more effort was required from the rowers and wine was distributed in the hope that it would stimulate them.[60] Meat virtually disappeared from their diet in the last quarter of the sixteenth century, when only eight stews a year included meat. The growth of population in the sixteenth century increased the demand for grain, and as cultivation of grain expanded, pasture lands were plowed under and the production of meat decreased accordingly. Before 1540, oarsmen aboard the Spanish galleys were allotted about four pounds of meat per month. By 1580, meat had been replaced completely by beans, which became the standard galley fare for the next two centuries.[61]

The actual distribution of food aboard the galleys left much to be desired, since the *chusma* did not always receive its full ration. Standards were set by royal decree, but short weighing, false measuring, cheating, and corruption characterized the system. At times, the penury of the royal treasury or difficulties with the food contractors caused a reduction in rations. In 1678, for example, the biscuit allowance was reduced from twenty-six to sixteen ounces because of a shortage of flour. The following year an additional eight ounces per man was removed from the bread ration, and chickpeas were introduced as a substitute. Reductions in the bread ration became so common in the last quarter of the seventeenth century that no attempts were made to substitute anything else, or to make up the losses after the scarcity had passed.[62]

The quality of the food on the galleys varied greatly. The biscuit was often hard and moldy and the stews full of vermin, because the pots were not cleaned thoroughly after their use so as not to waste the leftovers. Frequently the foodstuffs were of inferior quality, old, or spoiled, but since the galleys usually sailed close to shore and anchored at night in some coastal haven, fresh supplies could be taken on more often and there was less chance of spoilage. Rations were relatively fresh, at least in comparison to those found aboard transatlantic vessels.[63]

Attempts to vary the diet of the oarsmen proved unsuccessful. Shortages of beans at the end of the seventeenth century led to the introduction of rice as a substitute, but in the long run this measure increased the frequency of deficiency diseases such as beriberi and pellagra which, like scurvy, were always present. In 1680, galley officials in Cartagena complained that 257 oarsmen were ill as a result of the continued use of rice instead of beans.[64] In view of the inadequacy of rice and the total absence of meat it is not difficult to understand why for three centuries galley administrators considered beans (a cheap source of protein) as the essential food for the *chusma*.

It was also customary for the *forzados* and Christian slaves (Moslems who had been converted while serving on the galleys) to contribute regularly from their bread rations to the maintenance of religious services on the galleys. In the period 1665–74, their contribution amounted to two ounces per bench a day.[65] Free oarsmen gave a small sum from their salaries to this fund as well. When the ships were at sea, a special mass (*misa seca* or *náutica* without the consecration of the Host) was held on Sundays by the galley chaplain for all except the Moslem slaves, who were required to retire under their benches and cover their heads during its celebration. When in port, an altar was erected on the wharf near the galley anchorage for these services. In addition, all Christians on the galleys, whether *chusma* or galley personnel, belonged to a religious confraternity whose principal objective was to provide decent burials for its members. Two chapels were founded for this purpose in Puerto de Santa María and Cartagena, respectively, where masses were said for souls of deceased members and where some apparently were buried.[66]

Medical facilities aboard the galleys were the same for all oarsmen, but were completely inadequate. Aside from the fleet physicians (one per squadron), the regular medical staff of the galleys consisted of barber-surgeons and their assistants, either slaves or *forzados,* who treated the oarsmen at their benches (*en cadena*). They were assisted by the galley chaplains, who gave spiritual comfort to the dying. Despite these services, afflicted oarsmen generally expired, since most of the ailments—for example, scrofula, consumption, and tetanus—were incurable given their circumstances and the limited medical knowledge of the times. Hospitalization and an improved diet could have helped in some instances, expecially in the case of the common deficiency diseases, but even though two galley hospitals existed, one at Puerto de Santa María and the other at Cartagena, few oarsmen were treated there. Galley officials, ever alert against feigned illness, generally refused to allow the oarsmen to be taken to the hospital. Only in exceptional cases—instances of epidemic disease or incurable illness—did they permit removal for hospitalization. They believed that a stay in the hospital weakened the oarsmen, reducing their resistance to fatigue when they returned aboard.[67] There also was the problem of security. Despite elaborate precautions (numerous guards, prisoners chained to their beds), hospitals were not secure: in 1685, for example, a notorious robber band attacked the hospital at Cartagena with the (unaccomplished) design of freeing the *forzados* inside.[68] In order to avoid such occurrences and to prevent the removal of ill oarsmen ashore, one of the galleys belonging to the squadron of Spain was converted into a floating infirmary in the last years of the seventeenth century. In 1703, rules were adopted governing its organization and administration.[69] Whether or not floating infirmaries existed in other squadrons as well is not known, but it is quite clear that in the eighteenth century oarsmen still were being treated aboard the galleys, chained either to their regular benches or to those of the floating infirmaries.

The distribution of labor on the galleys provides one of the best examples of the overlapping between slavery and penal servitude. When at sea, the principal occupation of both *forzados* and slaves was rowing, and their placement at the oars reflected their physical strength rather than status. Slaves and *forzados* rowed side by side, but the slaves, reputedly of superior physical ability, usually occupied the places farthest inboard, which were considered the most fatiguing rowing positions. While the primary labor of the slaves was pulling the oars, they performed other services as well. Slaves customarily were sent ashore chained together in pairs and under guard to draw water and collect firewood. When the galleys were in port, slaves were used to haul and load supplies onto the galleys, and in the last quarter of the seventeenth century and in the eighteenth century they labored at other heavy tasks in the galley arsenals and ports.[70]

There were certain positions on each galley that were held principally by slaves. For example, slaves (almost always chosen from among those Moslems who had become Christians) served as assistants to the guards. Their main functions were to assist the guards in chaining and unchaining the *chusma* and to help them conduct the clothing and other inspections. Others, both Christians and Moslems, were personal servants of the galley officials. There also were the *barberotes,* or aides of the barber-surgeons, who helped to shave the hair and beards of the oarsmen every fifteen days and to care for the sick. While these posts could sometimes be held by *forzados* (but only those serving sentences of less than four years) slaves were preferred.[71] Regardless of whether they were slaves or *forzados,* men occupying these positions received better rations than their fellows, usually the regular seaman's rations, and went about their duties aboard the galleys either unchained or with light fetters.

In contrast to the varied activities of most of the slaves, most *forzados* and certain categories of slaves (Moriscos, renegades, and *arraeces*) were prohibited from performing any labor on the galleys except rowing. In practice, when the ships were in port, the oars-

men labored at such tasks as mending sails, ropes, and other equipment, or worked at their trades and handicrafts, since a substantial
proportion of the *forzados* were craftsmen or skilled laborers.
Numerous decrees throughout the sixteenth and seventeenth centuries reiterated the prohibition against allowing the *forzados* ashore
for any reason whatsoever until they had completed their sentences
and were given their freedom. This rule was established originally
so as to insure the proper expiation of their crimes in the manner in
which they had been sentenced, i.e., as rowers on the galleys. Later
it was claimed that the refusal to use *forzados* ashore was motivated
by the desire to protect them from exploitation and to preserve their
strength for the oars.[72] Fear of escapes was another factor, since it
proved impossible to guard slaves and *forzados* well enough to
prevent flights. Most of the successful escapes were accomplished
by slaves who managed to flee either while performing their regular
chores ashore or when laboring in the galley ports.[73]

When the galleys were at sea, mutinies and escape attempts were
infrequent, and those that have been recorded usually involved a
conspiracy between *forzados* and Moslem slaves. Although differences in religion might seem to have impeded such cooperation (and
sometimes probably did), for desperate men this too could be over-
come. In any event, it would have been useless for Christian *forzados* to mutiny and seize a galley unless they planned to take it into a
North African port. The assistance of the Moslem slaves was essential to any successful rebellion, especially since most of them were
professional corsairs who knew the routes and coastal waters well.
Mutinies were particularly likely when the galleys neared the North
African coast. Most of the recorded incidents occurred at that time
or during the course of battles between Spanish and North African
galleys.[74]

Notwithstanding the long-established policy of prohibiting the use
of *forzados* ashore, such labor became more frequent by the last
years of the seventeenth century, as the galleys gradually became
outmoded. In the eighteenth century, when the vessels spent most
of the year tied up in port, the *forzados* worked alongside the slaves
in the galley arsenals in a wide range of occupations, although most
performed heavy labor. They were used to move masts and other
stores around the arsenal and docks and to cut and transport timber

used in the shipyard. From 1716 they worked at dredging the port of Cartagena and cleaning the basins where the ships were built and launched. In addition, *forzados* and slaves from the galleys helped to build the pontoon bridge that served as principal access to the port of Cartagena, and worked at excavation for construction in the dockyard areas.[75]

The utilization of *forzados* from the galleys in unskilled labor in the arsenals and navy yards during the last years of the seventeenth century and the first half of the eighteenth century set the precedent for their use ashore in the second half of the eighteenth century. When the galleys were abolished in 1748, forced labor in the arsenals was substituted for galley service, and the navy yards and arsenals were transformed into penal establishments as replacements for the galleys. In the years 1749–87, a period of naval expansion, sentences to hard labor in the arsenals became the most common form of punishment as the government exploited the manpower of prisoners to perform the necessary heavy labor of construction and maintenance in the naval arsenals. As penal labor moved from the galleys, so did slavery. Slaves worked side by side with the convicts as the two systems of involuntary labor continued to coexist in the arsenals as they had on the galleys.

spiritual needs. *Forzados* who died before the termination of their sentences could not be replaced until affidavits were filed describing the causes of their deaths, and all requests for replacements had to be made directly to the king. Any prisoners who escaped through the negligence of the Fuggers or their employees had to be recaptured at their expense. Furthermore, the Fuggers were especially enjoined not to try to retain prisoners after the completion of their sentences, as was done on the galleys, but despite this prohibition, that is exactly what they did during the initial years of the grant. Complaints soon reached the court, and in 1569 a royal decree ordered the Fuggers to cease interfering with the normal release of prisoners and to free immediately all those who had completed their sentences.[3]

*Forzados* destined for Almadén were to be chosen from among the condemned criminals awaiting transportation to the galleys in the jail of Toledo. Preference was to be given to those serving limited sentences and who appeared to be most suited for work in the mines. Once selected, the *forzados* were handed over to an agent of the Fuggers and then placed in a chain destined for Almadén.[4] At the end of February, 1566, the first group arrived at Almadén to begin serving their sentences, and thus was inaugurated another experiment in the use of convict labor in early modern Spain.

At Almadén, as on the galleys, penal servitude and slavery coexisted throughout the early modern era. In this respect, Almadén was a faithful reproduction of the galleys, but on a more restricted scale, because only small numbers of slaves and *forzados* were utilized there. Aside from the reluctance of the government to allow the Fuggers control over more convicts than absolutely necessary, the enterprise did not require a large working force. What was needed at Almadén was a continuous supply of a limited number of workers who could be exploited without consideration of the hazards to health and life that existed in the mercury mines. While convicts were ideally suited to such circumstances, slaves generally were too valuable to be wasted in this manner, but this was not true for those at Almadén. These slaves, who were mainly North Africans, were purchased directly from private slaveholders for service in the mines. They were unwanted and rejected by their owners because they were insubordinate and rebellious or had committed misdemeanors that required punishment. Instead of donating them to the king for the galleys, which meant a total loss, owners could gain some compensation by selling them at lower prices for use in the mines of Almadén. Statistics for the sixteenth century are not available, but in the first half of the seventeenth century slaves were purchased for the mines at thirty to eighty ducats a head at a time when the common market value for an able-bodied slave was 100 ducats. Even in the second half of the seventeenth century, when slaves' prices rose on the Iberian Peninsula, recorded prices at Almadén were still below the competitive market price.[5] Given the circumstances, these slaves were as expendable as the convicts.

As in the case of the galleys, much of the source material for a study of penal servitude in the mines of Almadén has disappeared. One of the most valuable collections of extant documents can be found in the Archivo Histórico Nacional in Madrid. Among the papers belonging to the Order of Calatrava are three bundles of documents relating to an investigation of the mines in 1593 that was conducted by a royal commissioner who was none other than the famous sixteenth-century writer, Mateo Alemán, author of the picaresque novel *Guzmán de Alfarache*. This inquiry was occasioned by a steady current of complaints that reached the king in the 1580s about the treatment of the *forzados* at Almadén. The documents in this collection consist primarily of lists containing the names, sentences, dates of entry, and release or death of all *forzados* who served in the mines from 1566 to 1593. Transcripts of sentences, copies of appeals, and other legal papers belonging to the men provide further details about them. Additional information can be derived from the "Información Secreta"—some 189 folios of oral testimony taken from twelve prisoners still serving there in 1593.[6] There were actually thirteen prisoners, but one of them was unable to testify because of illness. That meant that there were twenty-seven vacancies (all caused by death) that the king refused to fill until the results of the investigation were known.

According to the official lists, some 220 convicts labored at Almadén during the period 1566-93 (including the men still there at the latter date). Given the loss of records for the early years, this figure represents perhaps some three-quarters of the men who served there; at least this is the impression that emerges from a study of the

sworn statements of the administrators of the mines in 1593. Moreover, several of the convicts noted in their testimonies that at times,
especially in the late 1580s when the Fuggers tried to increase
output, there were more than the stipulated number of *forzados*
working in the mines.[7]

The origins of the *forzados* are difficult to determine because only
one-half of them are listed with their places of birth or residence. It
does seem that most of the prisoners came from the big cities (with
over 2,000 householders) and the larger towns (fifty to 2,000 householders) of Castile, Andalusia, and Extremadura. There was also a
substantial group from the judicial districts of Ciudad Real and
Almagro, because justices in this region, due to the proximity of
Almadén, preferred to send men to the mines rather than to the
galleys. As for their professions, once again the lists seldom mention this kind of information, but on the basis of what information
does exist, it seems that most *forzados* belonged to the menial
trades, service industries, or unskilled working class of the towns
and cities. Some of the occupations frequently indicated are those of
carters, coachmen, barbers, bakers, blacksmiths, butchers, and
servants. There also were two notaries and four friars. Only four of
the *forzados* were of foreign origin (Flemish, German, Italian, and
Portuguese), and all had been condemned to Almadén for capital
crimes.[8]

More than half of the *forzados* at Almadén were serving sentences
of from four to six years; the remainder, from one to four years.
Only fourteen prisoners had been condemned for more than five
years (six to ten years), and in these cases homicides were involved.
Forty-two percent of the men completed their sentences and were
subsequently released, and 24 percent died before their release dates.
Some 8 percent were either freed before the expiration of their terms
(men who were still appealing their sentences or *en depósito*), or
escaped and, when recaptured, were executed or sent to the galleys.
Fourteen men (6 percent) were still serving their sentences. The fate
of the remaining 20 percent is unknown. It seems likely that some
died before completing their sentences, but their deaths purposely
were not recorded.[9]

Escapes were infrequent; during the twenty-seven-year period
from 1566 to 1593, there were only seven of them—two were

successful, and one, involving several prisoners, partially so. The convicts and slaves were well guarded and kept chained together when going to the mines from the building that served as their sleeping quarters. Once inside, the central chain that linked them together was removed (but not their individual chains), and it was not replaced until they were ready to leave the building to work in the mines. As on the galleys, guards and overseers were personally responsible for the loss of any of their charges, that is, they had to recapture them at their own cost or, failing that, had either to pay for slaves to replace them, or else serve in their stead.[10]

The only jailbreak involving a number of *forzados* took place in 1588 and provoked a serious controversy between religious and secular authorities over the right of sanctuary in church buildings. Four prisoners who were being forced to work in the mines at night overpowered their guards, killed an overseer, and then escaped through a ventilation shaft. They fled to a nearby Franciscan monastery where they asked for asylum. The friars not only honored their request, but also helped them to remove their chains and gave them new clothing to replace their prison garb. When the guards from Almadén arrived, the friars refused to surrender the prisoners to them. The administrator of the mines, fearful of the consequences of forcibly breaking the inviolability of church sanctuary, allowed them to remain there indefinitely. Eventually, two of the men were recaptured after they had voluntarily left the monastery, and one of them was subsequently tried and executed at Almadén for the murder of the overseer.[11]

The majority of *forzados* at Almadén were either thieves or men sentenced for both theft and vagrancy. Since work in the mines was considered less severe than on the galleys, murderers generally were not sent there. Only eight of the total number of prisoners had been convicted of homicide; two of them were wife-killers. Another prisoner serving a life sentence for murder was an Augustinian friar whose clerical status apparently saved him from the gallows. In the early years there were some *forzados* who had been sent to Almadén by the Inquisition for moral lapses and transgressions (bigamy, adultery, sodomy), but they were always an insignificant number. Ruffians, army deserters, bandits, Granadine Moriscos, and gypsies made up the rest of the convicts at Almadén.[12]

Among the prisoners, the most numerous were the cattle thieves, housebreakers, and burglars, followed by a substantial representation of pickpockets and sneak thieves. They included men of all ages. Pascual Abril, who was convicted of stealing two mules, is typical of the first category. At the time of his arrival at Almadén in 1586 to begin serving a six-year sentence, he was described in a notation on the official entry list as "a man of forty years of age with few teeth and a large knife mark on one cheek and a fierce expression."[13] Clearly a professional, Abril early attempted escape. Less than a month after his arrival he fled the mines, but got only as far as the town of Agudo (some twenty-two kilometers away), where he was recaptured after a brief struggle. Two years later, his death "from natural causes" was officially recorded, and within a month another thief was brought from the jail of Toledo to take his place.[14]

Among the best representatives of the sneak thieves and pickpockets were two boys who could have stepped out of any of the picaresque novels of the period. Francisco de Baena (alias Diego de Madrid) and Juan Martín had been practicing their professions at court in Madrid for some time before their arrest. Although the usual penalties for minors were flogging and banishment, the long criminal records of these two youths convinced the court that they were incorrigible and that sentences to the galleys were justified. It is not clear what tasks they performed at Almadén, because as on the galleys, minors could not undertake the hard labor assigned to the convicts. Both survived the rigors of their service at Almadén, four and five years, respectively, and they were released after completing their sentences.[15]

Almost none of the *forzados* at Almadén had been condemned there for simple vagrancy, although the laws provided for such sentencing. With only two exceptions, Almadén prisoners described as vagrants had been convicted also of some other crime, mainly theft, but this was true on the galleys as well. Contemporary opinion held that vagabondage and theft went hand-in-hand, and therefore those apprehended for the first offense also were accused of the second even when there was little basis for such a charge.[16] This was the case in regard to the gypsies, who also could be found at Almadén, although in fewer numbers proportionally than on the galleys. They were not usually sent to Almadén, because they were not considered suitable for labor in the mines, a belief well confirmed by their high mortality rate there. Indeed, most of those serving in the mines came from the surrounding judicial districts and were there *en depósito*. Typical gypsy *forzados* were Vicente Vizcaíno and Melchor del Campo, who were condemned to the mines on this basis for vagrancy, theft and resisting arrest. According to the transcript of their sentence, they were found hiding at night on the town commons of Almagro, and when ordered to surrender themselves resisted by throwing stones and shouting their defiance at the constables. What appeared to be stolen property was found on them. These charges resulted in a six-year sentence to be served at Almadén.[17]

Resisting arrest was a frequent charge connected with vagrancy for gypsies and others, especially those called *jácaros* or *rufos* (ruffians) in the official documents, who were among the most typical representatives of the underworld in this period. At their lowest level, *rufos* were nothing more than hired thugs and professional assassins who usually ended their lives on the gallows. Many of them also acted as procurers and lived off the earnings of prostitutes. This was the group most often seen at Almadén and on the galleys.[18] One of the first prisoners to arrive at the mines in 1566 was Antonio López Peláez, who was sentenced to six years at hard labor for being a ruffian and procurer. Like Morón (the protagonist in Francisco de Lugo y Dávila's novel of the underworld, *De la hermanía*), López Peláez "traveled around the country with his mistress and other women who supported him from their earnings in the brothels."[19]

Four members of religious orders served at Almadén during the years 1566-93 for crimes ranging from apostasy to murder. One of them, Juan de Pedraza, an Augustinian friar, had been convicted of murder and sentenced to the mines for ten years. The transcript of his sentence describes how, "consumed with passion for Elena de Portilla, an innkeeper's wife from the town of Ledesma, he waylaid her husband at night in the open countryside and killed him."[20] When the royal commissioner, Mateo Alemán, interviewed him in 1593, he had been in the mines for six years, an unusually long period of survival for a prisoner there (the average was four years).

The secret of his endurance was that he was not actually working in the mines. His labor services were being performed by a slave that his family had sent to him. Unfortunately for the friar, knowledge of this arrangement eventually reached royal authorities, who ordered the Fuggers to see to it "that he was put to work in the mines immediately, and if this was not possible, to send him to the galleys for life."[21]

A substantial number of *forzados* were Moriscos, some of whom had been condemned for actual crimes and others for having disobeyed the laws governing their relocation after the Alpujarras Rebellion of 1568-70. A special category among this group was the Valencian bandits—intransigent Moriscos who resisted the pressures placed upon them by taking to brigandage. For their crimes they were made royal slaves and sentenced to serve the rest of their lives in the mines. Two of them, Jerónimo de Valencia and Pedro de Meduar, who testified for Alemán in 1593, were the only survivors of a contingent of ten such Morisco bandits brought to Almadén in 1587.[22]

More numerous than the bandits were those Granadine Moriscos who had been resettled in the town of Almadén after the relocation of 1570, but had subsequently fled the district in an attempt to return to Granada. A royal decree of 1572 prohibited Granadine Moriscos from leaving their assigned places of residence and returning to Granada under the penalty of death or enslavement. Notwithstanding this legislation, the Almadén Moriscos (like their compatriots elsewhere) continued to abandon their new homes, and when recaptured were condemned by the justices at Almadén to serve in the mines, "in view of the pressing need for workers."[23] In addition to the Morisco *forzados,* there also were free Morisco laborers at Almadén who had been lured there by the promise of higher wages as recompense for dangerous work. They worked for short periods of time (twenty to thirty days) at the furnaces, where the risk of mercury poisoning was especially high. When they became ill, they left, often to return again after they had recovered. Other free Moriscos labored in peripheral jobs in and around the mines, such as clearing the land and preparing it for the excavation of mercury ore. Finally, there were Moriscos who were permanently employed at Almadén as guards and overseers—they accompanied the *forzados* into the mines and supervised their work.[24]

Living conditions at Almadén were, in the words of one of the prisoners interviewed by Alemán in 1953, "not such that a man could not survive."[25] The diet, for example, was far superior to that on the galleys. Instead of the beans, oil, rice, and biscuit that were standard fare on the galleys, the *forzados* at Almadén received a daily ration of meat, or fish on meatless days, two and one-half pounds of bread, and a pint and a half of wine.[26] The clothing allotment also was satisfactory—a pair of breeches, a doublet, stockings, two shirts, four pairs of shoes, and a hood were distributed to the men each year. Medical care was available at the infirmary, and all *forzados* questioned by Alemán declared that they were satisfied with its services. The staff consisted of a physician, a surgeon, and one or two male nurses. Medicines were readily supplied (the infirmary had its own apothecary), and special diets were prepared for the sick. One *forzado,* Miguel del Aldea, for example, told Alemán that when he was in the infirmary he had received four purges, several different kinds of medicine, and a light diet of chicken, eggs, and veal.[27]

Despite the existence of adequate medical services, the danger of death from mercury poisoning was always present, and few escaped its effects. All those interviewed by Alemán had spent time in the infirmary suffering from severe pains, which could afflict any part of the body. Some of the *forzados* and slaves trembled in every limb. Others lost their sanity, as did two men who died "foaming at the mouth and raving like madmen."[28] Work at the funaces was very dangerous, and this was one of the principal occupations of the *forzados*. Most of the men who labored continuously at the furnaces died from mercury poisoning. One even asserted that he saw as many as twenty-five men die there in the year 1590-91 because of overexposure to mercury through constant toil.[29]

Bailing water out of the mines to prevent flooding was another one of the tasks performed by the *forzados* and slaves. Although there was less danger of mercury poisoning, the work was so strenuous (even with an additional food ration) that many became ill from exhaustion or were so weakened that they easily fell victim to infectious diseases such as dysentery and tuberculosis. Many of the abuses that led to the royal investigation of 1593 occurred here or at the furnaces during the years 1589-91, when the production of mercury reached new heights. According to the declarations of the prisoners interrogated by Alemán, each work gang of four men was required to bail out 300 buckets of water without resting, and those who could not meet the quota were whipped. Even sick prisoners were treated in this manner—one *forzado,* for example, who fainted while bailing because he had not eaten for four days due to the sores in his mouth, was taken out twice within one hour to be flogged. Moreover, the men who customarily worked from dawn to dusk with one and one-half hours for lunch at noon were compelled to return to the mines and work at bailing all night without any opportunity for rest.[30] Under this treatment, the mortality rates among *forzados* and slaves soared to their highest levels.

For most of the prisoners, the rigors of their daily existence were somewhat ameliorated by the cultivation of their spiritual life within a religious confraternity to which all members of the Almadén community belonged. This confraternity was similar to the one that existed on the galleys. It was founded orginally to provide decent burials for its members, but it also supervised their religious life. Its operations were conducted by a prior—who was the administrator of the mines for the Fuggers—and several officials chosen from among the most devout *forzados*. The magistrates held nightly devotions and were charged with seeing that all brothers attended mass on Sundays and feast days. Nonattendance was punished by a fine of four maravedís. The activities of the brotherhood were supported by money collected from these fines, as well as from the proceeds of the sale of clothing worn by the prisoners at the time of their arrival and from the tallow made from the animals slaughtered for food. Most of the funds went toward the arrangement of elaborate funerals for brothers, and burial in the church of Almadén. In addition, the brotherhood paid for a specially sung mass to be celebrated on the third Sunday of each month and another high mass on the feast day of San Miguel, patron of the Confraternity, that included a procession and sermon. On that occasion, all the brothers received lighted tapers that they held in their hands during the divine service. The Confraternity also underwrote the cost of an additional food ration on the feast of San Miguel—another pound of bread, one-half pound of pork, and an extra pint of wine.[31]

The festivities and religious observances sponsored by the Confraternity brought a few bright moments into the lives of the *forzados,* but they could not change the basic realities of life in the mines. Although royal officials had assumed originally that being sentenced to the mines represented a less severe punishment than service on the galleys, the contrary proved to be true.[32] The better diet, living conditions, and medical services available at Almadén were cancelled by the constant exposure of the prisoners to mercury. As the convicts themselves realized, the chances of survival were far greater on the galleys than in the mines of Almadén.[33] For offenders in early modern Spain, consignment to the mercury mines of Almadén did not represent merely a term of years at involuntary servitude; it frequently meant condemnation to a slow and painful death. Yet, regardless of the cost in human lives, the convicts were deemed to be as necessary at Almadén as on the galleys. In both instances, the principal reason for their utilization was the problem of labor procurement. As the Fuggers stated in their original petition to the king and repeated often thereafter, it was extremely difficult to attract free laborers to Almadén, and those who were recruited either refused outright to work at dangerous jobs or would do so only for a short period of time and at high wages. Penal labor guaranteed a continuous supply of workers at reduced cost, and it enabled the Fuggers to work the mines profitably as well as to meet the growing demand for mercury. Figures for mercury production at Almadén illustrate this point. In 1565, one year before the introduction of the *forzados,* the mines of Almadén produced 1,000 quintals of mercury; seven years later, the yearly output had reached 2,100 quintals; and by 1594 production had tripled to 3,500 quintals.[34]

Despite the success of the Almadén mines in the last quarter of the sixteenth century, the demand of the New World mines for mercury soon began to surpass the ability of Almadén to produce it. In the first half of the seventeenth century production fluctuated greatly, and after 1630 it entered a period of steady decline.[35] There were many reasons for Almadén's difficulties—primitive technology, inefficient administration, the waning finances of the Fuggers—but one of the most important was the chronic shortage of labor.

Mercury poisoning caused high mortality rates and resulted in steady decimation of the labor force. At the same time, the king refused to increase the quota of *forzados* because of the continuing need for them on the galleys. The only solution was to make up the deficiency with slaves. By 1613, slaves already outnumbered *forzados* by a ratio of two to one.[36] Although slaves purchased for service at Almadén were cheaper than average, their expanded use at a time when the enterprise was beset with technical and organizational problems increased costs and reduced profits, which further depressed the industry.

In 1645 the Fugger concession was cancelled, and the mines were taken over by the state to be managed by royal officials. In 1648, there were 200 slaves and *forzados* working in the mines, but exact figures for each category are unknown.[37] In the eighteenth century, despite the declining need for *forzados* on the galleys there was no increase in their numbers at Almadén. Magistrates continued to sentence men automatically to the galleys and, whenever possible, to the North African presidios, where a continuous scarcity of workers and soldiers required the use of convicts. Labor shortages at Almadén resulting from the opening of new pits in the period 1696-1709 and in the following years were met by using more slaves. In 1701, the superintendent of the mines suggested that the *forzados* be replaced entirely by slaves, since they were better and stronger workers than the convicts and more docile. According to this plan, the slaves were to be promised their freedom after ten years of service so as to prevent them from committing desperate acts from fear of interminable labor. Although this idea was not accepted, the slave contingent at Almadén continued to grow in subsequent years. This trend continued until the abolition of the galleys in 1748, when it was decided to send a part of the *forzados* who remained on the galleys, that is, the most serious offenders, to complete their sentences at Almadén. In the following year, the courts were ordered to sentence all those guilty of capital crimes and meriting the penalty of the galleys to Almadén, while lesser offenders were to be sent to the North African presidios.[38] This legislation was in effect for two years, during which it became increasingly clear that neither the enterprise nor the facilities at Almadén needed or could accommodate a large convict population. Once the king became convinced that Almadén could not replace the galleys as a penal institution, he revoked the decree of 1749 and ordered that henceforth all prisoners sentenced to hard labor be sent instead to the naval arsenals or the North African presidios.[39] Magistrates, especially those in the neighboring Extremaduran judicial districts, continued to sentence men to Almadén, however, and several times during the course of the eighteenth century royal orders were issued directing the courts to send specially designated offenders to the mines of Almadén.[40] In 1755, two disastrous fires that caused widespread damage were blamed on the *forzados*. Consequently, they were removed from the underground operations and set to work above ground in such peripheral jobs as cleaning and excavation.

In the last quarter of the eighteenth century, the penal contingent at Almadén decreased sharply as the state satisfied its pressing labor needs in the naval arsenals, North African presidios, and public works projects with convict workers. In addition, improvements in technology during this period made the mines safer and reduced the hazard of mercury poisoning. It became possible to attract free workers, who gradually replaced the *forzados* and slaves. By the opening years of the nineteenth century it was no longer necessary to maintain a penal establishment at Almadén, and in 1801 it was closed, and the few remaining *forzados* were transferred to the presidio of Ceuta.[41]

Some Spanish penologists, notably Fernando Cadalso, have minimized the importance of Almadén in the history of penal servitude in Spain, mainly because the punishment of hard labor in the mines of Almadén never existed as a separate penalty in Spanish criminal law.[42] All those who served at Almadén were condemned originally to the galleys, and then in response to utilitarian needs their sentences were commuted to the mines of Almadén. Contemporary legal opinion held that, from the judicial point of view, sentences at Almadén and on the galleys were identical. The concept of Almadén as a kind of "terrestrial galleys," or the land equivalent of the galleys, was incorporated into the architecture of the building constructed to house the slaves and *forzados*. The interior of this edifice was designed in the form of a galley, with a long narrow central corridor in imitation of the midship gangway (*crujía*) and with the bunks of the inmates located on either side like the benches on the galleys. At night the men were chained to their bunks just as the oarsmen were attached to their benches. The building also contained an infirmary, chapel, and patio, and the whole complex was surrounded by a strongly fortified wall. In the eighteenth century the term *crujía* customarily was used to refer to this edifice, and it was not until the last years of the century that it became known as the "jail of the *forzados* and slaves of Almadén."[43]

Cadalso also has argued that Almadén was insignificant in the historical evolution of penal servitude in Spain because, unlike the galleys, only small numbers of convicts were employed there.[44] On the contrary, despite its limited penal population, Almadén played an important role, for it set the example for the kind of penal labor that reached its fullest development in Spanish America. In contrast to the galleys and the presidios, where prisoners labored in the service of the king and under direct military control, the Fugger concession at Almadén, 1566-1645, represented the exploitation of penal labor by private interests, which became one of the most characteristic forms of penal servitude in the New World.[45] In the Spanish colonies, royal judges sentenced men to terms of service at hard labor and then turned them over to private employers who used them in mines and factories just as had been done at Almadén. It seems likely, therefore, that the system of penal labor used in Spanish America for three centuries owed as much to the experiment at Almadén as it did to the galleys.

# 3

# The Presidios of
# North Africa

A third form of penal servitude developed in Spain in the early modern era was the presidio sentence. The origins of this penalty are difficult to determine, since there is no mention of it in Spanish law until long after it had been in operation. Legal writers of the sixteenth century claimed that it originated from the same source as did service on the galleys and in the mines of Almadén, that is, from sentences *ad metallum* and in *opus metalli* as found in medieval Castilian law. Modern penologists believe that there were other elements in its historical evolution as well.[1] Since the term *presidio*, derived from the Latin *praesidium*, means garrison or fort surrounded by protective walls, it is argued that this penalty also developed from the practice of keeping prisoners in custody in castles and fortresses in the Middle Ages.[2] In addition, banishment, which was widely utilized in the medieval period and the sixteenth century, represents another factor in the formation of this penalty. Significantly, all those who were condemned to the North African presidios were originally called *desterrados* (banished men), and this term was still in use in the eighteenth century. It seems likely that three different kinds of punishment, that is, banishment, confinement in a fortress or castle, and utilitarian service for the state, came together to form the presidio sentence. In the sixteenth century the presidio sentence meant service at arms in the North African presidios for nobles and rich men. It was not until the middle of the seventeenth century, when it was extended to poor commoners, that it took the form of either hard labor or military service depending on class and wealth. By the opening of the eighteenth century there were two kinds of prisoners: *desterrados*, who performed military service, and *presidiarios*, who were condemned to hard labor.[3]

The last step in the evolution of the presidio sentence as a penalty in Spanish law resulted from Spain's expansion into North Africa at the beginning of the early modern era. The same strategic and defensive reasons that motivated Spain to build a powerful galley fleet in the Mediterranean in the sixteenth century also led to a policy of intervention in North Africa. Although Melilla was captured in 1497, it was not until after Queen Isabella's death in 1504 that a series of expeditions was launched across the Mediterranean.[4] This campaign left Spain in control of several important points along the coast (1505, Mers-el-kebir; 1508, Peñón de Vélez; 1509, Oran), and in an excellent position to push into the interior. But the effort to penetrate the Magreb was not pursued, and the opportunity was soon lost as Moslem power in the region revived in the 1520s and 1530s. Two major expeditions against Tunis in 1535 and Mostaganem in 1558 did not alter the situation. After the failure at Mostaganem, the grandiose schemes for African expeditions did not completely disappear, but gave way to a policy of strengthening the positions held. The task of reinforcing and extending the fortifica-

Spanish presidios in North Africa, sixteenth-eighteenth centuries

tions of the coastal presidios began in the 1560s and continued for three centuries.

Despite the urgent need for workers, it appears that the building program of the sixteenth and first half of the seventeenth centuries was undertaken primarily by free labor. Diego Suárez, the soldier-chronicler who spent twenty-eight years in Oran (1577–1604), does not mention penal laborers. In his day the heavy labor of the fortifications was done by *gastadores* (pioneers) recruited from all over Spain.[5] There does exist a decree issued by Philip II ordering the transfer to Oran of a contingent of *forzados* about to embark on the galleys at Málaga, but it is not known how often this was done.[6] Given the demand for rowers on the galleys, it seems unlikely that the Spanish monarchs would have been willing to commit penal workers to the presidios on a permanent basis. If men condemned to the galleys or *forzados* already serving there were sent to the presidios during this period, it was done as an emergency measure only. In the sixteenth century the North African presidios, in contrast to the galleys, were not places of punishment for the general criminal population. Instead, they served as places of deportation and exile for nobles who could not be sentenced to the galleys and wealthy commoners who bribed their way out of serving on them. Many examples of banished noblemen could be given: among them, the grandson of Columbus, Luis, Duke of Veragua, who was condemned to ten years in Oran for trigamy and died there in 1573. Other *desterrados* in Oran were Felipe de Borja, brother of the Master of Montesa, and Don Gabriel de la Cueva, son of the Duke of Albuquerque.[7]

It has often been asserted that Spain did not adopt a policy of transportation of criminals as did other western European countries in the early modern era.[8] While this may be true in regard to the New World, it is not valid for North Africa. From the beginning, the North African presidios were authentic places of deportation (albeit for a select group) from which individuals were not expected to return. Cerdán de Tallada wrote in 1568 that it was common to sentence men to life terms at La Goleta and Oran during this period.[9] Later on, especially after the abolition of the galleys in 1748, the North African presidios became virtual penal colonies, where convicts drawn from all socioeconomic backgrounds worked for private individuals as well as for the state. Furthermore, in the eighteenth century some prisoners remained after the completion of their sentences, especially if they had skills that were needed.[10] In view of these circumstances, the North African presidios can be considered a Spanish example of transportation.

The gradual transformation of the North African presidios from places of deportation and punishment for nobles and rich men into penal establishments for all convicted felons—another version of the terrestrial galleys—began around the middle of the seventeenth century. Little is known about this development, because the sources available for a study of the North African presidios as penal institutions in the seventeenth century are meager.[11] It seems that the turning point occured in the 1640's, and that several factors stimulated this change. The extension of Spain's network of presidios in the seventeenth century brought about an increased demand for soldiers and laborers. By the mid-seventeenth century Spain held Ceuta, Melilla, Oran, and Peñón de Vélez. In addition to these possessions, there were Larache and La Mamora, but they were retained only to the end of the century.[12] At the same time, Spain's military needs in Europe grew enormously as a result of participation in the Thirty Years War and the Catalan and Portuguese revolts at home. Coincidentally, widespread epidemics and subsistence crises in this period brought about a decline in Spanish population, particularly in New Castile and Andalusia, which meant that fewer men were available for military service. The manpower and financial crisis of the 1640s and 1650s provided the impetus for the conversion of the presidios into general penal establishments equivalent to the galleys. In 1653 and 1654, the king directed magistrates to sentence convicted felons to Melilla and Larache.[13] In 1658, condemned prisoners in the Madrid jails who were skilled in building were ordered sent to Oran, where they were urgently needed. Finally, in 1677, all prisoners sentenced to less than three years on the galleys were to be sent instead to La Mamora. At the time of its capture in 1687, the whole garrison at La Mamora was made up of *desterrados*.[14]

Although it appears that the majority of convicts shipped to the presidios in the second half of the seventeenth century were destined to serve as soldiers at least most of the time, there were others sent there exclusively as laborers on the fortifications. Yet sentences to hard labor in the North African presidios, in contrast to sentences of miltary service, still represented commutations of galley service. It was not until after the abolition of the galleys in 1748 that the presidio sentence to hard labor became a separate penalty apart from that of the galleys. By the end of the seventeenth century the North African presidios were well on their way to becoming full-fledged penal institutions, but their formal organization as such had to wait until the eighteenth century.

# Part 2
# The Eighteenth Century

# 4

# Bourbon Reformism,
# Forced Labor, and
# the Penal System

In the eighteenth century, penal servitude reached the highest point in its development. The utilitarian spirit of the age and the reform program of the Bourbon rulers provided both a justification and a stimulus for its continued expansion. In the sixteenth and seventeenth centuries, penal servitude, whether on the galleys or in the mines of Almadén, was applied principally to hard-core criminals, although the laws of the period prescribed this penalty for vagrants, gypsies, and other "undesirables." Despite royal pressure to condemn as many men as possible to the galleys, magistrates continued to sentence vagrants and petty criminals to the traditional forms of punishment, that is, flogging and banishment. Vagrants and petty criminals who did serve on the galleys in this period usually were convicted of more than just vagrancy or were notorious recidivists. This also was true of the gypsies, except when they were conscripted en masse for the galleys, as, for example, in the seventeenth century.[1] In the Hapsburg period most vagabonds and petty offenders lived out their marginal lives freely, wandering about the country and subsisting off charity and crime. It was not a question of whether the laws were too lenient or too severe; rather, they were inconsistently enforced.

In the eighteenth century the campaign against idlers and delinquents had more effect. Under the Bourbons, the pressure of public opinion and the economic objectives of the government combined to produce a systematic plan of attack. Bourbon reformism was determined to eliminate or reduce antisocial and delinquent groups, or at least improve them by making them useful to society and the state. One of the most interesting characteristics of this movement was the support that it received from educated persons of differing intellectual views.[2] Benito Jerónimo Feijóo (1676–1764), a figure of the early Spanish Enlightenment, set the tone for the discussion by denouncing the willfully idle as a "pestilence" not to be tolerated by any rationally governed society.[3] As the century advanced, a stream of publications appeared lamenting the large numbers of vagabonds, beggars, and idlers and advocating decisive action to deal with the problem. Although their motives varied, the authors— churchmen, government officials, and "enlightened" writers—all denounced idleness and praised honest labor. While the clerics condemned idleness because it violated religious and moral norms, secular writers established a connection between labor and the volume of production. Gaspar de Jovellanos, for example, argued that idlers injured the economy and placed a heavy burden on the working part of the population. In the view of Lorenzo de Normante and others, the gravity of the offense demanded state action to compel the idle to work.[4]

The viewpoint of the state can be seen in the works of Pedro Rodríguez de Campomanes, Antonio Pérez y López, Nicolás de Arriquíbar, and others. They believed that every subject had an obligation to contribute to the well-being of the country; and the state, as the guardian of public good, had both the responsibility and the right to direct the population into useful employment. For the Count of Campomanes, work was "not a privilege but the obligation of every citizen"; and Arriquíbar believed that if a man was without an occupation, he was dead as far as the state was concerned.[5] Moreover, the attack against idleness was not made on exclusively economic or moral grounds, but was connected to a corporate interpretation of social organization. Society was based on the mutual interdependence of individuals. Most of the population was destined to provide food and clothing for the rest. Persons who did not work threatened the stability of the hierarchical social order.[6]

Idleness also was viewed as a source of social maladjustment and delinquency. It led individuals away from the obligations of a good Christian life to the disorders that accompanied a useless existence. Since idleness was conceived as the root of vice and delinquency, the state, by taking action against it, would extinguish the "seeds of most crime as well."[7] Given the connection between vagrancy, vice, and crime in the minds of the eighteenth-century thinkers, it is not difficult to understand the wide interpretation given to the term "vagrant" in the repressive legislation of the period.[8] In the category of "vagrants" was a large group of misbehavers who were not vagrants in the strict sense of the term. Since these elements threatened the social order, violated religious and moral concepts, and injured the economy, the state could suppress them by any means at its disposal.

The campaign against idlers and social outcasts began early. The proportion of vagrants had increased greatly during the last years of the seventeenth century and the War of Succession (1700–1713). In the reign of Philip V (1700–1746), several decrees were issued impressing vagabonds and idlers into the army, and similar legislation was repeated throughout the century. In the legislation of 1745, vagrants were defined as all those living without an honest and licit means of support, but as the years passed, the number of people included within this classification increased continuously. Decrees were issued against gypsies, wandering pilgrims, and others with similar nomadic lives, but these laws also allowed the authorities to impress drunks, men caught sleeping in the streets, artisans who refused to work, and sons disobedient to their parents. By the last quarter of the century, libertines, fornicators, and men who mistreated their wives or abandoned their families all were being prosecuted under similar legislation. On the basis of her data, María Rosa Pérez Estévez has concluded that only a small percentage of men impressed into the army during the eighteenth century were authentic vagrants. In the levy of 1759, for example, they represented 19 percent. Petty thieves made up 14 percent, and the rest had committed offenses against morality or had disturbed the public peace.[9]

The plan to derive utility from idlers and misbehavers resulted in their steady exploitation by the state throughout the eighteenth century. The able-bodied male vagrants were conscripted in the armed forces. According to a nation-wide sample for the years 1730–82 compiled by Pérez Estévez, of the 44,777 vagrants whose destinations are known, 24,899 (56 percent) went to the army and 11,664 (26 percent) to the navy.[10] In the 1740s, those who were not fit for military service because of age (over forty-four years old), youth (under sixteen), or physical defects were used as laborers on military fortifications. During those years the military plans of the government called for a program to strengthen the defenses of the Peninsula through the reinforcement and improvement of fortifications in addition to a reorganization of the army. Since the heavy work of construction and repair of fortifications in the North African presidios was being done by this time by penal labor, it was decided to apply the same system to the Peninsular presidios.

From the 1740s through the 1770s, forced labor contingents were organized in almost all the Peninsular presidios, but their quotas were small, ranging on the average from fifteen to sixty men. Two of the earliest establishments, created in the 1740s with forty and sixty men, respectively, were at Pamplona and Badajoz. La Coruña had the largest group, over 100 men, while San Sebastián, with fifteen, was the smallest. Other contingents could be found at Barcelona and Jaca; and the last-formed contingent (1776) was at Zaragoza.[11]

In the beginning, the forced-labor brigades in the presidios were made up of vagrants who were rejects from the armed forces. In addition to those who could not meet the age and physical requirements, there were chronic alcoholics, libertines, and petty thieves whose offenses automatically disqualified them from military service. In the 1750s the population of the presidios began to change. At mid-century the government inaugurated its program of naval expansion. Work was begun on the arsenals of El Ferrol (Galicia) and Cartagena, while the facilities at La Carraca (Cádiz) were expanded. During the important years of construction (the 1750s and 1760s) the main body of those disqualified from military service were sent into the naval arsenals to perform varied labor tasks.[12] Their places in the presidios were taken by smugglers and defrauders of the royal tobacco monopoly (minor offenders only), who by the late 1760s made up the majority of prisoners. It was not until the 1770s, when the naval arsenals were transformed into penal establishments for serious offenders, that vagrants and social outcasts were sent once again to the Peninsular presidios.[13]

In the 1770s there was little work to be done on the presidio fortifications, but their penal contingents continued to increase in disregard of official quotas. Prisoners from the presidios began to be used in municipal works projects. For example, in La Coruña in the mid-1770s there were 150 convicts, most of whom were utilized in street-cleaning and on bridge construction and maintenance. Conditions there, although not untypical, provoked royal intervention. In 1777 the king reaffirmed the established practice that men condemned to hard labor in the presidios could be used only in fortification work or in other tasks within the confines of the presidio.[14]

By the 1780s, a more flexible attitude began to be taken toward utilizing prisoners from the presidios outside the fortresses. As long as they performed work beneficial to the king or in the public interest, prisoners did not have to work specifically within the jurisdiction of the presidios. The new approach provided the basis for a proposal to establish a penal contingent of two brigades of fifty men each in the presidio of Alicante. There were to be used in the construction of a new customs house, to repair facilities in the port area, and to build a military hospital and barracks. Several budget estimates for this project were submitted to the king in the beginning of 1786. One of them, compiled in March of that year, is particularly revealing, since it purportedly represented the actual cost of the undertaking while the others underestimated it. Food and clothing were the principal expenses. The food ration alone cost 51,529 reales (at twelve cuartos or forty-eight maravedís per man), and this did not include bread. Had a bread ration been added, the cost would have risen substantially. As for the clothing allotment, the individual outfits amounted to an additional 140 reales per man every two years, or a total of 17,000 reales. Another large item in the budget was the expense of hospitalization, estimated at four and one-half reales per man for three hospital stays, or some 4,927 reales a year. The total cost of maintenance was 73,356 reales; still, this sum was less than the expense of hiring contract laborers. One hundred free workers at four reales a day per man for 244 working days a year amounted to 97,600 reales, or some 24,244 reales more than the total annual cost of the convict laborers.[15]

Despite the apparent financial benefits, the project to establish a penal contingent at Alicante was not adopted. The government was unwilling to organize a new establishment when it was dissatisfied with those that existed. Throughout the 1780s there were constant complaints against the administration of the labor contingents in the presidios, and in 1788 the king ordered an investigation.[16] It was found that the whole system was riddled with mismanagement, fraud, and abuse. In all of the presidios (the situation was particularly bad at La Coruña and Badajoz), passes were given to prisoners allowing them to return home temporarily or to live independently in the towns, practicing their trades. Some men from the Badajoz presidio were working in the surrounding countryside cultivating the land and caring for livestock belonging to presidio officers. Others were laboring in the town in the homes of those same officials as servants, or in like capacity in other private homes. At La Coruña, several convicts were employed as cooks and caterers for residents of the town and lived outside the presidio in rented quarters. In both La Coruña and Badajoz there were prisoners who were working as street vendors, and in 1788 a number of men from the Badajoz presidios were caught while engaging in their former profession of smuggling.[17] The conditions revealed in this inquiry led to the abandonment of the penal contingents in the Peninsular presidios. Their facilities were converted into *depósitos* or receiving centers for the temporary safekeeping of prisoners sentenced to the overseas presidios.

The eighteenth-century campaign against idlers and misbehavers reached its culmination in the last quarter of that century. The repressive legislation of the previous years had reduced the number of these elements, but since it affected only those who could be impressed into the armed forces as fighters or workers, many more remained. A large part of the pauper and idle population—women, children, the aged and physically handicapped—were untouched by the laws. It was at this time that the house of correction idea was adopted in Spain. These institutions were created elsewhere in Europe in the sixteenth and seventeenth centuries, but had long been rejected in Spain. Proposals to establish houses of confinement were made in the sixteenth century, but had little effect. In 1545, for example, a Benedictine monk, Juan de Medina, suggested the confinement of beggars, vagrants, and idlers. Medina's plan met with immediate opposition from the Dominican friar Domingo de Soto and others, who argued that confinement of the poor and indigent would deprive them of their God-given personal freedom, and that removal of mendicants from the streets would prevent the faithful from practicing charity necessary for their salvation.[18] In the eighteenth century, with the new emphasis on the economic benefits to be derived from welfare measures, the idea of confinement gained wide support. Advocates of the workhouses, like Bernardo Ward, whose writings on poverty and idleness enjoyed great vogue, emphasized the economic rewards to be gained by the state by putting the idle and poor to work.[19] In the period 1750–1800, workhouses were established all over the country. The essence of the houses of correction was that they combined the principles of the poorhouse, workhouse, and penal institution. Their objective was to force the poor, idle, and delinquent to work at useful tasks. It was hoped that the inmates, by being forced to work, would learn trades and form industrious habits at the same time.[20]

The House of Correction of San Fernando, located some eight miles outside Madrid, was a perfect example of this kind of institution. Established in the aftermath of the Squillace riots of 1766, it contained a mixed population of vagrants, beggars, and petty offenders of both sexes.[21] There also were paupers, orphans, and, at times, even the insane, but they were always in a minority (in the first six months of 1771, for example, of the 292 persons of both sexes who were sentenced to San Fernando, only 4 percent belonged to that category).[22] In the eighteenth century, these institutions typically combined several different functions within the same establishment. San Fernando was a refuge for orphans, the destitute, and the insane, as well as a penal institution.

From the beginning, all age groups were represented. Extant figures for the year 1771 give some idea of the age distribution.[23] At that date, 43 percent of the men sentenced to San Fernando were over fifty years of age: 29 percent between the ages of fifty and sixty-five, 10 percent in the sixty-five to seventy-five-year-old category, two men over seventy-five years old, and one eighty-four years old. At the other end of the scale, 29 percent of the male inmates consisted of children under fifteen and youths between fifteen and nineteen years of age. The remaining 28 percent were made up of men in the twenty to fifty-year-old group: twenty to thirty-year-olds accounted for 10 percent, thirty to fifty-year-olds for 18 percent. If these statistics are typical, and it seems likely that they are, the overwhelming majority of male inmates in San Fernando were men who were unable to serve in the army or perform hard labor on the fortifications or public works projects because of age or youth.

The female inmates were younger. Most of the women (over 81 percent) were between the ages of fifteen and fifty-five. The largest percentage of the total female population (55 percent) was made up of prisoners fifteen to forty, and the fifteen to twenty-five-year-old group alone accounted for 29 percent. There also was a substantial proportion (26 percent) of middle-aged women, forty to fifty years old. Beyond age fifty-five, the numbers decline sharply. Women in the fifty-five to seventy-five-year-old group represented an insiginificant 8 percent of the total.

The age distribution of the inmates corresponded closely to their offenses. Among the males, those over fifty years old were all beggars, while those in the twenty to fifty-year-old groups were either beggars or vagrants. Most of the children were orphans and paupers, but there were a few beggars as well. The fifteen to twenty-year-old category contained an equal number of beggars, vagrants, and orphans. Significantly, there were only three men who had committed real crimes. They included two youths (fifteen and seventeen years old) who were thieves and one mature man who was sentenced for assault and injury.

The female inmates were divided into two groups: the older women beggars, the younger ones prostitutes. Prostitution was not illegal in the eighteenth century, but periodically the authorities conducted a campaign to remove diseased women from the streets. Quite a few of the women in San Fernando were in the advanced stages of syphilis. Others were arrested on public scandal charges, that is, for having been caught *in flagrante* (conducting their business in public places, most typically the vestibules of private homes or public buildings).[24] Most of the prostitutes were between the ages of twenty and forty years, with the largest percentage in the twenty to twenty-five-year category. Among those fifteen to nineteen years of age there were prostitutes as well as vagrants and beggars. Similarly, the women thirty to fifty years old were either beggars, vagrants, or prostitutes. There also were some married women who had committed adultery and others who had been convicted of licentious behavior and concubinage.

While the majority of San Fernando's inmates in the 1770s were vagrants and beggars, the situation changed in the 1780s, when the Madrid courts began to sentence more delinquents there, especially women. In this period, male petty offenders normally were sent to the public works presidios, but there was no comparable place for women. The *galera,* a penal institution for women modeled after the galleys for men and in operation since the seventeenth century, held mainly major offenders and recidivists, and lacked the resources to receive others.[25] In 1783, when the English penal reformer, John Howard, visited San Fernando, women outnumbered men almost two to one. In the 1790s, the ratio was more than six to one.[26]

When the houses of correction like San Fernando began to take on an increasingly penal character, their original aim, the custody of vagabonds and beggars, was shifted to the *hospicios.* The former became institutions for the confinement and punishment of criminals. As penal institutions, they were not thought of as places where persons served sentences of imprisonment. Instead, they housed offenders sentenced to forced labor, and this concept was held until the end of the eighteenth century.[27] In this period, imprisonment as a punishment was still almost unknown in civil law, despite the efforts of the penal reformers (Cesare Beccaria and his Spanish interpreters, Manuel de Lardizábal, Gaspar Melchor de Jovellanos, and Juan Meléndez Valdés) to substitute it for capital and corporal punishment. Jails, as in previous centuries, continued to be detention centers for those awaiting trial or the execution of their capital or corporal penalties.

Conditions in Spanish jails, like those in other European countries, were notorious for centuries. Squalor, immorality, and idleness, as well as the deep-rooted corruption of wardens and subordinates, made them places of hardship and suffering. Yet, in the opinion of John Howard, one of the most notable penal reformers of the period, prisoners in Spanish jails seemed to have been somewhat better off than inmates in other countries. Howard, who visited a number of Spanish jails in 1783, was impressed with the fact that there existed separation of the sexes (introduced as early as 1519) in contrast to the indiscriminate mixing of male and female prisoners found in other European jails. In addition, he considered the architecture of Spanish jails to be well suited to the needs of the prisoners. Most Spanish jails were constructed with patios equipped with fountains and running water in the center and corridors for shade. Near the fountains were convenient stone troughs where the inmates washed their clothes.[28]

On the negative side, debtors in Spanish jails were not segregated from criminal prisoners, as they were in many other countries. All inmates, regardless of age, record, or type of offense, were kept together. The only separation was between those who had made their declarations and confessed, and those who had yet to do so. The latter were confined together in dirty, unventilated vaults (*encierros*). Frequently, those who persisted in protesting their innocence were laden with chains and placed in solitary confinement in *grilleros* (cages) until they had a change of heart.[29]

The principal officers in every jail were the jailers or keepers, and until 1840 these positions were sold by the Spanish crown to the highest bidder. Sometimes purchasers bought these posts as an investment which they subsequently leased out to others. On other occasions, they appointed deputies to perform their duties. Despite the small salary, the position of jailer was always popular, because it offered excellent opportunities for extortion and graft.[30]

The main source of remuneration for the jailers was the fees that they exacted from the prisoners. In order to secure their incomes, they ran their establishments like business enterprises. The jails functioned through a system of payments for services rendered. Everything the prisoners needed was available for a price. More spacious and cleaner quarters, beds, blankets, and mattresses were rented for a fee. The jailers also sold the prisoners their food and drink, as well as the fuel that they needed to prepare their meals. Prisoners could obtain more or less comfort and service depending on their resources. In addition, there were entrance and release fees.

Until 1788, discharge fees were paid by all prisoners regardless of the outcome of their cases, but in that year the king ordered that payments did not have to be made by persons who were acquitted of their crimes. Discharge fees reflected the socioeconomic status of the prisoners and their ability to pay. In the second half of the eighteenth century, common prisoners in the Madrid jails customarily paid eighteen reales, while the wealthier ones, who were lodged in the more comfortable parts of the jail, paid twenty-four reales. Those who rented rooms in the jailer's own apartment (the best accommodations in the jail) were charged two doubloons.[31]

The fee system in Spanish jails was justified as being the prisoner's contribution toward the cost of running those establishments. It was used to pay the salaries of the jailers, turnkeys, and guards, but also to cover the expenses of upkeep and repair. Authorities justified perpetuation of the fee system by claiming that they lacked sufficient funds to pay the prison staffs and maintain the jails. The most they could do was to keep the fees at reasonable levels. From the fifteenth century on, jailers were required to publically display tables of fees charged in their jails, and the sums that could be demanded were established by law. New fee tables were compiled in 1736, 1741, and 1781, and there were several revisions in the years before the end of the eighteenth century.[32]

In addition to the fees that prisoners had to pay for the services they received, they also had to make a peculiar form of payment, a kind of "garnish," when first admitted to the jails. Unlike the other jail exactions, garnish was arranged and collected by the prisoners themselves. Those who could not pay were liable to having their clothes stripped off them and being subjected to physical violence and ostracism by other prisoners. The most vivid accounts of the garnish system date from the sixteenth and seventeenth centuries and can be found in the picaresque literature of that period, especially Francisco de Quevedo's *El buscón,* but the same system was described by Ventura de Arquellada in 1801. Sporadic attempts were made to eliminate this practice, but most prison officials accepted it as an integral part of the prison life, and it continued well into the nineteenth century.[33]

Security in the jails was achieved through the use of a wide variety of irons, including manacles for the wrists, fetters and shackles for the feet, and iron collars for the neck. Any one of these contraptions could, if necessary, be attached to a ring or staple on the wall or in the floor. When ordered by the court, jailers could remove chains for a fee. The amounts charged were set in the fee tables, but as in the case of other jail payments, the sums varied depending on the circumstances and the ability of the prisoners to pay. In the Madrid jails of the 1780s, they ranged from thirty to forty reales.[34]

One of the best accounts of Spanish jails in the eighteenth century is that of John Howard. Among the jails and other penal institutions that he visited were those of Pamplona, Badajoz, Burgos, Valladolid, and Madrid. In Toledo he viewed two jails: one served as a detention center and the other as a central *depósito* for Castile. He found the *depósito* particularly dirty and crowded. Some 220 prisoners were confined to narrow corridors under a central courtyard, and all were heavily chained and looked unhealthy. The jailers informed him that the *depósito* usually held more prisoners, but that a hundred or more had been sent to the arsenal at Cartagena two weeks earlier. In contrast, the jail belonging to the *Chancillería* in Valladolid did not have any dungeons, and all the prisoners were kept together in one large room. As for the jail at Burgos, it was housed in a new edifice that was constructed especially for that purpose in 1778. It was built around a spacious courtyard with a fountain in the center. While he found it satisfactory from an architectural point of view, he described the cells and dungeons as unclean.[35]

Significantly, the jail in Burgos did not have any official torture chamber. Torture as a means of extracting evidence and confessions was very much a part of criminal procedure in Spain, as in other European countries in the early modern period. In Spain, some of the most common forms of torture—the rack, water torture, and hoist—fell into disuse in the last quarter of the eighteenth century. Indirect methods, such as confinement for long periods of time (often in various kinds of contraptions that hindered movement), took their place. They were used particularly against those accused of heinous crimes who persisted in denying their guilt in the face of incriminating evidence. These methods continued to be employed until 1814, when Ferdinand VII issued a decree abolishing the use of torture, both direct and indirect, to obtain confessions from defendants and evidence from witnesses.[36]

In Madrid, Howard visited the main jails as well as the Prado Public Works Presidio and the San Fernando House of Correction. The two principal jails were the Cárcel de Villa (City Jail) and the Cárcel de Corte (Court Jail).[37] The Cárcel de Villa was the original jail of Madrid. In the sixteenth century it was located in the Plazuela de San Miguel, but this site was abandoned by the end of the century. In 1619, part of a newly constructed city hall was set aside to serve as a jail. The main facade of the city hall opened on to the Plaza de la Villa. The jail was located in the rear of the building facing a narrow street called the Calle de Madrid. The City Jail remained at this site until 1833, when its deteriorated condition forced its closing and the transfer of its inmates to another location.[38]

The Cárcel de Villa was built around a courtyard and had a capacity of 150 to 200 prisoners. When Howard visited it is 1783, there were about 120 men and thirty women there. He described the rooms and dungeons as very dirty and offensive. The main dungeon, popularly called *El infierno,* was completely dark. In order to obtain some light, the inmates made candles out of filaments of thread unravelled from their clothing and lard taken from their food. Conditions in this jail were so bad that when it finally was abandoned in the nineteenth century, the authorities could not find any way to clean it up, and were forced to demolish the whole structure.[39]

The Cárcel de Corte was the largest jail in Madrid. It was located in the Plaza de Provincia in a building that was constructed in 1634 to serve as a courthouse for the *Sala de Alcades de Casa y Corte* as well as a jail. The *Sala de Alcaldes de Casa y Corte*, a committee of the council of Castile, exercised judicial control over the city of Madrid. It was divided into criminal and civil sections, and the Sala for crime had final jurisdiction over all crime in Madrid and its environs within a radius of five leagues.[40]

Originally, the Cárcel de Corte housed noble and distinguished prisoners, but in the eighteenth century there were all kinds of offenders. Even today the building's two storeys have an elegant appearance. The facade is flanked by two towers, and the main entrance is reinforced by a third section, the front of which runs the full height of the structure. An enormous royal coat of arms breaks up the cornice. In the eighteenth century there were spacious hearing rooms and court chambers on the top for the *Sala de Alcaldes de Casa y Corte*. The whole ground floor was given over to the Court Jail. There were two patios, one of which was paved and had arches on two sides and a fountain in the middle. Most of the male prisoners (all those who had completed their declarations) spent their days in this courtyard, and Howard was impressed when he saw many of them washing their clothes at the stone troughs near the fountain. At night, they were confined to dungeons some twenty-two steps down from the patio. In one of the dungeons there were beds that the jailer rented to prisoners who could pay him one and one-half reales a night. There also were rooms for which six doubloons were paid in advance, together with one and one-half reales per night. In addition, the jailer had accommodations in his own quarters that he could let out to selected wealthy prisoners at twenty-five doubloons per man for the period of their confinement. As for the women

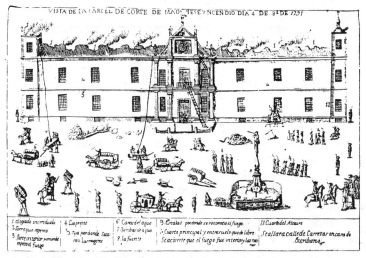

A view of the Cárcel de Corte in Madrid showing the fire of 1791. On the right-hand side of the illustration note the evacuation of the prisoners, male and female. Source: original in the Museo Municipal, Madrid; reproduced in Federico Sainz de Robles, *Historia y estampas de la villa de Madrid* (Madrid: Iberia-Joaquín Gil, 1933), vol. 1, p. 381.

prisoners, until the reforms at the end of the century, they were all confined together in one large room. None wore chains, since it was established practice in early modern Spain not to place irons on women. They had their own infirmary, as did the men. At the time of Howard's visit, the number of prisoners in the Court Jail totaled 180, with 140 men and forty women.[41]

Whereas the fee system allowed wealthy prisoners to obtain a scale of comfort and service graduated according to how much money they were paying, the poor lived out their days of incarceration in misery and squalor. Since there were no regular prison rations, penniless prisoners had to depend on charity and occasional free issues on religious holidays. More than one provision of this kind did exist. Although inmates ordinarily were not allowed to beg from the sides of the jails, a few inmates (on behalf of all) were permitted to do so on Thursday and Friday of Easter week. In addition, collection boxes were placed for this purpose outside the jails. This fund was administered by the jail chaplain and a specially appointed official known as the *procurador de pobres* who served as an attorney for the poor and destitute prisoners. The sums that were collected were distributed to the inmates either in cash or in food so as to provide them with additional nourishment for the Easter holidays.[42]

Poor prisoners also were assisted by individuals and societies that made charitable donations for this purpose. Many private persons, in particular the noble and wealthy, left them bequests in their wills. Furthermore, from the sixteenth century onward there existed in many cities charitable organizations that were devoted specifically to the assistance of poor and needy prisoners. In the eighteenth century other societies came into being, and two of the most important were in Madrid.[43] They were the Asociación de Señoras and the Asociación de la Caridad. The Asociación de Señoras, established in 1787, was an organization of noblewomen dedicated to the task of visiting the jails and aiding women prisoners, spiritually and materially. The Asociación de la Caridad, founded in 1799 by the Count of Miranda, performed the same services for male prisoners. Both organizations distributed alms, food, clothing, and blankets to prisoners, in addition to providing religious instruction.[44]

While the principal aims of these associations were religious and charitable, they also worked to effect reform of the jails. By this time, the ideas of Cesare Beccaria had entered Spain. Their most famous proponent was Manuel de Lardizábal, who in 1782 published his *Discurso sobre las penas* on the subject. This work constituted the doctrinal basis for Spanish penal reform. Like Beccaria, Lardizábal and other Spanish reformers rejected the death penalty in favor of punitive imprisonment and advocated the principle that the penalty must fit the crime. Lardizábal went further than any other reformer. While accepting the utilitarian and intimidatory purpose of the penalty, he emphasized the correction of offenders as the ultimate objective.[45]

The work of the Madrid associations must be viewed against the background of the writings of Lardizábal and the other criminal law reformers, but their main inspiration came from John Howard. Howard had a definite conception of how jails should be reformed. Prison buildings should provide sufficient security, but also have spacious rooms and sanitary conditions. Officials should be appointed and salaried under the supervision of some public authority. Inmates must be fed a healthy diet and given suitable education and religious instruction. Howard considered useful labor to be the essence of sound prison discipline, and believed that facilities for it should be provided in every jail.[46]

In the 1780s, the activities of the Asociación de Señoras were a faithful reflection of the ideas of Howard and the other reformers. Its earliest efforts were directed toward the classification and separation of prisoners to eliminate the pernicious effects of the indiscriminate mixing of inmates of all ages and crimes. This was done in the belief that segregation was the essential first step in bringing about the rehabilitation of offenders. The Asociación sponsored the establishment of a department for youthful female offenders (ten to sixteen years) in the Cárcel de Corte. This department, known as the *Sala de Corrección*, functioned on the principals of "seclusion, regulated labor and religious instruction." At the same time, another special department was set up in the same jail where pregnant women received special care.[47]

The Asociación de Señoras and, after 1799, the Asociación de la Caridad, believed like Howard that work was the main correctional tool. Both organizations introduced remunerative labor, which offered the inmates the opportunity to earn some money and to learn a useful trade. They purchased the necessary raw materials and set up workshops. Instructors and supervisors paid by the Associations were brought in to oversee the work. Finally, the Associations sold the goods that were produced and distributed the proceeds among the inmates.[48]

The work program initiated by the Madrid Associations was a voluntary one; prisoners could not be compelled to participate, because the jails were still detention centers. Only a small percentage of the inmates chose to work. For example, in the last six months of 1799, according to a report of the Asociación de Señoras, there were on the average ten prisoners enrolled in the program in the Cárcel de Corte out of a total of some fifty female inmates, and the ratio in the Cárcel de Villa was even smaller (three out of thirty prisoners).[49] After the turn of the century, when it became clear that the voluntary program was not successful, the Associations began to press for a reformed prison system based on compulsory labor as the principal means for rehabilitation. With the adoption of punitive imprisonment in the nineteenth century, the program of the Associations was enacted.[50] The prisons became workshops, and the forced labor characteristic of the houses of correction and the presidios became the rehabilitative labor of the modern prison systems.

# 5

# The Peninsular Naval
# Arsenals

Improvements in naval technology, rather than a change in penological methods, led to the abolition of the galleys in 1748. Compared with the sailing warships then in use, the galleys were no longer redoubtable. But the galleys were more than fighting ships, for they served the Spanish monarchy as an important penal institution—a place where large numbers of offenders could be confined to work for the benefit of the state. With their disappearance, some alternative had to be devised, since neither the mines of Almadén nor the North African presidios could take their place. The naval arsenals of the Peninsula eventually provided a replacement for the galleys, but this solution was not adopted immediately, even though a precedent had already been set at the end of the seventeenth century with the use ashore of *forzados* and slaves from the galleys. It was not until after 1765 that serious offenders began to be sentenced to the arsenals in substantial numbers, and their formal organization as presidios did not come until 1771.

The years immediately following the dissolution of the galleys were characterized by experimentation. Several expedients were tried, and a definite policy did not emerge until much later. To begin with, provision had to be made for the *forzados* and slaves still remaining aboard the now unserviceable galleys. A decree of January 1749 provided for a distribution of the *forzados*. Lifers were to be sent to the mines of Almadén, while those with term sentences of more than one year, or with the note of "retention" in their sentences, were assigned to the North African presidios. Finally, all prisoners with less than one year to serve were to be set free with the stipulation that they be banished for two years from the regions where they had committed their crimes. Despite this legislation, the courts continued to sentence men to the galleys, and in June 1749 (repeated the following October) the king ordered all offenders meriting the penalty of the galleys sentenced to the mines of Almadén while the rest were to be sent to the North African presidios.[1]

As for the slaves, the abolition of the galleys brought little change to their daily existence. The fact that they no longer had to pull the oars was meaningless, because in the eighteenth century the galleys went out on campaign infrequently. During this period the galleys remained in port almost all the time, and the slaves and *forzados* labored ashore in the navy yards and port areas. With the suppression of the galleys in 1748, the slaves continued to perform the same tasks as before, and in Cartagena were housed aboard the galleys now permanently moored as hulks in the harbor.[2] Their labor, supplemented by that of free contract workers, was considered sufficient to meet the normal needs of the navy.

The decision of the government in 1750 to begin construction on the naval arsenals of El Ferrol (Galicia) and Cartagena, as well as to expand the facilities at La Carraca (Cádiz), altered these plans. The new projects required the mobilization of large numbers of unskilled workers at the lowest possible cost, conditions ideally suited to penal labor. Because of security problems, the government was reluctant to send hard-core offenders into the arsenals. For that reason, it was not until after 1765, when problems in the North African presidios (overcrowding and desertion) came to a head, that a policy change was made.

In the 1750s and 1760s the government attempted to satisfy the labor needs of the arsenals with vagrants, gypsies, and other "undesirables" impressed into service in the forced levies (see table 5.1).[3] In September, 1749, an order was issued to send 600 gypsies, imprisoned in the castle of Alicante under the decree of 1749 providing for their arrest and application to forced labor, to work in the

Table 5.1. *Desterrados,* Slaves and Gypsies in the Arsenal of Cartagena, 1755–62

| Year | Number of Prisoners | Deaths (per year) |
|------|---------------------|-------------------|
| 1755 | 1,356 | 88 |
| 1756 | 1,300 | 36 |
| 1757 | 1,227 | 28 |
| 1758 | 1,496 | 70 |
| 1759 | 1,919 | 150 |
| 1760 | 1,814 | 86 |
| 1761 | 1,920 | 51 |
| 1762 | 1,814 | 32 |
| Total | 12,846 | 541 |

Source: AGS, Marina, leg. 708, Oct. 10,1773.

arsenal of Cartagena with the slaves already employed there.[4] The following year they were joined by the first contingents of vagabonds to arrive in Cartagena. During the initial two years of construction, the gypsies and vagrants worked as manual laborers, but after 1751 they began to be utilized in a variety of skilled and semiskilled tasks in the arsenal and navy yard, especially in the fabrication of materials necessary for sailing ships. To facilitate their use in a wide range of occupations in the arsenal, they were made to wear ankle fetters only. This was in contrast to the slaves and other prisoners who, in addition to their fetters, where chained together in pairs. The use only of ankle fetters encouraged escape, since the fetters could easily be removed and prisoners were able to slip out of the arsenal unnoticed among the free laborers, who served as foremen and master craftsmen, when they left their work at nightfall. Efforts to restrain the vagrants and gypsies through the application of chains in addition to the fetters proved unsuccessful. In the first place, it made them unserviceable for many of the jobs they were doing. Secondly, the legality of the practice was questionable, because customarily only serious offenders were chained in this manner. A flood of complaints led to the abolition of the practice in 1769.[5]

The failure to resolve the security problems involved in the use of vagrants and idlers led to their eventual withdrawal from the arsenals. Other factors that influenced royal policymakers to revise their plans concerning these elements included the poor quality of their work and the growing conviction that the program to convert them

flooding. In the 1760s and 1770s this was the principal occupation of the slaves, and the royal order of 1765 specifically stated that the strongest prisoners were to be assigned to the pumps. The labor of the pumps was so strenuous that eventually it became the maximum penalty in the category of hard labor and was reserved for slaves and for those found guilty of the most heinous crimes. Finally, in 1771 a decree formally established presidios in the naval arsenals and recognized them as being the replacement for the galleys.[9]

The law of 1771 not only had the immediate practical effect of creating presidios in the arsenals, but proved to be one of the most significant events in the history of Spanish penal legislation, because it incorporated key reform ideas current at the time. Most important among them was the separation of offenders into classes according to their crimes. Eighteenth-century penal reformers placed great emphasis on the need to separate prisoners so as to remove the lesser offenders from the hardened criminals. This was the message of Lardizábal's *Discurso de las penas*, which originally was prepared on royal orders in 1770, and served as the basis for the law of 1771. In the legislation of 1771, the principle of the separation of offenders was adopted mainly because it was considered to be the best means to deal with the problem of continued desertion of prisoners from the North African presidios to the Moslems. By dividing prisoners into classes according to the gravity of their crimes, and by assigning those of the first category (minor and first offenders) to North Africa and those of the second category (serious offenders and recidivists) to the arsenals, it was hoped that those thought capable of deserting to the Moslems and becoming renegades (second category) would be prevented from doing so.

The concept that the penalty must be commensurate with the crime also was incorporated into the legislation of 1771. Prisoners in the first category were to be applied to the labor of the fortifications and other similar tasks in the presidios. On the other hand, the most difficult and fatiguing work, such as the operation of the chain pumps, was reserved for prisoners in the second category, who were to perform it chained together in pairs.[10] As for the problem of indeterminate sentences, before 1771 they often were imposed, but desperation caused by fear of interminable imprisonment led to frequent escapes. In order to prevent prisoners from resorting to desperate measures, it was decided to restrict sentences to a ten-year maximum and to require judicial authorities to indicate fixed terms in their sentences. Finally, the legislation of 1771 established a system of distribution of prisoners among the three naval arsenals. Accordingly, offenders sentenced by the *Chancillería* of Valladolid, the *Audiencias* of Galicia and Asturias, and the Royal Council of Navarre, in addition to all other magistrates within those jurisdictions, were to be sent to the arsenal of El Ferrol. Prisoners from Andalusia, Extremadura, and the Canary Islands were destined for La Carraca, while Cartagena was to receive those originating from New Castile, Murcia, and the Kingdom of Aragon.[11]

With the law of 1771 the naval arsenals became the principal Peninsular penal establishments, and they remained so until their suppression in the early years of the nineteenth century. The number of prisoners who served in these arsenals can never be determined, but it is known that in the first seven years of operation a total of 12,846 men labored at Cartagena.[12] As for the prisoner population at any given time, only scattered statistics are available, and they are difficult to use because the categories employed to describe the prisoners are not clear. The terms *desterrados* and *presidiarios,* although clearly defined by the first half of the eighteenth century in the North African presidios, were still used interchangeably in the naval arsenals until the end of the century. In the beginning, vagrants and idlers impressed into forced labor in the arsenals by the levies were called *desterrados.* This term was the same used for those sentenced to serve at arms in the North African presidios in the eighteenth century. It was applied to the vagrants sent into the arsenals because originally they, too, were destined for military service, but were disqualified for reasons of age, poor health, or other factors. In the 1760s with the arrival of the serious offenders, the expression *desterrados por crímenes* was adopted to distinguish them from the *desterrados por la leva*—the vagrants and idlers. Finally, in the late 1770s the term *presidiarios* began to be applied to all prisoners with the exception of the remaining vagrants, who continued to be called *desterrados.* Nevertheless, in common practice, arsenal officials continued to use the two terms synonymously until the end of the century.[13]

In addition to confusing terminology, careless errors in calculation as well as purposeful distortion of the figures should be considered when analyzing prisoner statistics. Presidio administrators often changed the figures to suit their purposes. A good example of this occurred in 1761, when administrators were anxious to disprove the complaints by the North African states that Moslem slaves in the arsenal of Cartagena were being abused. By juggling the numbers for slaves and *presidiarios*, they could effectively lower the mortality rates for slaves, and then argue on the basis of the "figures" that the Moslem slaves were being treated well (compare the statistics in tables 5.3 and 5.4).

Despite the fragmentary nature of the quantitative data and the problems involved in its use, the figures in table 5.7 are useful for obtaining an approximate estimate of the prisoner population in the arsenal of Cartagena in the period 1761–1818. According to these figures, the number of *presidiarios* reached its highest point in 1786, when there were 2,530, after which there was a slow decline into the early years of the nineteenth century. Although the completion of the major construction work in 1782 and the abolition of the penalty of the chain pumps after 1787 reduced the need for penal laborers at Cartagena, this was not reflected in the figures, which remained at high levels. In the period 1786–1800, the courts continued to sentence convicted criminals to the arsenals, because they

Table 5.3. Mortality Rates at Cartagena, 1761

|  | *Presidiarios* (N = 841)* | Slaves (N = 982)* |
|---|---|---|
| Janurary | 7 | 4 |
| February | 7 | 2 |
| March | 4 | 4 |
| April | 7 | 6 |
| May | 4 | 1 |
| June | 5 | 2 |
| July | 4 | 1 |
| August | 3 | 3 |
| Total | 41 | 23 |

*These figures for *presidiarios* and slaves disagree with those in AGS, Marina (see table 5.4).

Source: AGS, Guerra Moderna, leg. 706, Aug. 24, 1761.

Table 5.4. *Presidiarios* and Slaves in the Arsenal of Cartagena, 1761–1818 (selected years)

| Year | Presidiarios | Slaves | Total |
|------|-------------|--------|-------|
| 1761 | 933 | 871 | 1,924* |
| 1767 | 1,461 | — | 1,461 |
| 1771 | 1,568 | 491 | 2,059 |
| 1779 | 1,621 | 223 | 1,844 |
| 1786 | 2,423 | 107 | 2,530 |
| 1800 | 2,114 | — | 2,114 |
| 1802 | 2,201 | — | 2,201 |
| 1807 | 1,000 | — | 1,000 |
| 1818 | 10 | — | 10 |

*Total for 1761 includes 120 gypsies.
Source: AGS, Marina, leg. 697, Feb. 16, 1779; leg. 699, Mar. 30, 1761; Apr. 1, 1767; leg. 700, Jan. 8, 1771; Sevilla y Solanas, *Historia penitenciaria*, pp. 204, 209; Lasala Navarro, *Galeotes y presidiarios*, p. 114; Salillas, *Evolución penitenciaria*, p. 14.

could not be accommodated in the North African presidios (especially after the loss of Oran in 1792), nor could they be sent to the public works presidios, reserved for minor offenders. This situation came to an end in 1807, when the king ordered that in the future no more offenders should be sent to the arsenals, because their labor was no longer necessary there.[14] Eleven years later, the naval presidios were abolished.

As for La Carraca and El Ferrol, the extant statistics are too few to permit analysis other than to state that the average *presidiario* population in both arsenals ranged from 500 to 800, and may have reached 1,000 at La Carraca (including prisoners in the *depósito*) by the end of the eighteenth century.[15] Both arsenals had *depósitos* that were centers of distribution for the New World presidios. The *depósito* at La Carraca was particularly important, usually holding 100 or more prisoners who were awaiting transportation from Cádiz to Spanish America. There also was a *depósito* at Cartagena which held prisoners destined for the presidios of North Africa and the New World; it served, too, as a "holding pen" for prisoners rejected from other presidios, or those not admitted to military or naval service for lack of qualifications.[16]

In the naval arsenals, as on the galleys, the main concerns continued to be security and utility. In the beginning, the same officials

A view of the city, port, and arsenal of Cartagena in 1778. The barracks housing the *presidiarios* can be seen in the upper right-hand corner (no. 8). From: Bernardo Espinalt y García, *Atlante español* (Madrid: P. Aznar, 1778), p. 74. Courtesy of the Hispanic Society of America, New York.

(*alguaciles*) who guarded the *forzados* and slaves on the galleys were transferred to the arsenals. As the prisoner population increased, the *alguaciles* proved insufficient in numbers to deal with the situation, while their notorious greed and corruption provoked criticism that led to an attempt to replace them. In 1754 a contingent of marine guards composed of veterans was established in the arsenal of Cartagena, and eventually similar units were formed in the other arsenals. While the purpose of this measure was to eliminate the *alguaciles*, it proved impossible to do so, and they continued to exist alongside the marine guards.[17] The new system provided some extra protection, but real security was impossible because of the disproportion in numbers between guards and prisoners. In 1761, for example, there were 154 guards for 1,942 prisoners at Cartagena, that is, one guard for every twelve prisoners, and at that time the arsenal was not completely enclosed. By 1773 a wall had been built around the whole arsenal complex, but the marine unit had been reduced to sixty men. If in the 1770s and 1780s there was a decline in the number of escapes, this was a reflection of the change in the kind of prisoners and the heavy application of chains rather than any increase in the effectiveness, or number, of the security force.[18]

In addition to security, another important concern on the galleys was utility. On oar-driven vessels, the physical condition of the prisoners was important precisely because they were needed to work the oars, that is, their utility depended on it. This was one of the most significant aspects of the galleys and distinguished them from other prisons in the period. No matter how debased it might have been in practice, this tradition was continued in the arsenals. Arsenal rules, like the galley ordinances, protected prisoners from arbitrary punishments and afforded equal treatment to all, regardless of status. Nevertheless, in the arsenals as on the galleys, there was more concern for the Moslem slaves than for the convicts. Although the motives were economic (convicts were expendable and slaves were not), in the 1760s they became political as well. The North African states made it clear that they would not honor their treaty commitments with Spain and would retaliate in kind against Spanish captives in North Africa in return for mistreatment of Moslems enslaved in Spain. As a result, conditions of Moslem slaves in the arsenals gradually improved. Bodily mutilations (cutting off of ears and noses) that were inflicted on slaves as punishments on the galleys and continued in the arsenals in the 1750s were eliminated, and the same penalties (mainly flogging) applied to slaves as the *presidiarios*. Slaves were allowed to correspond with families and friends in North Africa, and presidio officials were prohibited from interfering with the free flow of correspondence.[19] There also existed in Cartagena a cemetery for Moslem slaves. In addition, they were given the use of a building where they conducted the rites related to interment. Despite opposition from the town and ecclesiastical authorities, who claimed that it was really a mosque, it operated freely for thirty-seven years. In 1770 the Inquisition succeeded in having it torn down, but four years later, under pressure from the North African states who retaliated against Christian churches in their territories, it was rebuilt.[20] Given the circumstances, the remaining slaves in the arsenal in the 1780s were treated with far less rigor than were the *presidiarios*.

Although the arsenals continued the methods of administration used on the galleys, there were some changes. Among the most important was a reorganization of the "system of chains." Under the new system, troops accompanied the chains, and the conductors were always army officers in active service or veterans. The conductors were better paid. They received a salary of twenty reales per day for the round trip, and before leaving they were allotted an advance from the royal treasury calculated to cover all the expenses of the trip. Upon their return, an accounting was made, but with few exceptions the sums advanced were either adequate or only slightly less than the actual cost (see table 5.5). When there was a large disparity, padding of accounts can be assumed. This was not difficult to do, since mules and carts had to be rented and food purchased along the way, and prices varied in different regions. As for the food, the daily ration prescribed for the convicts was equivalent to sixteen cuartos (sixty-four maravedís) per man, but the actual amount of food they received depended more on its cost. When prices were high, they were given less than their standard allotment.

In addition to food and transportation costs, another large item in the total budget was salaries for the officers and troops accompany-

Table 5.5. Expenditures for Two Chains, Madrid–Cartagena, 1793 and 1797

| Item | Cost (in reales) | |
|---|---|---|
| | July, 1793 | July, 1797 |
| Food* | 7,873 | 2,528 |
| Carts and mules | 4,704 | 3,484 |
| Salaries | 5,999 | 6,085 |
| Other expenses | 2,956 | 5,438 |
| Total | 21,532 | 17,535 |
| Sum advance | 24,000 | 16,000 |
| Difference | 2,468 | 1,535 |

*Cost of food fluctuated in relation to the number of prisoners. July, 1793: Madrid–Toledo, 85; Toledo–Murcia, 187; Murcia–Cartagena, 186. July, 1797: Madrid–Toledo, 48; Toledo–Murcia, 57; Murcia–Cartagena, 58.

Source: AGS, Secretaría de Hacienda, leg. 978, July 26, 1793; July 27, 1797.

ing the chain. The troops were divided into cavalry and infantry units. Their numbers depended on the size of the chain, but on the average there was one soldier for every three convicts. In the case of larger chains, additional troops drawn from veteran units were added for increased security. The soldiers received sixteen cuartos and their officers four reales a day per man, respectively. Salaries also were paid to a cook (four reales a day) and to a functionary in charge of the chains and irons worn by the prisoners. The latter received six reales a day for forty days, since he was required to return the equipment to its place of origin.[21]

The chains were dispatched in the spring and fall of each year. May and October eventually were fixed as regular months of departure for the annual general chains, but smaller ones were sent out at other times whenever it was necessary to reduce the number of prisoners in the *depósitos*.[22] Lack of continuous records makes it difficult to determine mortality rates for the chains, but it seems likely that the average ranged between 1 and 3 percent. Instances of sickness and high mortality usually were related to poor health among prisoners as a result of long periods of incarceration in jails, or severe weather encountered along the route, rather than conditions on the chains themselves. For example, on the chain from Madrid to Cartagena in October 1797, out of a total of 242 prisoners, fifteen died en route and two remained hospitalized in one of the towns along the way. In this case, 158 convicts who were added to the Madrid chain in Toledo had arrived there only recently from Valladolid. Apparently they had contracted some infectious disease in the Valladolid jail. Two days after leaving Toledo, one of the prisoners from Valladolid died, and from that point forward every day brought another death.[23] Weather was another factor of great importance. Chains that were dispatched from Madrid to Cartagena during the summer months often met such extreme heat en route that prisoners had to be supplied with water jars so as to prevent them from fainting from heat prostration and lack of water. Such conditions forced a reduction of pace, and sometimes the trip lasted twenty-eight days.[24]

Despite reorganization and more careful supervision of the chains, it was difficult to eliminate the long-established abuses. Complaints by prisoners about bad treatment on the road, particularly about the malpractices of the conductors, were frequent. Conductors were accused of accepting bribes for better treatment, cheating on food rations, inflicting arbitrary punishments, and misappropriating funds. When investigations of complaints were conducted, they almost always resulted in the vindication of the conductors.[25] Hence, while conditions undoubtedly were better in the second half of the eighteenth century than before, prisoners still were at the mercy of the conductors.

The itineraries followed by the chains were the same as those used in previous centuries. Toledo remained the main *depósito* and distributing center for Castile, although most chains for Cartagena now originated in Madrid and contained a large number of prisoners from the jails of that city. Prisoners condemned to the arsenal of Cartagena from the north and northwest (Galicia, Asturias, Old Castile) were sent first to Valladolid, and from there, in company with those sentenced in Valladolid, they were dispatched to Toledo.[26] There they were placed in the *depósito* where they awaited the formation of a chain for Cartagena. Most often they were added to a chain from Madrid, and together, under the command of the Madrid conductor and his troops, they proceeded to Cartagena. From Toledo the chain moved southeastward through the bleak uplands of La Mancha to the town of Albacete—a trip of thirteen days. From there they traveled southward to Murcia (six days) along a road that dropped at one point some 2,000 feet within a distance of ninety miles. They covered the last part of the journey, from Murcia to Cartagena, in one day.

The trip from Madrid to Cartagena in the eighteenth century took twenty-four days, and given the distance between the two points (according to their route), it is possible to estimate an average daily march of twelve miles, weather and other conditions permitting. When crossing the dry rough plateau country between Toledo and Albacete the chain moved at a slower pace, however. By the time they reached Murcia, most prisoners experienced general physicial exhaustion. The gradual deterioration in the health and strength of the men is reflected in the steady increase in the number of carts utilized for the trip from Toledo to Murcia, especially after Albacete (see table 5.6). From Albacete to Murcia the speed was increased to seventeen miles a day, with the prisoners riding most of the time.

Finally, all prisoners rode in carts in order to cover the last thirty-one miles between Murcia and Cartagena in one day.

For men who survived the rigors of imprisonment and the long trek to Cartagena, conditions in the arsenals were harsh, but supportable. At Cartagena, before 1773 they were housed aboard the decaying galley hulks; in 1773 a barracks was built for them.[27] At El Ferrol and La Carraca they were lodged in barracks from the

Table 5.6. Carts, Mules, and Carriage Costs for the Chain, Madrid–Cartagena, July, 1793*

| Leg of Journey | Leagues** | Carts | Mules | Cost (reales) |
|---|---|---|---|---|
| Madrid–Getafe | 2 | 4 | 16 | 60 |
| Getafe–Torrejón | 2 | 3 | 20 | 75 |
| Torrejón–Yuncos | 3 | 5 | 20 | 112.5 |
| Yuncos–Cabañas | 2 | 7 | 28 | 105 |
| Cabañas–Toledo | 3 | 7 | 28 | 157.5 |
| Toledo–Almonacid | 3 | 8 | 32 | 180 |
| Almonacid–Manzaneque | 3 | 10 | 40 | 225 |
| Manzaneque–Madridejos | 5 | 10 | 20 | 225 |
| Madridejos–Villafranca | 3 | 10 | 20 | 135 |
| Villafranca–Campo de Criptana | 3 | 10 | 20 | 135 |
| Campo de Criptana–Pedro Múñoz | 3 | 10 | 20 | 90 |
| Pedro Múñoz–Socuéllamos | 3 | 10 | 20 | 90 |
| Socuéllamos–Villarrobledo | 3 | 10 | 20 | 135 |
| Villarrobledo–Minaya | 3 | 10 | 20 | 135 |
| Minaya–La Roda | 3 | 12 | 24 | 162 |
| La Roda–La Jineta | 3 | 11 | 22 | 148.5 |
| La Jineta–Albacete | 3 | 12 | 24 | 162 |
| Albacete–Chincilla | 3 | 12 | 24 | 108 |
| Chinchilla–Tobarra | 5 | 12 | 24 | 270 |
| Tobarra–Jumilla | 5 | 12 | 24 | 270 |
| Jumilla–Cieza | 5 | 12 | 24 | 270 |
| Cieza–Molina | 5 | 14 | 28 | 315 |
| Molina–Murcia | 2 | 23 | 46 | 207 |
| Murcia–Cartagena | 9 | 23 | 46 | 931.5 |
| Total, Madrid–Cartagena | | | | 4704.0 |

*Chain from Madrid to Toledo, 101 prisoners; Toledo–Cartagena, 187.
**One Spanish league = 5.5 kilometers.
Source: AGS, Secretaría de Hacienda, leg. 978, July 26, 1793.

beginning. Later on, an edifice called the Casa de Cuatro Torres (because of its characteristic four corner towers) was built at La Carraca to serve as their jail. This building, large enough to house 2,000 prisoners, was divided into two sections. The main part served as living quarters for the *presidiarios,* while the towers contained offices and rooms for the foremen and guards. Most of the area designed for the prisoners was taken up with lines of wooden bunks where they slept with their shackles fastened to chains attached to iron rings on the wall.[28] Some of the more fortunate had straw bedding, but because of the danger of fire the authorities were reluctant to allow straw beds. Only at El Ferrol, where climatic conditions kept their clothes permanently dampened, were the *presidiarios* given blankets. This was done so that they could remove their clothes at night to permit drying. As for sanitary conditions, at La Carraca, for example, the *presidiarios* shared their living space with six pigs that belonged to one of the guards.[29] Yet squalid circumstances of this kind were not unusual among the poor in the eighteenth century, and this was the class from which almost all of these men were drawn.

In the 1750s the diet of the *presidiarios* and slaves in the arsenals remained basically the same as on the galleys. Their daily fare still consisted of vegetable stews and bread in the form of biscuit, but there were two important differences. Rising bread prices by the mid-eighteenth century had caused a reduction in the daily ration from twenty-six to twenty-four ounces per man, while lower prices for wine led to its introduction (one pint a day per man) in place of water, the standard beverage on the galleys. Wine in the eighteenth century became a cheap foodstuff and an excellent source of calories when bread was expensive or unavailable.[30]

There was a slight improvement in the food ration in the last quarter of the century due to changes in the methods of distribution (see table 5.7). Originally, following the practice of the galleys, only two meals a day were provided, worth a total of twenty-two maravedís. The remaining twelve maravedís of the one real that the king had designated for the daily maintenance of the *presidiarios* was given to them in cash. It was expected that they would use it to purchase additional food, but most bought tobacco or gambled the money away. In order to provide them with a more balanced diet, the officials at Cartagena began to assign the whole sum of one real for food. In 1765 they introduced this practice for those working at the pumps, and by the early 1770s it was extended to the rest of the *presidiarios*.[31] In this way, they created a third meal (breakfast) out of the surplus twelve maravedís, but the sum total of food per day remained the same. The new system secured a better distribution of the same amount of edibles rather than providing better nutrition.

In contrast to Cartagena, the system of three meals a day was not introduced at La Carraca even though a commission investigating conditions there in 1777 urged its adoption.[32] The same committee reported that the midday meal at that arsenal consisted of a plate of beans that was full of worms and vermin. At night the prisoners received a stew of rice and chickpeas (reportedly "as hard as bullets"). There were many *presidiarios* who did not eat their daily ration, and instead purchased food with the twelve maravedís that they received in cash. In the opinion of the investigators, this was the cause of their chronic malnutrition and illness, because twelve maravedís could not provide sufficient sustenance. Despite the recommendations of this commission, the system of two meals a day was continued at La Carraca. At El Ferrol only one meal a day was

Table 5.7.  Diet of the *Presidiarios* in the Arsenal of Cartagena in the Eighteenth Century

| Year | Item | Daily Ration (per man) | Cost of Daily Ration |
|------|------|------------------------|----------------------|
| 1752 | Biscuit | 24 ounces | 22 maravedís* |
|      | Beans | 7 ounces | |
|      | (or Chickpeas) | 6 ounces | |
|      | Wine | 1 pint | |
| 1777** | Biscuit | 24 ounces | 1 real |
|      | Beans | 11 ounces | |
|      | Rice | 3 ounces | |
|      | Wine | 1 pint | |

*Until 1765, *presidiarios* were also given twelve maravedís in cash, for a total expenditure of one real.

**Records for 1792 show the same items, quantities, and costs as for 1777.

Source: AGS, Marina, leg. 694, Aug. 16, 1752; leg. 697, Aug. 30, 1777; Salillas, *Evolución penitenciaria*, 2:149.

provided, and prisoners were expected to purchase additional food with the rest of the sum allowed them.[33]

Although the presidio ration was based on bread and beans and was totally lacking in meat, this did not make it inadequate from a dietary point of view in the eighteenth century. In this period there were marked differences in meat consumption according to social classes, as well as variations among regions and between towns and countryside. Urban meat consumption totals tended to be higher than rural ones, but here, too, there was considerable variety. Vincente Vizcaíno Pérez, an eighteenth-century economic thinker, claimed that the unskilled working class as a whole lived permanently on a diet of bread and vegetables and rarely or never consumed meat.[34]

Some idea of how the presidio ration compared with the daily fare of free workers can be derived from a survey of conditions among the bakers of Madrid in the year 1767–1768.[35] Since the objectives of this investigation were fiscal, that is, to fix bread prices, a certain amount of exaggeration on the plus rather than minus side must be allowed. It was reported that all workers in the bakeries were given three meals a day in the form of identical stews. The average stew contained, per man, two ounces of meat, two ounces of chickpeas, one third of an ounce of bacon, and a sprinkling of olive oil plus seasonings. The stews of the workers, while slightly more varied and flavorful, were not much better nutritionally than those of the *presidiarios*.

As on the galleys, fraud and corruption reduced both the qaulity and quantity of the rations. In 1752 the prisoners at Cartagena claimed that they only received twenty-two ounces of bread, and that it was so hard and stale that they had to crush it with a stone or soak it before it could be eaten. They described their main meal as a watery stew with a handful of spoiled beans. Twenty years later the same complaints were being made. In 1772 the *presidiarios* at Cartagena asserted that their bread ration was short and that the stews contained fewer beans than required. They estimated that the individual stew rations were not worth more than two maravedís each— at least that was the price for which they were sold by those not able or willing to eat them.[36] In 1783 circumstances were still the same. In a petition of that year, prisoners complained that the food that they actually received was less than the official ration and that it was of inferior quality.[37]

While the presidio ration was supportable by eighteenth-century standards, it was nutritionally deficient, especially for the amount of labor being performed. Prisoners worked from dawn to dusk with a brief respite for lunch at midday. Frequently they were required to work on holidays, particularly in the early days of major construction at the arsenals and, later on, at such tasks as picking oakum in their barracks.[38] They performed their labor while wearing chains, that is, chained together in pairs and with fetters on their feet. These chains, weighing several pounds, hindered their movements and limited their output. In 1772 the intendant of Cartagena reported to the king that the labor of two *presidiarios* was scarcely equivalent to that of one free worker.[39] Any kind of work performed while wearing chains required extra food whereas the presidio ration only provided for the bare needs of existence.

The *presidiarios* and slaves who worked the chain pumps were an exception. In consideration of the severity of their work, they received a larger gratuity of twelve cuartos or forty-eight reales from the beginning, but only eight cuartos of this sum was invested in their food. In 1765, officials at Cartagena, convinced that this food allowance was inadequate, began to allot all twelve cuartos for rations. In that year there were 390 prisoners assigned to the thirteen chain pumps at that arsenal. Ten men worked each pump in three daily shifts of four hours. Every man labored a total of eight hours a day.[40]

The pumps had to be worked constantly. At Cartagena there was a leakage of some 3,690 cubic feet of water, and if it had not been for the steady movement of the pumps, the drydocks never would have been free of water. Prisoners and slaves were forced to work day and night, and when there were shortages of men due to illness or death, they were kept at this labor twelve to fourteen hours a day.[41] Like their working conditions, the circumstances under which they lived were harsh. To begin with, they were separated from the rest of the prisoners and housed aboard one of the galley hulks that had been set aside for them and anchored near the pumps. To achieve more security and convenience in 1771 they were moved into a subterranean chamber located under the pumps. There they

Sample of a petition and signature of prisoners in the arsenal of Cartagena complaining to the king about their treatment and living conditions, October 10, 1773. From AGS, Marina, leg. 696.

were confined to a small damp space without proper ventilation and subjected to the constant noise of the machinery. The pump room remained their quarters until 1773, when, in response to their numerous petitions, the king ordered them transferred to a nearby storehouse that was converted into a barracks for them.[42]

Despite the improved housing, conditions at the pumps continued to be the same. When the English traveler Henry Swinburne visited the arsenal of Cartagena in 1775, he observed that there were 800 *presidiarios* and 500 slaves assigned to the pumps, and that most labored there for a total of fifteen hours a day. He also reported that scarcely a day passed without some of them dropping dead at their work, and that suicides were frequent.[43] Twelve years after Swinburne's visit, the labor at the pumps ceased. In 1787 steam pumps were installed at Cartagena to replace the chain pumps, and in that same year the penalty of hard labor at the chain pumps was abolished.[44]

Two factors combined to bring an end to the presidios in the navel arsenals: the rising cost of maintaining them as penal institutions, and the decline of the Spanish navy after its defeat at Trafalgar in 1805. Originally, penal laborers were introduced into the arsensals to fill the immediate demand for cheap unskilled workers, but their continued use there depended on a combination of favorable economic factors. These circumstances existed in the period between 1749 and the 1770s, when it was financially advantageous for the state to utilize *presidiarios* to perform heavy labor in the arsenals because they were cheaper than free laborers. During those years their total upkeep, including food, clothing, and security, cost less than three reales a day per man as compared with the three and one-half reales (winter) and four reales (summer) in daily wages required by free workers.[45] In addition to the saving in wages, recruitment of free workers for unskilled jobs in the arsenals was difficult. In the planting and harvesting seasons contract labor was not available, and, regardless of the time of the year, free laborers could not be hired to work the chain pumps or to do any other disagreeable work. Even when slightly higher wages were paid as an inducement, as occurred at El Ferrol during the early years of construction, free workers still refused to labor there because of unfavorable working conditions.[46]

In the late 1770s the economic situation began to change. Sharply rising prices, particularly during the war period, 1778–83, increased the cost of maintaining the *presidiarios* and thereby reduced the economic benefits to be gained from their labor. From 1785 through the early years of the nineteenth century, a growing inflationary trend with a corresponding decline in wages (both real and nominal) completely reversed the economic balance. Maintaining the *presidiarios* in the arsenals became more costly than hiring free labor. In 1775 Swinburne observed that it cost the Spanish government five reales a day per man to support the *presidiarios*, while their work was estimated to be worth less than one tenth of what they ate. In 1800 the expenses of their maintenance had risen to eight reales a day per man, and the quality of their work when compared with that of free workers was calculated at the ratio of one to three, that is, three convicts did the work of one free laborer.[47]

As it became more expensive to feed and clothe the *presidiarios*, there was less need for their labor. The completion of major construction work in the arsenals and the installation of the steam pumps eliminated many of the difficult and distasteful jobs. Labor in the arsenals became more attractive to free workers. But despite these circumstances, there was no substantial decline in the arsenal prisoner population. There were 2,201 *presidiarios* in the arsenal of Cartagena in 1802, that is, some 491 more than in 1771, with "little or no work to do and idle most of the time."[48] In 1804 the king ordered the courts to refrain from sentencing criminals to the arsenals, especially Cartagena, but this decree, like previous ones in 1801 and 1802, had little effect. Aside from the crowded North African presidios, there was no other place where serious offenders could be sent. These circumstances, in conjunction with the penal reform ideas popular at the end of the eighteenth century and early nineteenth century, led to an attempt to preserve the naval presidios by transforming them into experimental correctional presidios.

In 1804 a new system of penal practice that combined the utilitarian needs of the state with the correction of offenders was established in the arsenals.[49] Inmate rehabilitation was to be effective through compulsory work in (and learning of) a special craft, with the end of making inmates useful to society and themselves. Prisoners had to pass through three progressive stages, each with its own system of rewards and punishments. In the first stage (corresponding to the first third of their sentences) they were assigned to hard manual labor in the arsenal, which they performed wearing heavy fetters and chained together in pairs. During the remainder of their terms, they were trained in seamanship and related crafts (second stage) and labored in these occupations (third stage). During this period their chains were lighter and fewer (those in the third category wore light fetters only), and they received a gratuity from one to three reales a day for their work. Although most of the money they earned was not given them until they completed their sentences, they could use 25 percent of it each month to improve their food and clothing. Under this system their labor was compulsory but at the same time educative and rehabilitative. It prepared them for re-entry into society by giving them a trade and some financial means to start a new life. In the opinion of the Spanish penologist Rafael Salillas, the legislation of 1804 for the arsenals laid the foundations for the progressive penal system adopted in Spanish correctional prisons in the nineteenth century.[50]

The naval disaster at Trafalgar in 1805 completed the ruin of the Spanish navy and brought a rapid end to the experimental presidios. In 1807 there still were a thousand prisoners in each of the three arsenals, but as a result of a decree of that year prohibiting further admissions, their numbers were reduced to a handful. In 1818 the presidios at Cartagena and El Ferrol were terminated when their remaining prisoners (ten and seven men, respectively) were transferred to other presidios. As for La Carraca, it continued to function as a military presidio for naval offenders, and continues to serve in that capacity today.[51]

# 6

# The Penalty of
# Public Works

In Spain the public works presidios were created in the second
half of the eighteenth century to meet the needs of the Bourbon
monarchs. During the reign of Charles III (1759–88), an extensive
public works program was inaugurated with the objective of improv-
ing transportation and communications within the country. The most
important innovations undertaken were the construction of paved
roads and canals. In 1761, construction was begun on a highway
system designed to connect Madrid with the periphery. The pattern
that was adopted reflected the prevailing concepts of political centralization. Madrid was to be the center of a radial system that
formed the circulation of the country. The new royal highways or
*caminos reales* followed the most direct routes from Madrid to their
peripheral destinations: Irún, Barcelona, Cádiz, Cartagena, Badajoz, and La Coruña. They were designed for efficient communications, and had little impact on the vast areas between them. Since
they were constructed in a straight line, some of the most important
interior towns, notably Toledo and Valladolid, were left out.[1]

These royal roads were planned on a grandiose scale, in terms of
cost and conception. The enterprise was so ambitious and it moved
so slowly that some thirty years later most of the work was still only
half finished.[2] In the last decade of the eighteenth century and the

first years of the nineteenth century, efforts also were made to build highways connecting the provincial and port cities. Some of the best roads were constructed in the Basque country and along the Mediterranean coast from Valencia to the French border. During those years, around 2,000 kilometers of new roads were added. By 1812, there were 12,700 kilometers of roads in Spain, a gain of 4,300 kilometers since 1758. Of this total, almost 4,000 kilometers could be found in Old Castile and León, with the rest distributed throughout the other northern and northwestern provinces.[3]

Like paved roads and highways, canals also were deemed necessary to stimulate economic development. A canal system was seen as the best means to lower the costs of transportation between the interior regions and the sea. By the 1780s, several canals were under construction, but the most impressive were the canals of Aragon and Castile. The canal of Aragon, based on a plan devised in the sixteenth century but abandoned because of engineering problems, was to run beside the Ebro River from Tudela to the Mediterranean Sea. A concession was given to a French company in 1768, but the enterprise soon failed, and the project was not revived until 1779, when the government invested large subsidies in it. By the end of the 1780s the canal of Aragon was completed as far as Zaragoza. Subsidiary irrigation canals for this region, for example, the canal of Tauste, also were part of the plan.[4]

The canal of Castile was to begin at Segovia, run northward past Valladolid and Reinosa, and enter the sea at Santander. Another branch of this system was to extend westward from Valladolid to Zamora. Construction began in the 1750s and continued intermittently until 1779, when the work was suspended pending further advancement on the canal of Aragon. When Townsend visited it in 1787, only a small portion of the canal, from Reinosa to Medina del Ríoseco, had been completed.[5] A third canal (the canal of Guadarrama) was to be build from Madrid southward through New Castile and La Mancha into Andalusia, entering the Guadalquivir River at Seville or Córdoba. It was hoped that this southern canal and the others would eventually form a national canal network comparable to the projected road system.[6]

Road and canal building, like the construction of naval arsenals and military fortifications, required the mobilization of a large labor force at minimum cost. Once again, the campaign to derive utility from marginal elements coincided with the public works program. As had occurred in the arsenals of Cartagena and El Ferrol, an attempt was made to supplement free contract laborers with forced workers. In the beginning, this was done with the use of slaves and gypsies. In 1763, three hundred Moslem slaves from the arsenal of Cartagena were sent to labor on the road being built from Madrid to Barcelona. Several gypsies who were confined to that same arsenal under the forced labor legislation of 1749 went along as foremen. The following year another contingent of slaves and gypsy foremen was transferred from Cartagena to construction work on the road from Madrid to Segovia.[7]

The experiment with slaves and gypsies was short-lived. In 1765, a royal decree repealed all previous legislation conscripting the gypsies for forced labor and ordered them freed from the arsenals and sent to their places of origin.[8] One year later a representative of the Moroccan government arrived in Madrid to negotiate a peace treaty and arrange for a mutual exchange of prisoners. He visited the Moslem slaves who were laboring on the Segovia road and secured the release of the Moroccans. From there he went to Cartagena, where he obtained freedom for the rest of the Moroccan slaves in the arsenal.[9] After the removal of the Moroccans, the remaining slaves working on the Segovia road (Algerians, Tunisians, and Turks) were returned to Cartagena. By that time the heavy work of excavation had been completed, and it was difficult to use the slaves in other tasks because of security problems. Moreover, frequent prisoner exchanges with the North African states from this time forward steadily reduced the number of slaves in Spain, and those still available were needed to operate the chain pumps at Cartagena.[10]

Simultaneously with the employment of slaves and gypsies, the government decided to conscript vagrants for public works. There existed a plan (originally conceived in the 1750s) to establish permanent brigades of vagrants assigned to public labor. These brigades, under the command of the military, were to be composed of one hundred men each. Their members were to be dressed in uniforms, housed in military barracks, and guarded by troops. In times of peace, they would be employed in constructing and repairing roads, building canals, and other kinds of hard labor. In wartime, they would be useful to the army as minelayers and sappers. But the companies were not formed, and because of the steady manpower demands of the armed forces, the majority of vagrants were destined for military service. Public works were reserved for vagrants who were too old for service at arms or whose physical condition was not satisfactory for work in the arsenals. According to Pérez Estévez, those destined for public works represented a mere 6 percent of her sample for the years 1730-82.[11]

In Madrid there was a special situation. As the center of the court and administrative capital, it had a larger number of vagrants than any other city in the country. Here the levies of vagrants were constant, especially after the riots of 1766. These conditions gave rise to a surplus difficult to accommodate in the jails.[12] In order to relieve the overcrowding, it was decided to use the vagrants destined for the armed services in public works while they were awaiting transportation to their units.[13] This decision also coincided with the initiation of a beautification program for Madrid. In its initial stages it involved the opening of new streets, the completion of the work of paving begun earlier, and the bettering of old promenades and the opening of new ones. In 1770, an order was issued transferring vagrants from the Madrid jails to a building specifically designated to serve as a *depósito* for them. This edifice, a former cavalry barracks, was located behind the Royal Granary near the Prado de San Jerónimo. For several years prior to this date, vagrants destined for the navy had been housed there and used occasionally in public works. This move marked the beginning of the first public works presidio of Madrid, known as the *Presidio del Prado*.[14]

The penal population of the Prado presidio in the early 1770s consisted primarily of vagrants, either those serving temporarily or those sentenced to public works because of ineligibility for military service. In general, the courts tried to take into consideration the age and physical condition of the vagrants, but since the objective was to secure the maximum number for the armed forces, many concessions were made. Consequently, the contingents of vagrants sentenced to public works were always minimal, even in a city like Madrid. For example, in the first six months of 1771, of the 192 vagrants imprisoned in the Cárcel de Corte, only thirty-nine were sentenced to public works.[15]

In addition to vagrants, the Madrid courts began to sentence petty offenders to the Prado presidio. During these years public works began to be championed as the best means of punishment for those convicted of minor crimes.[16] Traditionally, fines, banishment, and/or flogging had been applied to minor offenders, but the effectiveness of these penalties had long been questioned. The fines that were levied usually remained uncollected because the defendants, being poor men, could not pay them. As a result they remained in jails, causing overcrowding in those institutions and increasing the risks of disorder and disease. If applied to public works, indigent offenders could work off the fines and court fees that they owed. As for the municipality, it could utilize the prisoners in its building projects and in the regular tasks of street-cleaning and repairing, as well as in the upkeep of parks and promenades.[17] The convicts could be maintained at half the cost of wage laborers. From the early 1770s until 1805, two reales a day was the daily compensation per prisoner, whereas the rate for free contract laborers was at least four reales a day.[18]

Regardless of the advantages of sentencing minor offenders to public works, the number actually assigned there remained small. This was particularly true in the initial years. For example, in the six-month period from January to June, 1771, 147 prisoners were sentenced to the Prado presidio from all the jurisdictions of Madrid. Fewer prisoners completed their sentences. Of those sentenced in 1771, eleven were transferred from the Prado to other destinations (the *hospicios* or the navy), while nineteen were freed before the termination of their sentences. Discounting the five who died and the one who escaped, a total of thirty-seven completed their terms. At the end of June, 1771, the population of the Prado was seventy-four *presidiarios*.[19]

The year 1774 marked a turning point in the history of the public works presidio. The changes introduced in that year were related to the inauguration of one of the most important projects for the beautification of Madrid. It was decided to remodel the Prado Promenade, a favorite recreation spot for *madrileños* for centuries because of its rustic setting. The plans called for the transformation of this area into a vast public walk lined with trees and benches and adorned with statues, vases, and fountains. Although the project for the reconstruction of the Prado was devised in 1767 by the Count of Aranda, actual work did not begin until 1774.[20] In that year, prisoners from the nearby Prado presidio were used to perform the costly and heavy labor of clearing and leveling the land in preparation for construction. At the same time, the presidio was placed under the financial control of the municipality of Madrid. In the beginning, a part of the expenses of the establishment was paid from release fees extracted from the inmates, but with the abolition of these payments for presidio prisoners in 1776, funds had to be drawn entirely from city taxes.[21]

While the presidio was the financial responsibility of the municipality, it was run by the military. It was located in a converted military barracks, and its commander was an army officer attached to the garrison of Madrid. He was assisted by two other officers, a sergeant and a foreman. The sergeant was in charge of the custody and guard of the prisoners, while the foreman went out with them and directed their work. Troops stationed in Madrid were sent on a rotating basis to guard the *presidiarios* both when they were at work and when they were confined to the presidio barracks.[22]

In 1775, major offenders sentenced to the overseas presidios and naval arsenals (*rematados*) from the Cárcel de Corte who were awaiting the departure of the chain were sent to the Prado presidio.[23] This move was made because the relatively few prisoners regularly sentenced to the presidio could not meet the growing demand for workers. The *rematados* were to work on the Promenade and other public works during the interim period. When the chain was ready, they were to be returned to the jail where they would be subjected to the usual physical examinations and certifications prior to their departure. Although the use of *rematados* in public works was an innovation, a precedent had been set already in the temporary application of vagrants destined for the armed services. The transferral of the *rematados* to the Prado in 1775 converted it into a *depósito* as well as a public works presidio. In contrast to what occurred in other parts of Spain, the public works presidio of Madrid originated independently of the *depósito* rather than developing out of it. When John Howard visited it in 1783, he noted its mixed character. He saw three kinds of prisoners: those sentenced originally to public works, those destined for the navy, and *rematados*. There were around one hundred prisoners at that time.[24]

During the late 1770s there was an attempt to utilize *rematados* in public works projects on a more permanent basis. In 1777 the king authorized the tribunals of the kingdom to sentence offenders normally sent to the overseas presidios and arsenals to work on the Canal of Murcia.[25] The king took this action on the request of the company undertaking the construction of the canal. Its directors complained that the work was being delayed because of the difficulty of hiring laborers, especially during the planting and harvesting seasons. According to the terms of this concession, prisoners sent to labor on the canal were to be supported by the king, that is, given the usual presidio ration, and utilized principally in excavation work. There was a provision which permitted the distribution of gratuities in the form of cash to prisoners in reward for extra labor. It was hoped that this would stimulate them to work harder so that the project would advance more rapidly. At the same time, the extra money they gained could be used to improve their conditions.[26] This system proved too costly and was abandoned, but the idea of offering incentives to prisoners was retained. In future projects involving penal labor, reductions in sentences replaced money compensation.

In 1784 the government began construction of a new highway (the *Camino Imperial*) from Madrid north to the French frontier. This led to a new use of *presidiarios* from the Prado presidio. In September, 1784, the tribunals of Madrid were ordered to sentence as many prisoners as possible to forced labor on the new road. The only stipulation was that their sentences had to exceed fifteen days, because anything less was considered too short to be serviceable. Reductions in sentences were to be allowed as rewards for extra work, and the directors of the project were specifically enjoined to uphold this policy.[27] In the following years reductions were awarded periodically, and, on the average (depending on the gravity of the offense), ranged from three months for a six-month term and four months for a two-year sentence to eight months for a three-year term.[28]

In order to facilitate work on the *Camino Imperial*, the location of the presidio was changed. *Presidiarios* sentenced to this road were sent to new lodgings closer to the construction work. A few large decrepit barracks on the right side of the Toledo Bridge were outfitted for them. This establishment became known as the *Presidio del Camino Imperial* or *del Puente de Toledo*.[29] In 1785 the remaining prisoners in the Prado presidio (only twenty were left) were moved to the new location, and the old building was abandoned. A former washhouse located on the left side of the Toledo Bridge was appropriated for their use. This site came to be known as the *Presidio nuevo* or *del Prado* because it was considered the successor of the original Prado presidio.[30] From 1785 to 1798, the public works presidio of Madrid consisted of two establishments located on both sides of the Toledo Bridge. Their penal population labored on the *Camino Imperial* and other roads leading in and out of the city and performed municipal services such as street- and drain-cleaning, paving work, and the maintenance of parks and promenades.[31]

The use of prisoners from the Prado presidio in *Camino Imperial* work also brought about a change in the administration of the presidio. Since the *presidiarios* were to be used on a royal road, control over the presidio was transferred from the municipality of Madrid to the *Dirección General de Correos y Caminos*, a royal agency that supervised the construction and repair of roads and highways.[32] From 1784 to 1804 this agency directed the public works presidio of Madrid, but it did not finance it until after 1798. During the years 1784–98, the city government of Madrid supported the Prado establishment while the *Dirección General* maintained the Puente de Toledo. In 1798, the two presidios were merged and the Prado site abandoned. At the same time, the *Dirección General* assumed complete financial control over the new entity.[33]

While it is likely that the original Prado presidio in Madrid was the oldest of its kind on the Peninsula, similar establishments sprang up elsewhere in the 1780s. One of the most important, and probably the first created outside of Madrid, was located in Málaga. Similar factors contributed to its formation, that is, a surplus of prisoners and the inauguration of a public works program in the region. Málaga was the principal distributing center for the North African presidios, and its *depósito* was the largest in the country. Prisoners were brought to Málaga from all parts of Spain, and they often waited there for years before being transferred to their final destinations. Unserviceable *presidiarios* from the North African presidios also were returned to the *depósito* in Málaga, where they remained until they either were reassigned or died. In addition, prisoners from the North African presidios who were being transferred to the New World presidios and vice-versa were sent through Málaga. The volume of traffic, and the difficulties of transportation due to lack of money, and ships and interruptions because of wars, all combined to produce an excess of prisoners in the *depósito* at Málaga.[34] In the last two decades of the eighteenth century a rise in the level of criminal activity (especially property crime), reflective of the growth in population, along with more effective law enforcement and a decline in the death penalty, further increased the number of prisoners in the *depósito* and resulted in serious crowding.[35]

The glut of prisoners in the *depósito* of Málaga occurred precisely at a time when the government was beginning its road-building program in that region. Two new roads were projected, one from Málaga to Granada, and the other from Málaga to Antequera. In order to secure enough cheap laborers, the companies undertaking the two projects applied to the king for a grant of convicts. In 1780, a royal decree ordered the assignment of a part of the prisoners in the *depósito* of Málaga (the less serious offenders) to work on the two roads. The original contingent consisted of 100 men, but in December 1782 this number was increased to 200.[36] At the same time, the king approved a *Reglamento* for the governance of prisoners laboring on the Málaga roads. This code, a first of its kind, served as a model for other ordinances, notably that of the *Camino Imperial*. It incorporated the principle of reducing sentences in return for extra work, and in contrast to later ordinances it established a definite scale for them. A reduction in sentence of three months was to be given for every 1,000 *varas* of road completed.[37]

Although originally intended to labor on the royal roads, prisoners from the *depósito* were soon being utilized in public works projects sponsored by the municipality of Málaga. One of the most impressive was begun in 1786 when the city undertook to dam the Guadalmedina River, which frequently overflowed its banks and flooded the town. The labor on this project was performed by prisoners from the *depósito*. By that date almost all the prisoners received in the *depósito*, regardless of their sentences, were being applied to public works in Málaga.[38] Only the most serious offenders, that is, murderers, infamous thieves, and bandits, were sent on to their destinations in the North African presidios. While remaining a distribution center for the overseas presidios, the *depósito* at Málaga became a public works presidio as well.

The use of major criminals in public works created serious security problems. Escapes were frequent, and some escapees succeeded in joining the bands of smugglers who were particularly numerous in the mountains around Málaga. Others committed additional crimes—assaults, murders, and thefts. This situation influenced the king in 1787 to order the *depósito* officials to refrain from detaining prisoners destined for North Africa in Málaga and to ship there immediately all thieves, bandits, and habitual criminals. Only those who had been convicted of minor crimes or those whose sentences lacked a specific destination could be retained and applied to public works.[39]

Conditions in the *depósito* of Málaga were particularly bad in the 1780s. In 1781 there was a widespread outbreak of jail fever, with great loss of life. Jail fever (now believed to be a form of typhus) resulted from dirt, overcrowding, and lack of sanitary conditions, and was endemic to the jails. During the 1780s the *presidiarios* complained frequently about poor and insufficient food rations, as well as corrupt guards and overseers. Other complaints included accusations that some prisoners were employed illegally as assistants to the jailers and guards, and that they meted out arbitrary punishments to the others.[40]

Reports of abuses and mismanagement at the *depósito* of Málaga eventually reached the king, who ordered an official investigation. In 1795, new regulations were issued for the governance of the *presidiarios* at Málaga. The new rules once again forbade the retention in Málaga of prisoners sentenced to the overseas presidios, because this practice had continued despite the prohibition against it in 1787. Only those whose sentences bore the designation of public works could be used. According to the official explanation, the prisoners customarily sentenced to public works were minor offenders. This sentencing was done by the courts with the knowledge that minor offenders could be restrained by the limited security in the public works presidios. Other prisoners, the major offenders, needed the extra protection available only in the North African presidios, and (according to the new directives) should be dispatched as soon as possible to them. If by chance the transcripts of any sentences were missing, presidio officials were to direct the sentencing tribunals to replace them. Previously, transcripts had been purposely destroyed so as to justify illegal retention. Finally, presidio administrators were required to provide monthly accounts of deaths and desertions, so as to prevent cover-ups to hide faulty security and mistreatment.[41]

Another one of the abuses associated with the presidio at Málaga was the concession of inmates to private individuals, who used them as servants and employees. While this system was permitted in the North African presidios because of a lack of manpower, it was not allowed in the Peninsular presidios. The *Reglamento* of 1795 repeated the prohibition against the employment of convicts by private persons resident in Málaga or elsewhere. In addition, the directors of the private companies engaged in the public works projects lost their privilege to grant reductions in sentences.[42] It was felt that this authority in the hands of private individuals interfered with the government's sovereign power to grant pardons. The principal of distributing these rewards was not abandoned, but the power to do so was delegated to government officials.

Coincidentally with the emergence of the public works presidio at Málaga, the same transformation occurred at several other *depósitos*, namely Cádiz, Cartagena, and Barcelona. Like Málaga, all three were peripheral *depósitos* that served as main distribution centers. In addition, they were located in areas where there were extensive public works projects in the last decades of the eighteenth century and the early years of the nineteenth century. Prisoners were used to build the new Barcelona-Valencia highway in the 1780s and to improve port facilities in Cádiz, Barcelona, and Cartagena. They also were used in all three cities for repair and maintenance of the streets and public thoroughfares.[43]

In 1788 the Spanish government approved plans to build the Canal of Guadarrama, and construction was begun. The Bank of San Carlos agreed to advance money for the project and to supervise the work in return for a 10 percent commission and 4 percent per annum for all the money expended. After having difficulties recruiting free laborers, the directors of the Bank of San Carlos petitioned the king to grant them a contingent of prisoners. Following the precedent of the Canal of Murcia, the king ordered the assignment of offenders already sentenced and those about to be sentenced to the presidios or military service to the Canal of Guadarrama. Thieves, murderers, smugglers, and counterfeiters were excluded. In accord with this order it was decided to transfer prisoners from the public works presidio of Madrid to the canal. The directors of the project requested the use of 200 convicts immediately, but there were only seventy prisoners in the presidio of Madrid—twenty-one in the Prado and the rest in the Puente de Toledo. Furthermore, there were quite a few among them who had committed crimes that would prevent them from being used.[44]

Little is known about how the presidio of Madrid functioned during the years 1784–1804 while it was under the supervision of the *Dirección General de Caminos*. In that period the problem of security was foremost. Escapes were common, despite the guards and chains. Even the introduction of the penalty of 200 lashes for those caught had little effect. One of the most serious incidents occurred in 1788, when a group of *presidiarios* who were being taken out to work attempted to overpower their guards. In the resulting struggle several prisoners escaped, and there were deaths and injuries on both sides. This event was blamed on the presence in the presidio of army deserters who had been sent to work on the *Camino Imperial*, but their subsequent removal did not improve the situation.[45] One year later there was a full-scale revolt in which the prisoners almost succeeded in seizing the presidio. An investigation of this uprising resulted in accusations of laxity and favoritism against the presidio officials. It was claimed, for example, that some prisoners were allowed to remain without chains, while others left the presidio daily to go into Madrid on errands for themselves or presidio administrators.[46] In the 1790s, special efforts were made to enforce discipline and curb corruption, including several changes in command at all ranks. But conditions did not improve substantially.[47] In the early 1800s, while the total inmate population was about the same as in previous years, the escape rate had doubled. Similarly, charges of maladministration continued to be directed against the presidio officials.[48]

Extant data in the municipal archives of Madrid allow a quantitative analysis of prisoners in the public works presidio for selected years. The collection of documents in the Archivo de Villa consists of a series of prisoner lists for the years 1794–1802, when the presidio was under the direction of the *Dirección General de Caminos*.[49] Some of these records contain crimes and sentences. Others give an account of the number of deaths, completed sentences, and releases. A substantial number of transcripts of sentences also have been preserved for the years 1796-1800, yielding additional socio-demographic data. They represent a scattered and fragmentary collection for the most part, with the exception of the years 1799 and 1800, which seem to be complete.[50]

Table 6.1 shows that in the period 1794–1802, 81 percent of the presidio population was being confined there for one year or less: 52 percent were sentenced to terms of less than one year, while 29 percent were serving one-year sentences. Some 14 percent had been condemned for two years. Convicts serving terms of three years or more, transients, and others made up the remaining 5 percent.[51] Among the prisoners serving less than one year, 92 percent were sentenced to terms lasting from one to six months. Sentences of two, four and six months were the most common penalties, while terms of less than one month were rare (see table 6.2).

Statistics for releases and completion of sentences can be deduced from these same sources, but the sample is smaller. There is an uninterrupted series of figures for the years 1797–1802. During that period, 37 percent of the men confined to the presidio completed their terms (see table 6.3). A somewhat higher ratio (41 percent) were released before the termination of their sentences. The rest (22 percent) either died, deserted, or were transferred. In the less than

Table 6.1. Distribution of Sentences, Presidio of Madrid, 1794–1802

| Length of Sentence | Number of Prisoners | Percentage |
|---|---|---|
| Less than one year | 341 | 52 |
| One year | 190 | 29 |
| Two years | 94 | 14 |
| Three years or more and other | 33 | 5 |
| Total | 658 | 100 |

Source: AGV, Secretaría, sec. 2, leg. 323, no. 15; sec. 2, leg. 323, no. 19.

Table 6.2. Distribution of Sentences of Less than One Year, Presidio of Madrid, 1794–1802

| Length of Sentence | Number of Prisoners | Percentage |
|---|---|---|
| Less than one month | 4 | 1 |
| One month | 43 | 12 |
| Two months | 100 | 27 |
| Three months | 22 | 6 |
| Four months | 72 | 20 |
| Five months | 0 | 0 |
| Six months | 100 | 27 |
| Not stated | 24 | 7 |
| Total | 365 | 100 |

Source: AVM, Secretaría, sec. 2, leg. 232, no. 15; sec. 2, leg. 232, no. 19.

Table 6.3. Completions, Releases, and Deaths, Presidio of Madrid, 1797–1802

| | Number of Prisoners | Percentage |
|---|---|---|
| Completed sentences | 220 | 37 |
| Released before termination | 242 | 41 |
| Died | 20 | 3 |
| Other | 115 | 19 |
| Total | 597 | 100 |

Source: AVM, Secretaría, sec. 2, leg. 323, no. 15.

one-year group, slightly more men completed their terms than were released (47 percent vs. 38 percent; see table 6.4). For those serving one-year terms the situation was reversed; 27 percent completed their sentences, while 48 percent were released before the end of their terms. When dealing with convicts sentenced for one year or more, mortality and desertion rates must be considered. There was a 6 percent mortality rate among one-year prisoners in the period 1797–1800. Although figures are missing for the number of men who escaped, other sources indicate higher desertion rates among inmates serving one year or longer.[52] Among those in the two-year category, the percentage of prisoners who completed their terms was sharply reduced (only 15 percent). There was an 8 percent death rate as well.

The release of a substantial proportion of prisoners before the termination of their sentences was not unusual in a public works

Table 6.4. Completions, Releases, and Deaths within Sentence Categories, Presidio of Madrid, 1797–1802

| Length of Sentence | Completed Sentences | | Released | | Died | | Other | |
|---|---|---|---|---|---|---|---|---|
| | No. | % | No. | % | No. | % | No. | % |
| Less than one year | 161 | 47 | 130 | 37 | 3 | 1 | 51 | 15 |
| One year | 48 | 27 | 86 | 48 | 11 | 6 | 35 | 19 |
| Two years | 11 | 15 | 26 | 52 | 6 | 8 | 28 | 39 |

Source: AVM, Secretaría, sec. 2, leg. 323, no. 15.

presidio in this period. Since many of the men (in particular, those serving one year or less) were convicted of very minor offenses, especially those related to disturbing the domestic or public peace, they were considered candidates for early release. One-year sentences of these offenders usually bore mandatory terms of six months, but they also contained a proviso allowing for parole upon completion of the minimum mandatory term. At the appropriate time, wives or parents petitioned the sentencing tribunals to parole prisoners in consideration of the lightness of their offenses and the urgent need for them at home. The majority of those released early belonged to this group. Severe illness or total physical incapacity was another cause for early release, but these cases were rare. Indisposed and sick *presidiarios* were treated in the presidio and, if necessary, were transferred to a military hospital where special quarters were reserved for them.[53]

The public works presidios were established primarily as places of confinement for two kinds of offenders: disturbers of the domestic and public peace and petty thieves. In the period 1799–1800, 63 percent of the men sentenced to the presidio of Madrid belonged to these two categories (see table 6.5). The largest number (34 percent) were convicted of offenses against good customs and morals and disturbing the peace. These delicts included vagrancy, drunkenness, and licentious behavior. Vagrants made up 21 percent of those sentenced for disturbing the peace, while chronic alcoholics accounted for 10 percent. Libertinism, i.e., concubinage and sexual misconduct, represented 19 percent of this category. More numerous (30 percent) were the men sentenced for mistreatment of their wives and failure to support their families. Often these same individuals were convicted of drunkenness and libertinism as well. They served sentences ranging from two months to one year, with an average of four months. They also were the group most likely to be paroled after completing their mandatory sentences. The courts were anxious to return these offenders to their homes as soon as possible so as to prevent destitution and degradation of their wives and families.

The second largest contingent of convicts in the presidio (29 percent) was made up of men convicted of crimes against property. Almost all were sentenced for petty larceny, that is, small thefts involving objects of limited value. Objects stolen were mainly food products and pieces of clothing, usually the most accessible kinds, such as hats, shoes and handkerchiefs. A considerable number of these prisoners were convicted of pilfering from their places of employment—for example, masons who removed building materials and tools from construction sites, or workers in a meat-salting plant who stole pieces of bacon and lard.

Only 13 percent of the men were confined to the presidio for crimes against persons. Punishment for offenses of this kind depended on many factors, in particular, the severity of the injury and the status of the individuals involved. Serious injuries and injuries inflicted on persons of high social position brought sentences to North African presidios. Those serving in the public works presidio for violent behavior were men of low social status (as were their victims), and the injuries inflicted were slight or insignificant. Some were there because they could not pay the damages and fines

Table 6.5. Classification of Offenses, Presidio of Madrid, 1799–1800

| Nature of Offense | Number of Prisoners | Percentage |
|---|---|---|
| Crimes against persons | 35 | 13 |
| Crimes against property | 80 | 29 |
| Crimes against good customs and morals, disturbing the domestic peace | 63 | 23 |
| Disturbing the public peace | 31 | 11 |
| Swindling, fraud, and counterfeiting | 17 | 6 |
| Offenses related to forests | 30 | 11 |
| Not stated and other | 21 | 7 |
| Total | 277 | 100 |

Source: AVM, Secretaría, sec. 2, leg. 323, nos. 9–11, 19.

assessed in these cases. There also were a considerable group who were convicted of attacks against their wives or other members of their families.

The remainder of the population of the Madrid presidio consisted of a small percentage of prisoners sentenced for swindling, fraud, and forgery, as well as offenses related to the forests. In this period the courts were indulgent toward the more intelligent kinds of crimes (except counterfeiting) if they involved men of status and wealth. Few of these offenders were ever prosecuted, as can be seen in their low representation in the North African presidios. The prisoners in the public works presidio of Madrid were all poor men, and their offenses were minor. For example, there were frauds connected with the exercise of their trades: a shopkeeper who sold several people small amounts of adulterated olive oil, or a carpenter who used inferior materials in a commissioned work. There also were a few men condemned for offenses related to the forests. The forests traditionally were sources of food supply during times of shortage. Gleaning and the collection of firewood were still popular and collective acts, as witnessed by the fact that thirteen men were serving six-month sentences each for collecting firewood and acorns from royal and municipal lands. Poaching was a more serious offense that usually resulted in a longer overseas presidio sentence. There were four men in the presidio convicted of poaching. One was sentenced to Puerto Rico, and was at the presidio temporarily until the departure of the chain, while the others were first-time offenders whose crimes were so minor that they did not merit a more severe sentence. They were serving one-year terms each at public works, but their sentences carried the warning that in case of recidivism they would be condemned to eight years in a North African presidio.

Table 6.6 reveals an apparently older convict population. While men under thirty were numerous (31 percent of the sample), they did not predominate. The largest percentage (41 percent) was made up of mature men aged thirty to forty-five years. In addition, there was a substantial proportion of men between the ages of forty-five and fifty-five. After fifty-five, the pyramid declines rapidly. Similarly, there were few young prisoners (under twenty years), since youthful offenders normally were sent to either the *hospicios* or the houses of correction.

Table 6.6. Age Distribution, Presidio of Madrid, 1799–1800

| Age Group | Number of Prisoners | Percentage |
|-----------|---------------------|------------|
| Under 15 | 1 | 1 |
| 15–19 | 5 | 4 |
| 20–24 | 19 | 14 |
| 25–29 | 23 | 17 |
| 30–34 | 19 | 14 |
| 35–39 | 14 | 11 |
| 40–44 | 21 | 16 |
| 45–49 | 12 | 9 |
| 50–54 | 10 | 7 |
| 55–59 | 5 | 4 |
| 60–64 | 3 | 2 |
| 65–69 | 2 | 1 |
| Total | 134 | 100 |

Source: AVM, Secretaría, sec. 2, leg. 323, nos. 9, 19.

With their population of mature prisoners, the public works presidios stand in sharp contrast to the North African presidios. There were several reasons for this. The North African presidios had a large number of military prisoners, and soldiers were in the youngest age groups. Moreover, the very nature of the public works presidios as places of punishment for minor offenders tended to exclude younger men. In the eighteenth century, as today, each age group was associated with a specific type of crime. Violent crime seemed to have been more closely associated with younger men, and these offenders were normally confined to the North African presidios. Crime among middle-aged and mature men was somewhat different. Among the prisoners in the Madrid presidio, those in their thirties and forties seem to have been involved more often in sexual misconduct, while those in the forty to fifty-five-year-old category mistreated their wives and engaged in public drunkenness. The oldest criminals were vagrants, who often were convicted of small thefts as well. Younger men (the twenty to thirty-year-old group) committed most of the crimes against persons, while theft was common among all groups.

Marriage and celibacy rates among the prisoners correspond to their age groups and types of offenses. The majority of convicts were married (65 percent, as compared with 28 percent unmarried and 7 percent widowed), but most of the younger men (under twenty-five years) were single (see table 6.7). Between ages twenty-five and thirty, the ratios of married to unmarried are close (about two to one). Beyond age thirty, the incidence of celibacy drops sharply. Eighty-four percent of the men between thirty and forty-five were married. The number of celibates among those aged forty-five and older was negligible. These figures are consistent with what is known about eighteenth-century marriage patterns. In this period, the average male age at marriage fluctuated between twenty-five and forty years.[54] Given the character of the public works presidios, a married older penal population was typical.

From 1798 to 1803, the presidio of Madrid known as the Puente de Toledo was located in a converted barracks on the right side of the Toledo Bridge. Because of their restricted numbers (usually fifty or sixty), most *presidiarios* labored in road-building and repair. Few were available to the city for use in street-cleaning and the maintenance of parks and promenades, as had been done in the past. In April, 1803, in order to obtain more penal workers for municipal duties, the city decided to reestablish the Prado presidio. Its former site on the left side of the Toledo Bridge was rehabilitated, and by the summer of 1803 it was in full operation. In the following year, control over the Puente de Toledo presidio was transferred from the *Dirección General de Caminos* to the city of Madrid. The municipal corporation henceforth assumed responsibility for both presidios.[55]

At the time of the transfer, there were 136 prisoners in both presidios: sixty-three in the Prado and seventy-three in the Puente de Toledo.[56] Most men in the Prado (46 percent) were convicted of offenses against good customs and morals and disturbing the domes-

Table 6.7. Percentage of Married, Single, and Widowed Convicts, Presidio of Madrid, 1799–1800

| | Age Group | | | | | | | | | |
|---|---|---|---|---|---|---|---|---|---|---|
| | 15–19 | 20–24 | 25–29 | 30–34 | 35–39 | 40–44 | 45–49 | 50–54 | 55–59 | 60–65 |
| Single | 100.0 | 53.0 | 43.0 | 9.0 | 17.0 | 5.0 | 29.0 | 0.0 | 0.0 | 0.0 |
| Married | 0.0 | 47.0 | 52.0 | 91.0 | 83.0 | 80.0 | 57.0 | 60.0 | 80.0 | 100.0 |
| Widowed | 0.0 | 0.0 | 5.0 | 0.0 | 0.0 | 15.0 | 14.0 | 40.0 | 20.0 | 0.0 |

Source: AVM, Secretaría, sec. 2, leg. 323, nos. 9, 19.

tic and public peace. Crimes against persons in which the attack was incidental or the injury superficial made up 21 percent of the total, while crimes against property represented 14 percent. In contrast, 59 percent of the prisoners in the Puente de Toledo had been sentenced for property crimes. Offenses against morality and disturbing the public and domestic peace totaled 21 percent, while personal crime made up 10 percent. The majority of men in both presidios were sentenced to terms of one year or less, but in the Puente de Toledo, a larger percentage of prisoners were serving sentences of two years or more.

The Puente de Toledo was above all a presidio for thieves, while the Prado contained vagrants, drunks, wife-beaters, and sexual misbehavers. The difference between the two presidios was manifest in the kind of work the prisoners did. Contingents from the Prado regularly cleaned the streets and performed other tasks within the city limits. Men from the Puente de Toledo, being property offenders, were considered too dangerous to be used in the city proper. They worked on surrounding roads and other projects on the outskirts of town.[57]

A considerable number of men in the Puente de Toledo presidio were convicted of serious thefts. In the past they would have been sentenced to a North African presidio, but during these years the government was attempting to reduce the population of the North African presidios. Consequently, the Madrid courts were asked to assign these offenders to public works presidios, and this practice was continued in subsequent years.[58] In this way the public works presidios began to take on the form that was fully developed in the nineteenth century, that is, as places of punishment for more substantial property offenders as well as petty thieves.

One year after the city assumed responsibility for the public works presidios of Madrid, there occurred a decisive change in their administration. In 1805, control over them was transferred from the city to the state even though the municipality of Madrid was still required to finance them.[59] With the change in status came new rules and regulations for their governance. The *Reglamento* of 1807 (originally approved in 1805) provided for the creation of the post of director of presidios, a royal appointee directly under the Ministry of Justice.[60] The director was responsible for the administration of the two presidios. He was assisted by the presidio commandants, who supervised the day-to-day operations of their establishments. The powers of the commandants, who were to be retired army officers, were limited. They could no longer exempt prisoners from any labor or remove their chains. Nor could they select their subordinates, because all the presidio officials were appointed by the director. Finally, only the director had the authority to reduce sentences in return for extraordinary work, in accord with standard practice in the public works presidios.

The daily routine of the *presidiarios* was carefully defined. They were required to labor on all public works financed by the municipality, and specifically on highways, public thoroughfares, and crossroads in Madrid and its vicinity. They were to be used in construction work in the cemeteries and in the preservation of the Prado and other promenades and parks. Finally, they were to do street-cleaning, paving, and other tasks related to municipal repair and sanitation. All work was to be performed in chain-gangs and under heavy guard, but with the proviso that those condemned for theft or like crimes could not be used in street-cleaning or other labor within the city proper. In the winter, when bad weather prevented them from laboring outside, they were to be employed indoors making brooms, baskets, and similar items.

For their maintenance, each man received nineteen cuartos (four reales) a day, which was divided into six cuartos for lunch, three cuartos for dinner, and ten cuartos for bread. For the first time, prisoners were required to wear uniforms. Uniforms were not used previously because they were considered too expensive for men serving short sentences, but the poor security record of the presidio while it was under the *Dirección General de Caminos* influenced the municipality to adopt a uniform.[61] In addition, the hair of prisoners serving sentences over six months was shaved in a further attempt to reduce escapes. Finally, deserters were to be punished with additional sentences of six months.

The *Reglamento* of 1807 established the basic rules and regulations for the use of penal labor in public works in the nineteenth century. It incorporated the fundamental methods used in the eighteenth century, but also adopted new ideas reflecting changing concepts of penal organization in the early years of the nineteenth century. The public works presidios originally were military establishments at the service of the city and state. They were directed by military officers and guarded by troops. The *Reglamento* of 1807 changed their character. Their director became a civilian government employee with wide powers of supervision, while the authority of their commandants, previously unlimited, was sharply reduced. Even though the participation of the military was not completely eliminated, since troops were still used to guard the prisoners, for all practical purposes the public works presidios were transformed into civilian institutions.[62]

When they became civilian institutions, the objectives of the public works presidios changed. In the eighteenth century penal labor had two main purposes: utilitarian, that is, the exploitation of convict labor for the state; and vindictive—the expiation of crimes through suffering. Under the *Reglamento* of 1807, the public works presidios became correctional presidios, a change reflected even in their titles (*presidios de corrección*). The name-change implies that the vindictive purpose was no longer to be stressed. Despite the intent, the idea of rehabilitation did not become fully operative until much later; but at least in a theoretical way, the new aim was to reform the inmates through productive labor.

The *Reglamento* also provided for changes in the kind of work that the prisoners did. In the eighteenth century, *presidiarios* performed unskilled labor only, and this was considered particularly appropriate for the punitive objectives of their sentences. Because of their chains and the security problems involved in their use, they were held to be unserviceable for other jobs. Moreover, they were always utilized as auxiliary workers (at times when free laborers were not available or too expensive), or else in combination with contractual workers. In contrast to eighteenth-century practice, the aim of the *Reglamento* of 1807 was to convert the *presidiarios* into a permanent force of unsalaried city workers. They were to be employed in a variety of municipal jobs, a few of which required a little skill, such as pruning of trees and plants, gardening, and irrigation works in the parks and promenades. The utilitarian aspects of this plan were obvious. By utilizing the convicts, the city did not have to pay salaries to workers to perform necessary municipal tasks, and could effect large savings. In addition, under the *Regla-*

*mento* the presidios became industrial workshops with the *presidiarios* producing various items during the off-seasons. The sale of these products could help defray the cost of their upkeep, but aside from economic reasons, there was a rehabilitative element also. By turning the prisoners into gardeners, pruners, irrigation workers, and industrial producers, their work ceased to be, as in the past, simply hard labor, forced and punitive. The work was compulsory, but at the same time useful and remunerative, for when prisoners worked on special assignments they received a gratuity. It also was to be educative, in accord with the modern concept that rehabilitation was the ultimate aim of the penal system.

One of the most important aspects of the *Reglamento* of 1807 was that it was supposed to serve as a model for other municipalities. But its extension elsewhere in the country was prevented by the Napoleonic invasion of Spain and the subsequent war and occupation (1808–14). Political problems afterwards caused additional delays, and it was not until 1822 that further steps were taken to reform the presidios. In that year a new Spanish penal code included, for the first time, the punishment of forced labor on public works, but this was really a redefinition of the old penalty. It further called for the establishment of a network of public works presidios.[63] Once again, changes in the political situation prevented further action. Finally, in 1834, the *Ordenanza General de Presidios* reorganized the entire penal system, and the public works presidios were incorporated into the new organization as correctional presidios and designated as places of punishment for offenders sentenced to terms of two years or less.

idlers and delinquents and to derive utility from them. The vagrants were sentenced to terms ranging from two to four years, but, as on the galleys, retention was common. In 1706, it was reported that more than 200 men in Oran had already served two to three years more than their original sentences, and that they could not be released because of the lack of replacements.[3] Following the practice of the galleys, the retainees automatically were converted into volunteers, and in that status they were applied to fortification work at a salary of two reales a day per man.[4]

In addition to the vagrants, there was a gradual increase in the number of serious offenders sent to the North African presidios in the 1720s and 1730s, but the transformation of these presidios into general penal establishments was a slow process, not completed until after the abolition of the galleys in 1748. In the first half of the eighteenth century the galleys continued to absorb the majority of felons convicted in Spanish courts, and sentences to the presidios for commoners still represented commutations of galley sentences.[5] For this reason, the presidios continued to be viewed as places of confinement for the privileged, and this attitude was reflected in the way in which they were administered. They were not governed by any formal code of rules, but rather by customs and observances developed over the course of the centuries. Their governors had wide and almost unlimited powers, and they used them to punish and reward prisoners at will.[6] They often freed men before the termination of their sentences, or allowed them to return home on temporary passes. When crimes were committed by prisoners in the presidios, the governors frequently permitted them to be transferred to other presidios instead of sending them to the galleys, as was required for commoners. In effect, they had complete freedom of action, despite repeated royal decrees prohibiting such practices.[7] Given the circumstances, prisoner escapes were common, and many escapees succeeded in reaching Spain. In the first decade of the eighteenth century, the judges on the *Sala de Alcaldes de Casa y Corte* often complained to the king about the number of criminals that they had condemned to the presidios who had escaped and returned to Madrid. They blamed these conditions on the laxity and indifference of the presidio administrators and, in particular, on their ineffective security measures.[8]

In 1716 the Spanish Government attempted to improve discipline by introducing into the North African presidios the military reform measures being adopted in Spain at that time. Special legislation (a *Reglamento*) was drafted for the presidios applying for the first time the brigade structure for the organization of prisoners. The brigades were to be composed of fifty men each commanded by officers called *reformados*. In addition, the *Reglamento* of 1716 made a clear distinction between the two kinds of prisoners: *desterrados*, men sentenced to the service of arms, and *presidiarios,* those condemned to hard labor on the fortifications. There were to be separate brigades for *desterrados* and *presidiarios*.[9]

While there was some improvement in conditions in the presidios after the *Reglamento* of 1716, the situation did not change substantially until the 1740s. In conjunction with the creation of penal contingents in the Peninsular military presidios, it was decided to reorganize the North African presidios as well. The *Reglamento* of 1743 represented the first formal code of rules and regulations for the governance of the penal establishments in the North African presidios.[10] It became a model upon which all subsequent legislation for those institutions was based. The first part of this ordinance provided for the assignment of duties and the delineation of authority among the several officers of the presidio. Under its provisions, the powers of the governors were reduced and divided among the members of a governing junta composed of a comptroller and a chief military engineer, in addition to the governor. The brigade structure introduced in the *Reglamento* of 1716 was retained, and the individual brigades were enlarged to consist of eighty to one hundred men. The brigade commanders, now called brigadiers, still had complete authority over their men, but their actions were made subject to review by a new group of officers known as inspectors. All these officials were appointed by the governing junta and were under its supervision.[11]

The second part of the *Reglamento* of 1743 dealt with the daily regime of the prisoners. The administration and distribution of their food rations was reorganized. In the sixteenth and seventeenth centuries, prisoners in the North African presidios were not given any food rations except their daily allotment of bread. Instead, each received a daily cash allowance of three cuartos (twelve maravedís) to purchase food. By the opening years of the eighteenth century this sum was grossly inadequate.[12] The *Reglamento* of 1716 called for the distribution of food to prisoners in addition to their bread rations, but it did not specify how this was to be accomplished. In 1738 a system was introduced by which the food allotments were combined (in quantities for eleven men) and prepared in the form of stews by camp cooks, usually prisoners.[13] This practice received official sanction in the legislation of 1743, and the daily menus were described in detail. The food in the two daily stews cost seven cuartos (twenty-eight maravedís) per man—five cuartos (twenty maravedís) for lunch and two cuartos (eight maravedís) for supper. The remaining one cuarto (four maravedís) of the eight cuartos (32 maravedís) of the prisoners' allowance was retained to cover the cost of washing their clothes, providing oil for the lamps in their quarters, shaving, etc.[14]

The food distribution system adopted in the *Reglamento* of 1743 was introduced to effect economies. This was necessary because the provisioning of the North African presidios was very difficult. All food supplies and munitions had to be brought from Spain. Only Oran could obtain its basic provisions through tribal allies in the neighborhood. Food was scarce, and the garrisons usually were demoralized by the irregularity with which supplies reached them. Under the system established in 1743, savings could be had by preparing food in large quantities, while at the same time the quality of the meals was improved. In addition, the legislation of 1743 stipulated that *presidiarios* who were employed as servants of presidio officials and town residents could not receive presidio rations. They had to be supported by their employers.[15] This reduced the number of men to be fed and clothed with presidio funds. Despite the reorganization, however, the food allotments in the North African presidios continued to be meager. Not surprisingly, the lack of food was one of the principal factors behind the high desertion rate in the North African presidios for both soldiers and *presidiarios* throughout the centuries.

Dependence on supply ships from Spain was only one part of the problem. As on the galleys and in the Peninsular presidios, there were constant complaints concerning the quality of food as well as the way in which it was actually distributed. The *Reglamento* of

1743 gave the brigadiers control over the distribution of food and clothing to the prisoners. On the first day of each month, the brigadiers received the monthly allotments (in cash) due the men under their command. These payments had to be exchanged immediately for their equivalents in food, including the bread ration.[16] From the beginning, this system engendered fraud and corruption, and most of the abuses originated with the brigadiers. They developed the practice of illegally advancing the prisoners their monthly allowances in consideration of retaining eight to ten reales for themselves. Since the *presidiarios* usually spent most of this money on alcohol, tobacco, or gambling, they often suffered hunger and malnutrition. Many resorted to theft to obtain food, or ended up in the hospital suffering from illnesses caused by lack of proper nourishment. In Ceuta and Oran there also was the long-standing custom by which the *presidiarios* turned over their monthly allowances to the brigadiers in return for permission to work in town at their trades, or as street vendors and porters, instead of laboring on the fortifications.[17]

In the years after 1743, attempts were made to reduce the powers of the brigadiers and to deprive them of their control over the monthly cash allowances. On several occasions, a paymaster was appointed and charged with the receipt and distribution of the payments. And, it was decided to make these payments every fifteen days (on a bi-monthly basis) so as to reduce the sums available for malversation.[18] Nevertheless, pressure from the brigadiers doomed all efforts to failure, and the abuses continued unabated throughout the period. They were, after all, inherent in the system.

Regardless of the *Reglamento* of 1743 and all subsequent legislation (most notably the *Reglamento* of 1791, which included tighter controls and more restrictions), the North African presidios were never as effectively governed and administered as the Peninsular naval arsenals.[19] One of the main reasons for this was their distance from Spain and their precarious position as Christian outposts in a Moslem world. This situation was perfect for the growth of indiscipline, fraud, and corruption. An official investigation of the Alhucemas presidio in 1778 found that bribes and special favors were rampant at all levels of the administration. Similar inquiries at other times showed that the same circumstances existed in other presidios.[20] Moreover, criminals were quite aware of the more "flexible" conditions in the North African presidios, and despite the obvious inconveniences, many preferred to be sent there rather than to the naval arsenals. In 1767, when prisoners at the arsenal of Cartagena were given the choice of remaining at that presidio or being transferred to North Africa to complete unfilled quotas there, 923 out of 1,464 asked to be sent to North Africa.[21]

With the abolition of the galleys in 1748, the penal population of the North African presidios underwent a sudden rise. The remaining *forzados* on the galleys were distributed between the mines of Almadén and the North African presidios. Prisoners with term sentences of more than one year, or with the note of retention, were destined for the North African presidios. In order to accommodate the increased numbers, new brigades were created and the old ones enlarged, but these measures were temporary because circumstances changed rapidly.[22] As more convicted criminals were sentenced to the arsenals in the late 1750s and early 1760s, serious manpower shortages developed in the North African presidios. After 1765 the situation deteriorated further, largely as a result of legislation in that year which ordered that all those guilty of crimes meriting presidio punishment be sent to the naval arsenals.[23] Also, in the late 1760s and early 1770s the North African presidios had to compete with the presidios of the New World for convict laborers. In 1766, the Spanish government decided to strengthen the defenses of the Spanish Empire in America by rebuilding the fortifications of Havana and San Juan. Part of the plan was to sentence military deserters and civilian smugglers, who normally would have been sent to the North African presidios, to the Caribbean presidios.[24] In 1766 and 1767, the lack of manpower in the North African presidios became so severe that 1,214 prisoners serving at Cartagena were removed from the arsenal and distributed between the presidios of Ceuta and Oran.[25]

A new era for the North African presidios began in 1771 when, as a result of the legislation of that year, prisoners were divided into categories according to the severity of their crimes. Minor and first offenders were assigned to the North African presidios, while recidivists and major offenders were sent to the naval arsenals. Although available statistics are few and incomplete, some general trends can be ascertained.[26] The 1770s and early 1780s were a period of accelerated growth for the North African presidios, due to the resumption of hostilities with the Moslems (see table 7.1). The peace treaty of 1767 with Morocco was short-lived, and in 1773, Ceuta, Melilla, and El Peñón were attacked. The elevated population figures reached during the late 1770s and early 1780s coincided with the period of war. High levels continued to be maintained throughout the 1780s in the larger presidios of Oran and Ceuta, while El Peñón and Alhucemas registered a decline. Melilla, after reaching a peak in the late 1770s, declined somewhat in the early 1780s, but recovered by the end of the century. When Oran was captured by the Algerians in 1792, its prisoners were distributed among the remaining presidios, mainly Melilla and Ceuta.[27]

In the eighteenth century the Spanish government made strenuous efforts to restrict the population of the North African presidios to soldiers and *presidiarios*. This policy was based on military and financial considerations—the high cost of defense and provisioning. Legislation throughout the century prohibited the wives and children of soldiers and *presidiarios* from residing in the presidios.[28] On the other hand, their governors had the authority to grant special permits for temporary residence, on condition that family members could be supported.[29] Table 7.2 shows that in 1774 women and children made up 16 percent of the total population at Melilla and 22 percent at Alhucemas. Among the *presidiarios*, dependents of those serving in the fixed regiments (*fijos*) were among those favored for these permits. In 1774, at Melilla, for example, thirty-three out of ninety men in the fixed regiment had their wives with them. Occasionally, permission was given to the wives of *presidiarios* working in the presidio shops or offices or plying their trades in the town. Some of these women worked as servants in the homes of presidio officials, and their permits for temporary residence were based on this arrangement.[30]

The same financial and military considerations that influenced the Spanish government to limit the population growth of the presidios also motivated it to try to prevent them from becoming penal colonies. To that end, *presidiarios* were prohibited from remaining after the completion of their sentences. But there always were exceptions. Many former prisoners who performed work in necessary or special-

Table 7.1. *Presidiarios* in Three North African Presidios, 1772–88*

| Year | Oran** | Melilla | El Peñón |
|------|--------|---------|----------|
| 1772 | 2,810 | 730 | — |
| 1773 | — | — | — |
| 1774 | — | 808 | 249 |
| 1775 | — | 725 | — |
| 1776 | 2,055 | 998 | 266 |
| 1777 | — | 1,330 | 260 |
| 1778 | 2,941 | — | 276 |
| 1779 | — | 1,023 | 296 |
| 1780 | 3,024 | — | 285 |
| 1781 | 2,888 | — | 282 |
| 1782 | 2,629 | 726 | 164 |
| 1783 | 1,598 | 850 | 209 |
| 1784 | 2,582 | — | — |
| 1785 | — | — | — |
| 1786 | 2,616 | — | 205 |
| 1787 | 2,379 | — | — |
| 1788 | 2,532 | — | — |

*Ceuta and Alhucemas have been omitted from this table because of insufficient data.
**Figures for Oran are averages calculated on the basis of monthly reports.
Source: AGS, Guerra Moderna, Legs. 4898, 4913, 4934, 4935, 4951, 4955, 4959, 4968, 4972, 4975, 4977, 4981, 4982, 4986.

ized trades or professions received permission to remain temporarily and even permanently. By the end of the eighteenth century, there existed the nucleus of a permanent resident Spanish population made up of former *presidiarios* and their families.[31] In this way, the foundations were laid for the eventual transformation of the North African presidios into penal colonies in the nineteenth century.

As for the convict population of the presidios, it was not determined by changes in the Spanish penal code or by need alone. Two key factors influencing prisoner statistics were death and desertion rates (see table 7.3). Desertion, in particular, was a constant problem. In the sixteenth and seventeenth centuries, men frequently deserted because of scarcity of food and other provisions, and these same miserable conditions continued to motivate desertion in the

Table 7.2. Total Population of the Presidios of Melilla and Alhucemas, 1774

| | Melilla | | | Alhucemas | | |
|---|---|---|---|---|---|---|
| Status | Men | Women | Children | Men | Women | Children |
| Military staff | 19 | 6 | 21 | 5 | 3 | 2 |
| Accounting dept. staff | 3 | 2 | 2 | 2 | 2 | 3 |
| Ecclesiastics | 3 | — | — | 3 | 1 | 3 |
| Regular garrison (*fijos*) | 90 | 33 | 59 | 67 | 13 | 12 |
| Arsenal personnel | 20 | 14 | 28 | 8 | 6 | 9 |
| Navy personnel | 45 | 7 | 13 | 25 | 10 | 19 |
| Hospital staff | 6 | 5 | 8 | 3 | 5 | 9 |
| Widows, orphans | — | 4 | 8 | — | 3 | 2 |
| Private individuals | 5 | 12 | 16 | — | — | — |
| Rotating battalions | 539 | 9 | 8 | 122 | 3 | 2 |
| Supply dept. | — | — | — | 1 | 4 | 3 |
| *Presidiarios* | 808 | 14 | 20 | 174 | 2 | 2 |
| Total | 1,538 | 106 | 183 | 410 | 52 | 66 |

Source: AGS, Guerra Moderna, leg. 4923, Melilla, June 13, 1774; Alhucemas, June 7, 1774.

eighteenth century.[32] The conversion of the North African presidios into general penal establishments in the eighteenth century further aggravated the situation, but it is not correct to assume that desertion was a problem mainly involving *presidiarios*. On the contrary, soldiers (those belonging to the rotating regiments that were stationed temporarily in the presidios) as well as the *presidiarios* deserted throughout the eighteenth century. At times, the desertion rate of the soldiers was much higher than that of the *presidiarios* (see table 7.4).[33] The prisoners serving at arms (*desterrados*) were especially inclined to desert. Most of these men had committed offenses, usually desertion, while stationed in Peninsular Spain. After being tried by courts martial, they were condemned to serve in the fixed regiments in the North African presidios. The military courts customarily meted out long-term sentences (eight years or more) or life sentences to deserters. In addition, before 1771, indefinite sentences in such cases were frequent. A high rate of desertion is not suprising among men who already had a high recorded rate of desertion and who, besides, were made desperate by the fear of indeterminate punishment.[34]

Both the location of the presidios and conditions in them favored desertion. These fortresses were enclaves in a hostile countryside, and once prisoners were outside the walls, desertion and capture by the Moslems was easy. Since the fixed regiments customarily served as guards in advance posts and strongholds *extramuros*, there were ample opportunities for desertion. These regiments also helped to guard the cattle and flocks of sheep belonging to the presidio that were pastured in the surrounding countryside.[35] As for the *presidiarios* assigned to the labor brigades, traditionally a greater part of them were left unchained. Only those condemned for heinous crimes wore chains and fetters. In the 1780s, the practice of chaining those sentenced for theft was introduced as a means of reducing the high

Table 7.3. Deaths and Desertions in the Presidio of Oran, 1768*

|           | Died | | Deserted | | Total | |
|-----------|----------|--------------|----------|--------------|----------|--------------|
|           | Soldiers | *Presidiarios* | Soldiers | *Presidiarios* | Soldiers | *Presidiarios* |
| January   | 21 | 13 | 2  | 1  | 23 | 14 |
| April     | 5  | 11 | 10 | 12 | 15 | 23 |
| June      | 3  | 4  | 12 | 11 | 15 | 15 |
| July      | 13 | 6  | 18 | 16 | 31 | 22 |
| August    | 8  | 4  | 4  | 3  | 12 | 7  |
| September | 7  | 2  | 4  | 4  | 11 | 6  |
| October   | 3  | 1  | 3  | 6  | 6  | 7  |
| November  | 7  | 3  | 6  | 4  | 13 | 7  |
| Total     | 67 | 44 | 59 | 57 | 126 | 101 |

*Figures for February, March, and May are unavailable.
Source: AGS, Guerra Moderna, leg. 4700.

Table 7.4. Desertions from Ceuta and Oran, 1742–50

|          | Soldiers | *Presidiarios* | Total |
|----------|----------|--------------|-------|
| 1742–44  | 149 | 40  | 189 |
| 1745–47  | 262 | 123 | 385 |
| 1748–50* | 90  | 72  | 162 |
| Total    | 501 | 235 | 736 |

*Through the first six months of 1750 only.
Source: AGS, Guerra Moderna, leg. 1532.

rate of crimes against property in the presidios. Although it did accomplish its purpose (theft declined somewhat), presidio officials considered such punishment excessive and, in the long run, unwise. They believed that it made prisoners more inclined to desert and more willing to take any risks. Chained prisoners were used in fortification work exclusively, and could not be removed from it.[36] As for the rest of the *presidiarios*, some were employed in presidio offices and shops. Others labored at their trades and other occupations in the town. The relative freedom of movement enjoyed by many *presidiarios* made desertion an ever-present possibility.

Although statistics are fragmentary, available data suggest that desertion rates began to rise sharply in the 1750s, coinciding with the abolition of the galleys. Desertion reached its highest levels in the last years of the 1760s and in the decade of the 1770s. In the 1780s there was a tendency toward stabilization, with a gradual decline in the late 1780s and into the 1790s (see table 7.5).

Alarmed by the increase in desertion in the second half of the eighteenth century, the Spanish government restudied the problem

Table 7.5. Desertion Rate for Selected Years, Oran, 1760–88*

|  | Percentage of *Presidiarios* Deserting |
|---|---|
| 1760 | 3.6 |
| 1766 | 5.1 |
| 1767 | 2.1 |
| 1768 | 7.1 |
| 1772 | 7.6 |
| 1773 | 6.7 |
| 1776 | 6.8 |
| 1780 | 3.8 |
| 1781 | 4.0 |
| 1782 | 4.1 |
| 1783 | 3.3 |
| 1784 | 3.7 |
| 1785 | 5.4 |
| 1786 | 3.4 |
| 1787 | 2.5 |
| 1788 | 3.1 |

*No figures are available for years not shown.
Source: AGS, Guerra Moderna, legs. 4860, 4889, 4894, 4898, 4913, 4919, 4951, 4955, 4959, 4964, 4968, 4972, 4976, 4985.

and developed new approaches to it. Several methods were devised and utilized to combat desertion. To begin with, there was a modification of the penalties previously inflicted on deserters. Traditionally, all those who deserted from the presidios and were apprehended were subject to the death penalty.[37] In 1765 (and again in 1769) it was decreed that the death penalty would be commuted for deserters who returned voluntarily before surrendering to the Moslems or being captured by them. Instead, they would be sentenced to serve at the chain pumps in the arsenal of Cartagena for five years. After that, they would be returned to a North African presidio to complete their original sentences, but with the proviso that the total time served could not exceed ten years. In the 1780s, after the abolition of the penalty of hard labor at the pumps, many deserters, in particular recidivists, were sent to the presidios of the New World.[38]

Most of the men who were penalized for desertion either had been captured in the act or had returned voluntarily. Most had deserted in the hope of somehow finding their way back to Spain. After successfully eluding capture by the presidio forces and the Moslems, they hid in the surrounding countryside for a short time. When they finally realized the hopelessness of their situation, they returned voluntarily to the presidio. In general, the period of desertion was short, usually a few hours or days. Extant data also suggest that drunkenness and the perpetration of crimes in the presidios by the *desterrados* and *presidiarios* were frequent causes for desertion.[39]

The deserters who returned to the presidios from Moslem captivity made up a special category. To encourage these men to return, it was established that, in such cases, the penalty of five years at the pumps would be commuted to the same length of time in a North African presidio. This was done in consideration of their sufferings in captivity. It also was assumed that their devotion to the Christian faith had motivated their flight, a claim which they all made, even though most had converted to Islam. Despite the modification of punishment, such cases do not seem to have been numerous. The few examples that have been recorded involve men who had been in captivity for a long time—on the average, from ten to twenty years—and who were renegades. In such instances, the procedure called for a period of interrogation and quarantine in the presidio, after which the returnees were sent to Spain to be reconciled by the Inquisition.

Once absolved by the Holy Office, they were returned to a North African presidio to complete their sentences. In certain cases of old age or physical incapacity, they were freed.[40]

Another method of combating desertion was the deployment of troops from the presidio to patrol the immediate area surrounding it. In Ceuta, a presidio with one of the highest desertion rates, for years there was a special cavalry unit for the sole purpose of seeking out and capturing deserters. When in the 1760s it became impossible, for fiscal reasons, to maintain it, a small number of *presidiarios* ("trusties") were assigned to lookout posts in the area for the same purpose. In return for their services they were offered a partial or full pardon, depending on their crimes and the amount of time remaining in their sentences.[41]

The payment of bribes and rewards to Moslem chieftains and others in the frontier zones surrounding the presidios was another approach to the problem. This system was utilized in Ceuta and Melilla in the 1760s, but was not introduced into Oran until the 1780s. It was particularly effective in the years following the treaty of 1767 with Morocco, which ushered in an era of greater cooperation between Spain and Morocco. This treaty provided for mutual restitution of deserters, and a considerable number of men were returned under this provision. Nevertheless, the Moroccans eventually adopted the practice of allowing deserters who converted to Islam to remain. The rest were forcibly turned over to the presidio officials. In the 1770s, in order to encourage the frontier Moors to return even those deserters who had been willing to convert, the Spanish government offered them payments at thirty to forty pesos a head for each deserter that they returned.[42] Frequent references to these payments in the records indicates that the system was somewhat effective.

The reform legislation of 1771 represented the most comprehensive and far-reaching plan to combat desertion in the eighteenth century. Here the emphasis was on prevention rather than control. Major offenders and recidivists, the group thought to be most capable of deserting and becoming renegades, were not to be sent to North Africa. Only minor offenders were to be assigned to the North African presidios. In addition, the elimination of indefinite terms and the establishment of a ten-year maximum for all sentences were conceived as a means to prevent desperation, which was considered to be one of the main causes of desertion. Finally, the legislation of 1771 called for a softening of treatment, since it was believed that the cruelty to which prisoners often were subjected influenced them to desert.[43]

The gradual decline in desertion rates in the late 1770s and in the 1780s seems to have been closely related to the legislation of 1771. Perhaps just as important was the cooperation of the Moroccans and Algerians (the treaty of 1785 with Algiers included a restitution provision) in returning deserters. But in the last analysis, desertion could be reduced but not prevented. As one presidio official stated in 1780, "once a soldier or *presidiario* decides to desert, nothing can stop him. He is not deterred by fear of captivity, punishment or anything else."[44]

An extensive quantitative analysis of prisoners in the North African presidios is not possible because of lack of data. With the exception of selected years and a few presidios, the registers of prisoners in the North African presidios are no longer in existence.[45] Although the complete series seems to have disappeared, the data that remain facilitate at least a partial statistical analysis. Some of the most useful extant material relates to the presidio of Oran in the 1780s. This collection consists of lists of prisoners received in Oran during the years 1781–86, together with their crimes and sentences. In addition, there are five separate lists for the years 1785–89 with the names of 1,579 men and their social and occupational status.[46]

As can be seen in table 7.6, the majority of prisoners in Oran in the years 1781–86 were property offenders, smugglers, and soldiers. These three groups represented 71 percent of the sample of 3,477 men. Soldiers made up 26 percent of the total. The North African presidios, like those of the New World, served as military prisons in the second half of the eighteenth century. For 28 percent of these soldiers, a presidio sentence resulted from such common-law offenses as homicide, theft, or robbery, while 60 percent were condemned for infractions against military discipline. Property crimes alone made up 24 percent of the total number of military delicts.

There were several categories of military offenses. Two of the most usual were abandonment of guard duty and sale of military property (clothes, munitions, and provisions). Violence against fel-

Table 7.6.  Classification of Offenses, Oran, 1781–86

| Nature of Offense | Percentage |
| --- | --- |
| Crimes against persons | 10 |
| Crimes against property | 32 |
| Crimes against good customs and morals; disturbing the domestic peace | 3 |
| Disturbing the public peace | 10 |
| Smuggling | 13 |
| Swindling, fraud, and counterfeiting | 2 |
| Military offenses (all kinds) | 26 |
| Others | 4 |
| Total | 100 |

Sample: 3,477 men.
Source: AGS, Guerra Moderna, leg. 4934.

low soldiers and officers also was a frequent offense, and carried with it a ten-year presidio sentence. Of all the military infractions, desertion was the most common. Some 39 percent of the soldiers condemned to Oran were deserters. Of this total, less than one quarter were repeat offenders, since it was customary during these years to send recidivist deserters to the presidios of Spanish America.[47] As for the others, with the abolition of the chain pumps in the arsenal of Cartagena, most first-time offenders were sentenced to North Africa.

Despite their large representation, soldiers were not the most numerous group in the Oran presidio. The largest category of prisoners was civilian property offenders, who accounted for 32 percent of the total inmate population. On the basis of this sample, without additional data, it is not possible to say whether or not property crime increased during this period, but the evidence seems to indicate that it may have become more violent. Significantly, men convicted of robbery, banditry, burglary, and housebreaking (crimes that involved violence or the threat of it) represented the majority of prisoners sentenced for crimes against property (a total of 52 percent). These statistics agree with what is known about property crime in town and countryside in this period. Banditry, for example, endemic to many parts of Spain in the seventeenth century, became particularly intense in Andalusia and Extremadura during these years. Within the urban centers—in Madrid, for example—robbery cases represented a large proportion of the property delicts coming before the *Sala de Alcaldes de Casa y Corte* in the 1780s.[48] The rest of the property offenders in the Oran presidio sample included an assortment of thieves, particularly horse and cattle thieves, and those who specialized in stealing from churches. All were men who had committed serious thefts (in number and value) or were notorious recidivists. There were few petty thieves in the North African presidios at this time, since they were being absorbed almost entirely by the Peninsular public works presidios. When they did appear, their sentences included other crimes in addition to theft, most often resistance to arrest.

Among those sentenced for property crimes there was a small percentage of cases of swindling and fraud. Most involved office-holders who had been convicted of malversation in the performance of their duties. While peculation and fraud were common occurrences among government officials in the early modern era, few of these officials, protected as they were by their privileged status, were ever prosecuted. This explains the small representation of these offenses. Similarly, only 3 percent of the men sentenced to Oran in this sample had committed crimes against good customs and morals. In the 1780s, most sexual offenses were punished by fines and short sentences in the public works presidios.

Offenses against the public order constituted a somewhat larger percentage of the sample (10 percent). Most common was the use of prohibited arms, which was the charge against 32 percent of the offenders in this category. Men who disregarded the laws against the possession of various kinds of knives and firearms were sentenced to four to six years in an overseas presidio. In 1771, the North African presidios were specifically designated as their place of reclusion.[49]

The third largest group in the Oran presidio were the smugglers. They represented 13 percent of the total inmate population. Among the smugglers, 87 percent were defrauders of the government tobacco monopoly, who were serving terms that averaged between four and six years. Tobacco fraud was one of the most frequent offenses in eighteenth-century Spain, and it involved individuals from all socioeconomic groups. The most common form of fraud was the sequestration of tobacco from factories and warehouses by employees. Although tobacco workers were carefully searched when leaving their work, it was impossible to prevent small amounts of tobacco from being removed. Workers convicted of these offenses were subject to presidio sentences, and they were among the prisoners at Oran. Nor was it unusual for officials of the government monopoly to be involved in the theft of tobacco from warehouses and engaged in its illegal sale. Some of these men ended up serving long sentences in the presidios.[50]

While the amount of tobacco pilfered from factories and storage facilities was large, it was insignificant when compared with the quantity of foreign tobacco brought into Spain clandestinely. Most of this tobacco originated in France, and was smuggled across the Pyrenees into Spain. Spanish tobacco in the form of powder or snuff (its most solicited variety in the eighteenth century) was finer than the French type, but popular opinion, dominated by French styles in this period, preferred the French powder, known as *rapé*. Because of the incessant demand for *rapé*, all laws against its illegal importation proved ineffective. Finally, in 1786, the Spanish government authorized the manufacture of the French-style powder in Spanish factories; but by that time tastes had changed, and smoking tobacco had become more popular than snuff.[51] The conversion of Spanish factories from the manufacture of snuff to that of smoking tobacco took a long time. The process required a large number of specialized laborers who did the work by hand, and for many years production was limited. At the same time, demand rose sharply in the last years of the eighteenth century and the first decades of the nineteenth century. During that period of restricted Spanish output, contraband tobacco helped to satisfy the expanding market.[52]

The most numerous group of tobacco defrauders in the presidios were the smugglers who specialized in bringing foreign tobacco into Spain. Predominant among them were the smugglers of Aragon, Catalonia, and Navarre who operated in the Pyrenean region along the Franco-Spanish frontier. These men worked in groups and spent most of their lives in desolate and mountainous areas living in caves and huts. They brought their merchandise to isolated roadside inns whose owners served as intermediaries between them and prospective purchasers. These bands were equipped with all kinds of weapons, including harquebuses, and they fought standing battles with frontier guards and army troops that were occasionally sent out to capture them.[53]

In Andalusia and Extremadura the smugglers operated in a similar manner. The Extremaduran smugglers brought Brazil-tobacco into Spain from Portugal, while the Andalusians obtained their contraband from Gibraltar and North Africa. In certain Spanish towns around Gibraltar, smuggling was organized in an almost capitalistic manner. Individuals came together and formed companies with the objective of making a profit. Some invested capital and others their labor. Those who did the actual smuggling were considered employees of the company and were paid salaries. Spanish popular opinion was favorable toward the tobacco smugglers, especially in Andalusia and Extremadura, where poverty and unemployment forced many into this activity. Regional folklore bears eloquent testimony to the popular exaltation of the smugglers and the legends that were created about them.[54]

Only 10 percent of all *presidiarios* in Oran in the 1780s had been sentenced for crimes against persons, most of them for murder and

Tobacco smugglers. Reproduced in José Pérez Vidal, *España en la historia del tabaco* (Madrid: Consejo Superior de Ethnología Peninsular, 1959), p. 360.

manslaughter. Since the trend in the second half of the eighteenth century was toward the substitution of presidio sentences for capital punishment, and homicide is one of the better-reported crimes, the number of sentences for it bears a close relationship to its actual incidence.[55] In the 1780s a good number of these offenders were being sentenced to the North African presidios rather than the naval arsenals. On the other hand, whether the low percentage is indicative of a real decline in personal crime in Spain in the last quarter of the eighteenth century (as seemingly occurred in other western European countries) is questionable. The re-establishment of the galleys in the years 1784–1803 may be a determining factor. In 1784, the king directed the courts to sentence all serious offenders to the galleys, as had been done in the past.[56] This would include most of those convicted of crimes against persons, but how many offenders were actually sentenced to the galleys or were ever received there is not known. In 1787, a scarcity of rowers moved the king to issue another decree offering those *presidiarios* already serving in the arsenal of Cartagena reductions in sentences to volunteer for the galleys. Two years later further incentives were offered, and in view of these circumstances, it is likely that volunteers of this kind made up the main body of rowers.[57] Since the degree to which re-manning of the galleys affected the distribution of prisoners to the North African presidios cannot be determined, the question of whether or not personal crime declined in the last years of the eighteenth century remains unresolved.

An occupational analysis of prisoners in Oran can be made on the basis of extant data for the years 1785–89 (see table 7.7). Although the period covered is short, the size of the sample is considerable, at least when compared with the dearth of like information for the galleys or the arsenals. This kind of data presents many difficulties, however. To begin with, the occupational lists were compiled separately from those containing crimes and sentences. Since the names on the two sets of lists do not correspond, there is no way to determine what crimes were perpetrated by specific offenders. Secondly, soldiers and smugglers were listed in separate categories without any indication of their former or original occupations. Smuggling in this period was clearly just as much of a profession as soldiering. Moreover, both groups are under-represented in these data, because the lists contain only the names of prisoners transported to Oran on the regular monthly supply ships sent out from Málaga and Cartagena to the North African presidios. For security purposes, military prisoners and smugglers usually were grouped together and shipped to North Africa separately from other prisoners, whenever possible on warships. In addition, no divisions were made between journeymen and master craftsmen. Only in a few instances do journeymen appear as a separate category, and then there is no indication of their trade or occupation.[58]

Classifying the peasantry proved even more difficult. Since only one term, *labrador*, is used throughout the data to describe all farm workers, it is impossible to distinguish among them. In the eighteenth century, those peasants who worked their own land were commonly called *labradores* in contrast to the *jornaleros* or day laborers.[59] But it is not clear whether or not those who compiled this data were using the term *labrador* all-inclusively, because on two of the lists (for the years 1788 and 1789) the expression *del campo* ("from the countryside") also appears. Since the problem is unresolvable, I have simply placed all those described as *labradores* and *del campo*, together with shepherds and gardeners, in the broad category of rural workers.

The fact that almost half of the *presidiarios* in this sample (45 percent) came from the countryside seems to indicate that crime in the late eighteenth century was no longer as markedly an urban phenomenon as surviving records for previous centuries imply. The increase in the number of criminals from rural areas may be accounted for by an enlarged population, since the bulk of the

Table 7.7. Occupational Distribution of *Presidiarios*, Oran, 1785–89

|  | Number of Prisoners | Percentage |
|---|---|---|
| Rural workers | 705 | 45 |
| Urban trades and services | 591 | 37 |
| Professional and privileged group | 75 | 5 |
| Soldiers | 103 | 6 |
| Smugglers | 105 | 7 |
| Total | 1,579 | 100 |

Source: AGS, Guerra Moderna, leg. 4985.

demographic expansion in the second half of the eighteenth century came among the peasantry in the countryside. Another possible explanation is that it reflected changes in land cultivation and tenure occuring in this period as a result of the movement toward market agriculture. In most regions there was an effort to reverse terms of rent for peasant properties, taking advantage of the price rise and the increase in land values. In the southern and south central regions the trend was to evict peasant renters in order to form single-bloc farms and carry on large-scale cultivation. Property also was rented to wealthier peasants who sublet it to poorer peasants or hired laborers to cultivate large tracts for them. By the end of the century, according to the census of 1797, only a little more than 20 percent of the peasants were listed as property holders, while one-third were classified as renters and one-half as *jornaleros*.[60] Given these circumstances, the increase in the number of rural criminals was, to a considerable extent, a matter of growing poverty and necessity.

Some 37 percent of the *presidiarios* came from the world of the crafts, trade, and domestic service. Within this category, artisans were the most numerous. They were the same group that predominated on the prisoner lists of previous centuries, and that had the highest rate of offenses against persons as well as a high rate of theft. In the sample data, cloth and clothing workers—tailors, hosiers, hatters, weavers, carders, and shearers—appear most frequently. Shoemakers are particularly conspicuous, but this is not surprising, since their craft is usually described in eighteenth-century sources as being one of the most miserable and poor.[61] Among construction workers, masons and carpenters have equal representation, while in the metallurgical trades, ironsmiths predominated. The food, service, and transportation industries were represented principally by bakers, innkeepers, and muleteers and coachmen, respectively.

Professionals and those belonging to the privileged classes made up the smallest percentage of *presidiarios*. This group, representing 5 percent of the total sample, included doctors, lawyers, notaries, officeholders, students, and noblemen. Some in this category appear on the lists with their professions, while others are listed by name only, but with the honorific title of *don*. In this period (unlike in previous centuries), the title *don* was not reserved for nobility, but was applied to all men of wealth and position. Those whose names appear with the title *don* and the notation *sin oficio* (without occupation) were the real noblemen.[62]

Not all the prisoners in the sample data were being shipped to Oran directly from Peninsular jails. Quite a few were being transferred from other presidios to Oran. *Presidiarios* who committed crimes while confined to the presidios were tried by court martial and, except in extraordinary cases where the death penalty was required, were sentenced to serve additional sentences in other presidios. Prisoners from Melilla, Alhucemas, and El Peñón were transferred regularly to Ceuta and Oran, while the latter sent their offenders to the minor presidios. In 1786, because of overcrowding and lack of security in the minor presidios, the king ordered presidio officials at Oran and Ceuta to refrain from sentencing prisoners charged with new crimes to Alhucemas, Melilla, or El Peñón. Instead, prisoners were to remain where they were for punishment.[63] The common penalties used in these cases included additional sentences, often to be served in chains and fetters, in addition to flogging or "running the gauntlet."[64] Available documentation shows that most of those who were convicted of crimes in the presidios had committed theft or had killed or wounded a fellow prisoner.

The exchange of prisoners among different presidios was not confined to the North African establishments. Until the late 1780s, it was standard procedure to send deserters from the North African presidios to the chain pumps at the arsenal of Cartagena, after which they were returned to North Africa to complete their original sentences.[65] The movement of prisoners extended across the Atlantic as well. In addition to the regular shipment to the New World of offenders who were sentenced there (in particular, recidivist deserters and some kinds of tobacco defrauders), exchanges of military prisoners between the presidios of North Africa and Spanish America were common. The most frequent transfers were between Havana and San Juan on the one hand and Oran and Ceuta on the other, but there are examples of military prisoners being sent from New Orleans, Pensacola, and even Manila to North Africa and vice versa.[66] The ports of Cádiz in Spain and Havana in the New World were the principal receiving depots for the transatlantic prisoner traffic, while Málaga served as the distribution center for North Africa. Prisoners from the North African presidios being transferred to the New World were shipped first to Málaga and from there to Cádiz. At Cádiz, they were placed aboard ships once again and transported across the Atlantic to Havana, Cuba, where they either remained permanently or were sent on to their final destinations. The trip from the New World to North Africa followed the same route. There thus existed in the last quarter of the eighteenth century a network of penal institutions encompassing the Spanish empire.

In the eighteenth century, the North African presidios went through the last stages in their transition into full-fledged penal institutions. The laxity and maladministration of the previous centuries were not totally eliminated, but changes in governance gradually effected improvement. Desertion continued to be a problem, but here, too, there was some amelioration, particularly after the reform statute of 1771 and the restitution treaties with the North African states. By the end of the century, the conditions had been laid for the transformation of the North African presidios into penal colonies in the nineteenth century.

# 8

# Overseas Presidios:
# The Caribbean

Little attention has been given to the role of penal servitude in the history of the Spanish Empire, for historians traditionally have been more interested in other forms of coercive labor. With the exception of the textile industry, the systematic exploitation of convict labor in Spanish America has remained a relatively unexplored field of investigation.[1] Yet throughout the colonial period, prisoners were an important source of cheap labor, and their utilization by the state as well as by private interests merits close attention by those interested in colonial labor systems. Moreover, the history of penal servitude presents a good opportunity for the approach to colonial Spanish American history suggested by the Belgian historian Charles Verlinden some years ago.[2] Although Verlinden stressed the continuity between medieval European societies based on classical origins and Spanish American colonial societies, he also placed emphasis on the reciprocal contacts between colonies and metropolises. Penal servitude, like slavery, is an excellent example of the survival of classical and medieval influences, but both institutions also existed simultaneously on the Peninsula and in the New World during the colonial period. Thus, penal servitude, with its long history in the Mediterranean world, was transplanted to the New World, where,

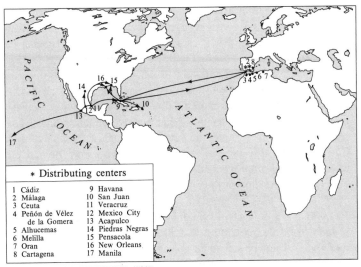

* Distributing centers

| | |
|---|---|
| 1 Cádiz | 9 Havana |
| 2 Málaga | 10 San Juan |
| 3 Ceuta | 11 Veracruz |
| 4 Peñón de Vélez | 12 Mexico City |
|    de la Gomera | 13 Acapulco |
| 5 Alhucemas | 14 Piedras Negras |
| 6 Melilla | 15 Pensacola |
| 7 Oran | 16 New Orleans |
| 8 Cartagena | 17 Manila |

CARTOGRAPHIC LABORATORY, UNIVERSITY OF WISCONSIN – MADISON

Movement of *presidiarios* between Spain, North Africa, and the New World in the eighteenth century

like its Peninsular counterpart, it reached its most extensive development in the eighteenth century.

In Spanish America penal servitude followed the Peninsular model, except that the line between public and private interests was blurred. In Spain, convicts could be used only in projects deemed to be in the interest of the state; for example, they labored on the galleys and in the presidios in the service of the king, and were under military control and jurisdiction. In the New World there was no such distinction, and anything that helped to further develop the economy was deemed in the public interest. Faced with a severe shortage of labor because of the decline in Indian population from the middle of the sixteenth century, the colonial courts sentenced men to terms of service at hard labor and then turned them over to private employers who used them in mines, factories, and mills.[3] The growth of population in the eighteenth century reduced the need for such labor in the private sphere, but the demand in the public sector continued to increase in response to the requirements of imperial defense.

Spain's losses to England during the Seven Years War (1756–63) convinced the Spanish government that the defenses of the New

World had to be reinforced. In the postwar years a plan was devised for strengthening and fortifying American ports, in particular Havana and San Juan, Puerto Rico, as a first line of defense. Havana had long been considered essential to the preservation of Spain's control over America, and its temporary loss to the British in 1762 was a severe blow. As for San Juan, the abandonment of the convoy system and adoption of a more flexible strategy of defense increased its importance. In the hands of the enemy, either of these ports could serve as a base for an attack on Spanish shipping in the Caribbean and threaten the security of Veracruz and Mexico. The rebuilding and improvement of their fortifications was therefore vital to the protection of the Spanish Empire.[4] A subsidy of 300,000 pesos a year was assigned to the fortifications of Havana, and 100,000 pesos to that of San Juan (both sums to be paid for the *situado* from Mexico), but it was clear from the beginning that these funds would not be adequate unless expenditures were kept low.[5] The success of the project therefore depended on the maintenance of a steady supply of workers at minimum cost. In the opinion of the planners, this problem could be resolved only through the use of penal labor, as had been done in Spain in the construction of the naval arsenals of Cartagena and El Ferrol. Thus, *presidiarios* came to play as important a role in the execution of Spanish defense plans in the Caribbean as they had performed on the Iberian Peninsula.

The improvement of the fortifications of Havana began immediately after the British returned it to Spain in July, 1763. The new governor, the Count of Ricla (1763–65), who arrived in June to supervise the transfer of power, had instructions to repair all fortifications and defenses on the island, to rebuild whatever had been destroyed, and to add whatever was needed as rapidly as possible. The reconstitution of El Morro and the erection of the forts of San Carlos de la Cabaña and Atarés were begun in July with a work force consisting of black slaves, free laborers, and some local prisoners.[6] Most of the black slaves were recent imports from Africa who had been introduced on the island during the British occupation. They were purchased by the governor specifically for this project from private owners at 150 pesos each, making a total investment of 954,000 reales for the original group of 795.[7] As far as can be determined, black slaves made up the largest percentage of workers during the first two years of construction, but later their number decreased sharply. Available statistics show that a total of 4,198 of them worked on the fortifications during the years 1763–65, and that they reached their highest number (1,967) in 1764. Figures for 1766 and 1767 are nonexistent, but those for 1768 and 1769 show a decline in the number of slaves and a steady increase in *presidiarios*. In January, 1768, there were 636 *presidiarios* and 1,136 black slaves out of a total of 1,977 workers; but by the following January, of a total work force of 2,030, the number of *presidiarios* had risen to 1,115, while the black slaves had declined to 766.[8]

In a letter to the king in May, 1769, Governor Antonio María Bucareli explained the apparent shift away from the use of black slaves to that of *presidiarios*. According to his account, the progress of the work had reached a critical point. The black slaves were proving too costly because of their high mortality rates, while free laborers required a daily expenditure of three reales per man in wages. The only way to keep costs down and to stay within the 300,000-peso annual subsidy was to replace the slaves and free workers with *presidiarios*. In August, 1769, the king ordered Bucareli to sell the remaining black slaves and to dismiss the free laborers in numbers equal to those of *presidiarios* arriving from Spain and Mexico.[9]

In contrast to Havana, in San Juan a labor force made up predominantly of *presidiarios* was projected from the beginning. In September, 1765, when the king approved the plan to repair and reconstruct the forts of San Felipe del Morro and San Cristóbal, he authorized the use of 445 *presidiarios* from Spain, Cuba, and Venezuela, although it was expected that the majority would come from Spain. The shortage of available manpower on the island and the unwillingness to utilize black slaves because of the unhappy experiences with them in Cuba motivated this decision. Initially it was thought that the *presidiarios* could be supplemented by soldiers from the San Juan garrison, who were to be paid two reales a day for their services.[10] Apparently some were employed in the early days of construction, when there were few *presidiarios,* and later, when the pressure of work demanded extra laborers, but aside from these special occasions, the work force consisted of *presidiarios.*

Work on the fortifications of San Juan began in January, 1766, but the period of greatest activity was 1769–83, during which the forts of San Felipe del Morro and San Cristóbal were converted into powerful strongholds. Statistics are lacking for the years 1766–70, but it appears that fewer than the assigned number of 445 *presidiarios* worked on the fortifications in that period, and the higher quota of 600 that was enacted after 1771 was never reached.[11] It is possible to estimate the actual representation of *presidiarios* on the basis of existing data (see table 8.1). In the years 1771–76, there were an average of 476 *presidiarios* in the San Juan presidio; from 1778 to 1780, 446; from 1781 to 1783, 260; and from 1784 to 1786, seventy-seven (after 1785, the quota was reduced to 300). According to these figures, the number of *presidiarios* peaked in July, 1773, at 557; by December, 1783, there were only 163. These statistics coincide perfectly with the different periods of construction. The largest contingents of *presidiarios* appear during the years 1771–83, which was precisely the most intense stage of the work, while the sharp decline in 1783 and after reflects the completion of the major undertakings.

These figures are somewhat misleading, because they reflect the total number of *presidiarios* in the presidio without adjustment for the number of those unable to work because of illness. The actual

Table 8.1. Number of *Presidiarios* in the San Juan Presidio, 1773–83*

| Month | 1773 | 1774 | 1775 | 1776 | 1778 | 1779 | 1780 | 1781 | 1782 | 1783 |
|---|---|---|---|---|---|---|---|---|---|---|
| January | 480 | 517 | — | 467 | — | 479 | — | 338 | 286 | 251 |
| February | — | — | — | 466 | 539 | 477 | 402 | 338 | 275 | 233 |
| March | 459 | 500 | — | 455 | 541 | 475 | 396 | 341 | 273 | 266 |
| April | 436 | — | 438 | 434 | 526 | 465 | — | 341 | 294 | 170 |
| May | — | — | 430 | 432 | 517 | 472 | 387 | 345 | 282 | 148 |
| June | 447 | — | 479 | 432 | 513 | 459 | 378 | 331 | 260 | 142 |
| July | 557 | — | — | 431 | 459 | 448 | 376 | 321 | 258 | 144 |
| August | 504 | — | — | 417 | 483 | 447 | 352 | 323 | 265 | 150 |
| September | — | — | 439 | 413 | 480 | 447 | 367 | 318 | 268 | 163 |
| October | 504 | — | 442 | 421 | 477 | — | 362 | 315 | 282 | 170 |
| November | 479 | — | 443 | — | 472 | — | 357 | 306 | 276 | 169 |
| December | 528 | — | 460 | — | 480 | — | 349 | 306 | 272 | 163 |

*Figures for the year 1777 are missing.
Source: AGI, Santo Domingo, legs. 2504–11.

number working at any given time was much smaller than appears from these statistics. Inaccuracies and inconsistencies in the official monthly reports make it difficult to calculate more than a rough estimate of the number of *presidiarios* who were incapacitated due to poor health. In a normal year (one in which there were no major infections), an average of some 10 percent of the *presidiarios* of San Juan were idle each month for health reasons (see table 8.2).[12] In times of widespread illness, the lack of *presidiarios* brought the work to a virtual standstill; for example, in October, 1773, at the height of an outbreak of scurvy in the San Juan presidio, some 361 men were incapacitated—72 percent of the labor force.

The physical health of the *presidiarios* was closely related to their diet and living conditions. Climatic considerations were another factor, for life in the tropics, with its constant heat, frequent storms, and hurricanes, in addition to infectious disease, took its toll. The diet of the *presidiarios* in the New World was similar to the ration distributed in the Peninsular presidios (in particular, the naval arsenal of La Carraca). Modifications of the basic presidio diet in Spanish America resulted from two factors: the unavailability of wheat on the islands, and the greater supply of other food, especially meat. Biscuit made of cassava flour in the form of hard round cakes supplanted the hardtack of the Peninsular presidios, and the daily

Table 8.2. *Presidiarios* Ill or Incapacitated in the San Juan Presidio, 1776*

| Month | Hospitalized | Confined to Quarters | Total Number of *Presidiarios* | Percentage of *Presidiarios* either Hospitalized or Confined to Quarters |
|---|---|---|---|---|
| January | 22 | 33 | 467 | 12 |
| February | 22 | 33 | 466 | 12 |
| March | 22 | 51 | 455 | 16 |
| June | 8 | 64 | 432 | 17 |
| July | 8 | 16 | 431 | 6 |
| August | 11 | 16 | 431 | 6 |
| September | 11 | 18 | 413 | 7 |
| October | 10 | 19 | 421 | 7 |

*Figures for April, May, November, and December are unavailable.
Source: AGI, Santo Domingo, leg. 2506A.

allotment was reduced from twenty-four to twelve ounces per man. The reduction of the bread ration was made possible through the addition of meat (either fresh or salted) to the stews. Since meat was plentiful and cheap in the New World, eventually it replaced beans as the standard fare in the American presidios. The stews also contained a sprinkling of vegetables, such as potatoes and squash, missing from their Peninsular counterparts, all of which meant that the diet of the *presidiarios* in the New World was better balanced and more nutritious than in the Old, while the cost was the same (one real).[13] In addition to wine, the *presidiarios* in Spanish American received a daily ration of brandy that was distributed to stimulate greater activity in a kind of "morning break" between breakfast and lunch.[14]

Although the food ration in the New World presidios was better than in the Peninsula, it still was insufficient, and therefore created a state of chronic malnutrition. Lack of fruits and vegetables in sufficient quantity resulted in the constant presence of deficiency diseases, especially scurvy. Furthermore, malnutrition made for lowered resistance to infections. As in the Peninsular presidios, the existence of scrofula and consumption in endemic form among the *presidiarios* can be attributed in part to their deficient diet. Poor living conditions were another factor in the incidence of disease. Lack of personal hygiene, infrequent changes of clothing, and crowding contributed to the high incidence of diseases such as scabies.[15] More serious were body lice, which carried typhus fever, a frequent cause of death in jails, presidios, and wherever the unwashed were crowded together.

Besides the *presidiarios* who were genuinely sick, there were those who feigned illness to avoid work. In 1770 this problem was serious enough to spur the presidio officials in San Juan to take measures against it. Since the guards and overseers could not readily ascertain who was genuinely ill, the doctor of the presidio hospital was engaged to examine daily the *presidiarios* who claimed that they were indisposed.[16] Many of the imposters probably were discovered by this means, but it was impossible to eliminate them all, and absenteeism of this kind continued to be a problem. In view of this situation, it is easier to comprehend the repeated complaints of the presidio administrators in their correspondence with the king as to the scarcity of *presidiarios*.

In addition to those with temporary indispositions (whether real or feigned), the category of unserviceable *presidiarios* also included those who were permanently incapacitated through disease or injury. The principal source of information about this group is a list compiled by the San Juan officials in 1773 with the objective of securing their release so as to replace them with fresh contingents. It contains the names of sixty-five men classified as incurably ill. Most of these men were suffering from scrofula and consumption; the rest were incapacitated because of hernias or paralysis. Although this list covers a substantial period of time (1768–73), it does not correspond to the years of most intense activity, and therefore its statistical value is limited.[17] It seems likely that the number of incurables increased substantially when both the population of the penal contingents and the difficulty of work-loads reached their maximums.

The decision in 1773 to release the unserviceable *presidiarios* raised the question of what to do with them, as well as what to do with others in the same category in the future. Castilian law specifically required the return of former prisoners after the completion of their sentences to their places of origin, where they were known to authorities and could be under constant supervision. In practice, it was difficult to enforce this provision, because when prisoners were returned to Spain, few went back to their home districts. Most tended to congregate around their ports of entry, or to migrate to the larger towns and cities in these same regions. Many government officials blamed the high levels of crime in coastal Andalusia and Valencia on this situation, and believed that it was necessary in the interests of law and order to decrease the number of such elements being brought back to the Peninsula.[18] This idea accorded well with one of the objectives of eighteenth-century Bourbon reformism—the elimination, or at least reduction, of criminals, social deviants, and other "undesirables." It ultimately prompted the royal decision in 1774 to resettle *presidiarios* on the island of Puerto Rico rather than having them returned to Spain. This measure further stipulated that they should be settled in groups in sparsely inhabited parts of the island and given some kind of supervision.[19] Although Spain, unlike other western European countries such as England and France, never adopted the policy of transportation of criminals, the attempt to settle released *presidiarios* on the island of Puerto Rico in 1774 manifested a similar approach and, in effect, accomplished the same objectives.[20]

In Spain, the collection and distribution of convicted criminals sentenced to the New World presidios was the same as for those condemned to the Peninsular and North African presidios. Local justices first sent them to the central prisons of their respective judicial districts, and from there they joined the chains destined for Cádiz, the main distribution center for the presidios of America.[21] Once in Cádiz, they were placed in a jail (*depósito de presidiarios*) that was maintained for them in the naval arsenal of La Carraca to await shipment to the New World. Since, for purposes of security, *presidiarios* could be sent only on warships carrying troops, they often waited in the *depósito* for years before they finally were sent to their destinations.[22]

At La Carraca, prolonged incarceration in crowded and unsanitary conditions took its toll of the prisoners—many of those who survived were so weakened as to be unserviceable by the time they were ready to be sent to America. Men in feeble health were shipped out regularly, notwithstanding the requirement that they be examined and officially approved by the arsenal doctors. In practice, only in cases of obvious incapacity—for example, blindness or paralysis—were men rejected; the remainder, regardless of age or infirmities, were sent. This was especially true in the years 1771–80, when the demand for *presidiarios* in San Juan was so great.[23] In 1773, for example, the officials there complained to the king that most *presidiarios* coming from Spain arrived on the island in such poor health that they were "permanently incapacitated" or at least "temporarily unserviceable."[24] Four years later, conditions among the prisoners destined for Puerto Rico in the *depósito* of La Carraca were so deplorable that the chaplain of the arsenal wrote the king's confessor asking him to intervene with the king to provide for their immediate transport to the New World. Apparently nothing came of this appeal, because two years later they were still awaiting shipment; the only difference was that those who were able were being employed in the work of the arsenal.[25]

The exploitation of prisoners while they were in the *depósitos* was a departure from accepted procedure, which specifically prohibited their use except at their assigned destinations. This practice was introduced at La Carraca as a temporary expedient to serve the interests of both prisoners and the state. For the prisoners, it offered relief from constant incarceration, while the king benefited from the utilization of additional workers. While this system was introduced at La Carraca to meet a special situation, changing circumstances in the late 1770s and early 1780s led to its adoption in other *depósitos* as well. By the last decades of the century, this system was firmly established on both sides of the Atlantic.[26]

Although Cádiz was the principal port of embarcation for *presidiarios* being shipped to the presidios of Spanish America, prisoners from the northern and northwestern regions of the Peninsula (Galicia, Asturias, Basque Provinces) often were taken to the naval arsenal at El Ferrol in Galicia or to the port of La Coruña.[27]

The principal sources of *presidiarios* for both San Juan and Havana were Spain and Mexico, although it is impossible to determine exact numbers. In most instances, transcripts of sentences bore the designation "either Havana or San Juan," thereby allowing officials to assign *presidiarios* according to need. This practice gave rise to abuses on the part of the officials in Havana, since all *presidiarios* bound for the Caribbean from either Spain or Mexico had to pass through Havana before they could be sent to their ultimate destinations. Havana was the main distribution center for the New World presidios, and a *depósito* was maintained there for *presidiarios* in transit. The administrators of the Havana presidio made it a practice to retain prisoners destined for San Juan, on the grounds of acute labor shortages in Havana and lack of the necessary funds to cover the cost of their shipment to Puerto Rico. On this pretext, they detained prisoners "temporarily" and utilized them in the work of the presidio in the same manner as if they actually had been sentenced there.[28] Once these prisoners were incorporated into the work force of the presidio, the Havana officials applied to the king to sanction their actions. Since royal approval usually was forthcoming, the retention of these prisoners became permanent.[29]

From the beginning, fear of disorders arising from prisoner escapes dictated that the penal laborers sent to the New World be restricted to military deserters, and they continued to be in the majority to the end of the century. Later, prisoners who had committed other crimes, for example, homicide, assault, and theft, were added, along with a category of civilian prisoners—smugglers and violators of the royal tobacco monopoly.[30] Sentences for deserters ran from eight years to life (in the case of recidivists, the life sentence represented a commutation of the death penalty), while smugglers and tobacco monopoly defrauders averaged terms of four to six years.

In 1772, as a follow-up to the legislation of the previous year eliminating indefinite sentences, maximum terms for the New World presidios were lowered to six years with the exception of those individuals whose sentences specified "retention."[31] Dissatisfaction with the law of 1772 led to its early modification. The presidio administrators in Havana complained that because of the six-year maximum, too many men completed their terms within a relatively short time, and there were not enough prisoners to replace them. In 1778 it was decided to apply the six-year maximum to those with terms of over eight years. For prisoners within this category who had committed heinous crimes, presidio officials were given the authority to determine on an individual basis whether or not they merited the reduction of their sentences. These new regulations still did not satisfy the Havana officials, and in response to further pressure from them, the king declared in 1780 that the previous decrees represented a special royal concession only, and were not designed to establish a general rule.[32] Thus, the law restricting presidio sentences in the New World to a six-year maximum was duly abrogated.

Whereas the *presidiarios* sent to Havana and San Juan from Spain were almost all military men, those destined for the same presidios from Mexico were, with few exceptions, civilians. A large body of prisoners sentenced by the two principal judicial bodies in New Spain, the *sala de crimen* of the audiencia in Mexico City and the tribunal of the *acordada,* received presidio sentences, but it is difficult to determine what proportion of them served their terms in Veracruz (the most important Mexican presidio), Havana, or San

Juan. The majority of *acordada* prisoners, for example, served their terms in Havana or Veracruz, but significant numbers also went to Acapulco, Piedras Negras, Pensacola, and, in rare instances, the Philippines.[33] In 1773, for example, among the hard-core offenders in Havana serving terms of over six years, 486 came from Mexico out of a total of 586 in that category. The remainder came from Spain (all military deserters), Cuba (military prisoners), and Cartagena de Indias (murderers serving ten years to life).[34] As for San Juan, certainly not more than a small percentage of those shipped to Havana from Mexico were destined originally for San Juan; and of these, even fewer arrived there, because of the practice of retaining them in Havana.

Since the Indians, except in rare instances, usually served their sentences in Veracruz or some other presidio within the jurisdiction of modern Mexico, those sentenced by the Mexican courts to Havana and San Juan were Spaniards, mestizos, and mulattoes.[35] Almost all had committed capital crimes meriting substantial sentences. According to the data of 1773, 15 percent of the Mexican offenders were sentenced for crimes against persons, some 13 percent for homicide alone. Among the property offenders, who composed 34 percent of the total sample, horse and cattle thieves, bandits and robbers predominated. A considerable number of these men had committed homicide as well. There were few petty criminals sent from Mexico to Havana, because in Mexico a substantial proportion of cases involving minor crimes were settled by local officials with short-term punishment. The regular judicial system came into play only when a case involved a serious crime that merited a public display of judicial authority.[36]

In the 1780s and 1790s, the labor demands of the Havana presidio far exceeded those of Veracruz and San Juan. During that period, officials undertook improvements of the port, the harbor, and the fortifications. The Castillo del Príncipe and the Battery of Santa Clara, both considered vital to defense, were completed during those years. In 1787, the governor of Cuba blamed the slow work on the Castillo del Príncipe on the lack of *presidiarios,* and he requested the Viceroy of Mexico to send 2,000 *presidiarios* to Havana to satisfy the requirements of the new fortifications alone.[37] As for the needs of the port and arsenal, *presidiarios* manned the crews of the twelve pontoons and barges engaged in dredging the harbor and formed the work gangs employed in excavation work for construction projects around the port area. They also were used to cut and transport timber needed in the shipyard and to move heavy equipment around the docks and arsenal. In addition, a steady supply of *presidiarios* was required to move the chain pumps that prevented the dry docks from flooding. As in the Peninsular presidios, this labor was so arduous that only men who had committed the most serious crimes were subjected to it, and their sentences always specifically assigned them "to the pumps."[38]

In contrast to the men condemned to work the pumps, the remaining prisoners could be utilized in any kind of presidio labor, since their sentences stated simply that they were destined for the "arsenal and fortifications of Havana." It became customary in this period to define work categories more carefully so as to achieve a better distribution of *presidiarios*. The inauguration of a municipal improvement program for Havana during those years (street paving, a water supply system, new buildings for the government) resulted in keen competition for penal labor. In order to secure an adequate supply of *presidiarios* for the presidio as well as the public works projects, the courts were asked to specify in their sentences the kind of labor to be performed by the prisoners, that is, either "arsenal and fortifications" or "public works."[39]

The shortage of *presidiarios* in Havana in the last decades of the century was not only the result of the volume and intensity of the work. Attrition rates from desertion, death, and releases also must be considered. Figures for Havana are lacking for this period, but the official correspondence between Havana and Madrid contains repeated reference to losses because of frequent escapes and completion of sentences by prisoners. Some statistics are available for San Juan during the years 1778–82 (see table 8.3). In this period, some 40 percent of the working force was lost through death, desertion, and releases, and it is likely that this ratio increased in the 1790s. Most surprising are the figures for releases, which show that twice the number of men completed their sentences and were freed than died during these years. It seems that the survival rate was higher during the last decades of the century than in the previous period, but there is no evidence to suggest that this change resulted from better treatment or improved conditions for the *presidiarios;* on the contrary, the opposite was true.[40] The decline in the death rate and the increase in the number of those completing their terms was more likely a reflection of the tendency in the last decades of the eighteenth century to reduce the length of sentences while at the same time extending presidio punishment to a greater number of offenders. A survey of extant data from the *Sala de Alcaldes de Casa y Corte* shows the degree to which the judges, influenced by the ideas of Beccaria, Lardizábal, and others, were using their discretionary powers to modify and change penal law. Presidio sentences (generally from four to six years) were given for serious crimes, while lesser offenses were punished with short terms at hard labor in the public works projects (six months to two years). The death penalty is infrequent, and only in cases of the most heinous crimes. A similar pattern of sentencing can be found in the data published for the tribunal of the *acordada* (Mexico) during the years 1782–1808.[41]

Throughout the colonial period, the exploitation of penal labor was an essential part of the Spanish American labor system. In private industry, colonial employers regularly utilized penal labor, and some enterprises, notably those in the textile industry, were always associated with it. In the eighteenth century the military needs of the empire took precedence over private interests, and convicts began to be sent en masse to the presidios. By the end of the century, the state had become the principal employer of penal labor in the New World as in Spain.

Table 8.3. Deaths, Desertions, and Releases in the San Juan Presidio, 1778–82

| Year | Deserted | Died | Completed Sentences | Total Number of *Presidiarios*\* |
|------|----------|------|---------------------|-------------------------------|
| 1778 | 52 | 37 | 18 | 499 |
| 1779 | 66 | 28 | 85 | 463 |
| 1780 | 63 | 27 | 108 | 373 |
| 1781 | 42 | 37 | 66 | 327 |
| 1782 | 55 | 36 | 59 | 274 |

\*Figures are averages calculated on the basis of monthly reports.
Source: AGI, Santo Domingo, legs. 2507, 2508; monthly reports, years 1778–82.

# 9

# Conclusion

Prison, as a means by which society deals with criminal behavior, has come into widespread use only within the last three centuries and is the result of penal practices that have developed over a long period. In the history of penal administration, several periods can be identified in which different systems of punishment were prevalent. In the early Middle Ages, penance and fines were the preferred methods of punishment, but in the later Middle Ages they were gradually replaced by capital and corporal penalties. While capital punishment and bodily mutilations continued to be used in the sixteenth century, there also developed the practice of exploiting the labor power of prisoners in the interests of the state. The idea of penal labor was not new; its prototypes had already been created in the *opus publicum* of antiquity. The reappearance of this practice in western Europe in the early years of the sixteenth century was closely related to the military needs of the emerging national states. For the Spanish rulers, the demand for rowers on the galleys became particularly urgent at this time, with the onset of a period of naval wars in the Mediterranean. In the reign of Ferdinand and Isabella penal servitude was introduced as an alternative form of corporal punishment more useful to the state than other existing afflictive penalties. As the years passed, a continuing need to fill the galley benches made galley service the most common form of punishment.

148

By the end of the century, free oarsmen had virtually disappeared, and laws had been enacted extending service at the oar to all kinds of offenders. The usual terms were from two to ten years, but experienced oarsmen customarily were illegally retained after completing their sentences.

While convicts made up one part of the galley *chusma,* slaves— purchased, sentenced, or captured in war (these were Moslems)— constituted the rest. Their numbers gradually increased in the seventeenth century, and by the 1660s they represented almost one-half of the *chusma.* Slaves received the same food and treatment as the convicts, but their duties were more varied. Their principal occupation was rowing, but they regularly were sent ashore chained together in pairs to draw water and collect firewood. They also served as assistants to the guards and as servants of the galley officials.

Life on the galleys for both slaves and convicts was below subsistence. The rations, consisting of biscuits and vegetable stews made of beans and/or rice and water, were sometimes putrid and usually short. Lack of meat and fresh fruits and vegetables made deficiency diseases endemic. Oarsmen were always chained, and when ill were not permitted hospitalization but were treated at their benches by barber-surgeons. Even so, life on the galleys could be preferable to incarceration (given jail conditions in this period) or freedom in poverty and destitution. When sailing ships replaced the galleys in the eighteenth century, the former oarsmen were used ashore as laborers in the ports and arsenals.

In the 1560s, sentences to the mines of Almadén, whose mercury was needed to refine Mexican silver, were introduced as an alternative to the galleys. The Fuggers of Augsburg, administrators of the mines, asked the king to grant them convict labor when they failed to meet their production quotas in 1566. Here, as on the galleys, the use of convicts and slaves was dictated by the fact that free labor could not be obtained at reasonable cost.

Living conditions at Almadén were better than on the galleys. Meat, bread, and wine were rationed daily in sufficient quantities, clothes were issued, and hospitalization was provided. On the other hand, mercury poisoning was endemic, especially at the furnaces, and many men died insane or in agony. The chances of surviving one's sentence were considerably better on the galleys, in spite of conditions there that appeared to be far worse. Historically, Almadén is important because it set the example of turning convict labor over to private contractors for exploitation, a system that reached its fullest development in Spanish America.

Another form of penal servitude that developed in Spain in the early modern era was the presidio sentence. It arose in the sixteenth century as a means of providing garrisons for the Spanish presidios in North Africa. In the beginning, noble and wealthy offenders were sentenced there to serve at arms (*desterrados*), but a change occurred around the middle of the seventeenth century. During those years, Spain was extending its network of North African presidios, and there was a great need for soldiers and laborers. Coincidentally, war, revolts, epidemics, and famines at home and abroad created a severe population and financial crisis. To fill the manpower gap, felons of all kinds began to be sentenced to the presidios in North Africa to work on the fortifications and to fight. By the end of the seventeenth century the character of the North African presidios had already been set, although they were not formally organized as penal institutions until the eighteenth century.

After the abolition of the galleys in the mid-eighteenth century, their place was taken by the peninsular naval arsenals. A reform statute of 1771 formally created an organization of arsenal presidios, and for the first time separated prisoners and assigned labor to them according to the gravity of their crimes. After 1771, the arsenal presidios of Cartagena, La Carraca, and El Ferrol became the principal Spanish penal institutions. They were finally abolished in 1818—some thirty years after the completion of major construction—because with the ruin of the Spanish navy at Trafalgar there was no longer need for forced labor drafts. Furthermore, by this time convict labor had become more expensive than free labor.

In the history of penal servitude as a punishment in criminal law, the naval arsenals occupy an intermediate stage between the punitive hard labor of the galleys and the rehabilitative labor of the modern correctional prisons. In the beginning, the system of the galleys was carried over into the arsenals, but gradually, under the influence of the eighteenth-century penal reformers, changes were introduced. Finally, in 1804 a system of penal practice was adopted that combined the utilitarian needs of the state with the object of correction. The naval arsenals thus preserved the legacy of the galleys, but at the same time laid the foundations for the progressive penal systems of the modern era.

The North African presidios also assumed their final form as penal institutions in the eighteenth century. The distance of these presidios from Spain resulted in a chronic situation of loose administration, fraud, and corruption, while desertion was a constant problem. In 1743, a formal code of rules and regulations (the first of several such ordinances) was introduced, with the result that conditions slowly improved. There was some progress in the reduction of desertion resulting both from a series of innovative measures to combat it and more importantly, in the last years of the century, from a series of restitution treaties with the North African states. Official attempts to limit the population growth of the presidios because of financial and military reasons could not prevent some former *presidiarios* from staying on, especially if their skills were needed. In this way, the groundwork was laid for the transformation of the North African presidios into penal colonies in the nineteenth century.

Like the construction of naval arsenals and military fortifications, the public works envisioned by the Bourbons, especially Charles III (1759–88), required the mobilization of a large labor force at minimum cost, and, once again, convict workers were used. The practice began with the impressment of gypsies and vagabonds and the sentencing of minor offenders. It grew with the contractors' petitions to employ penal labor, especially on the highways around Madrid and Málaga, districts where there was an overflow of prisoners in the jails. The public works presidios were urban and metropolitan, and therefore only petty offenders were sentenced to them; the rest were sent to the arsenals and North Africa.

This system was given definite organization by the *Reglamento* of 1807, which removed the public works presidios from military control and placed them under civilian direction. With the change to civilian status, the presidios became institutions of correctional (rather than expiatory) labor, in which the aim was to reform the offender through useful work. This reform was completed in 1834, when the public works presidios were incorporated into the new penal code as correctional presidios for minor offenders.

In the New World, as in Spain, convicts were an important source of cheap labor. Penal workers were regularly hired out to private employers, but in the eighteenth century their major sphere of employment was in the public sector. After the Seven Years War (1756–63), Spain strengthened the defenses of San Juan and Havana, where *presidiarios* were imported to replace black slaves, who were too expensive. Prisoners were shipped from Mexico and Spain to the Caribbean presidios, and there also existed a steady exchange of convicts among the presidios of North Africa, Spain, and the Caribbean. In the last quarter of the eighteenth century these presidios formed a network of penal institutions that embraced the Spanish empire.

Penal servitude, which reached its highest point of development in the eighteenth century, was stimulated by the utilitarian spirit of the age and the reforms of the Bourbon rulers. In previous centuries forced labor was used primarily for serious offenders, but in the eighteenth century it began to be applied to all antisocial elements and delinquents with the objective of making them useful to the state. Influenced by corporate interpretations of the good society, which included the belief that every subject had an obligation to contribute to the well-being of the country and the state and that idleness was the root of all vice, the government vigorously pursued vagabonds, minor offenders, the unemployed, and the destitute. Large categories of antisocial offenders, from vagrants to disobedient sons to fornicators, were impressed under antivagrancy laws into the armed forces. The unfit were sent to labor in the presidios and arsenals.

In the last quarter of the eighteenth century, the idea of the house of correction for paupers who could not fight or work—the aged, cripples, women, and children—was adopted in Spain. These institutions, common to the rest of Europe in the early modern era, had long been opposed in Spain on the grounds that removal of mendicants from the streets would prevent the faithful from fulfilling their religious obligation to dispense charity, and would deprive persons not accused of any specific offense of their right to personal liberty. In the eighteenth century, with the new emphasis on the economic benefits to be gained by the state from forcing the poor and idle to work, the principle of confinement gained support. From the 1750s on, workhouses were established where it was hoped that forced labor would teach the poor skills and the habit of industry. Despite the importance that the supporters of the workhouses placed on them as institutions of social transformation, their penal aspects were obvious from the beginning. They held a mixed population of vagrants, beggars, and petty offenders, but there also were orphans, the crippled, and the insane, many of whom were incapable of learning a trade and were simply confined there for most of their lives. In the 1780s the workhouses began to house more and more minor offenders, particularly women (mainly thieves and syphilitic prostitutes).

The houses of correction were not thought of as places of imprisonment; rather, they held prisoners sentenced to forced labor. Imprisonment in this period was little used in Spanish civil law, and jails were detention centers for persons awaiting trial or the execution of their sentences. Conditions in Spanish jails, as in jails in other parts of western Europe, were appalling for most prisoners. Jailers purchased their positions from the king and supported themselves by charging prisoners for their food, drink, and other necessities. In addition, there were special fees levied for such things as better quarters, removal of irons, entrance, and release. Destitute prisoners had to depend on charity—in particular, charitable societies organized specifically for that purpose—and it was through these associations that the idea of confinement to correct offenders rather than punish and exploit them came into being.

In the last two decades of the eighteenth century the Asociación de Señoras of Madrid was propagating the views of Cesare Beccaria, John Howard, and their Spanish disciples, especially Manuel de Lardizábal. In accord with Howard's idea that useful labor was the principal regenerating tool, the Associación de Señoras introduced a program into the Madrid jails whereby young females were segregated and placed under a regime of seclusion, work, and religious instruction. A similar plan was introduced for men by the Asociación de la Caridad, also of Madrid. In the beginning, the work programs were voluntary, but when they proved unpopular, the

Associations began to advocate a reformed prison system based on compulsory labor to bring about rehabilitation. When imprisonment as a punishment was introduced in the nineteenth century, this program was adopted, the prisons and presidios became workshops.

The rapid growth of penal servitude in the eighteenth century can be viewed against the background of a conjunction of socioeconomic factors such as the decline of slavery, an increase in the number of convicted criminals, and a rise in the demand for unskilled workers in the public sphere. By the last quarter of the eighteenth century, slavery was in its final stage on the Iberian Peninsula. High prices for black slaves had limited their presence to a few noble houses, where they served mainly as objects of decoration, while frequent prisoner exchanges between the North African states and Spain had decreased the number of Moslem slaves to a negligible figure. At the same time that slaves were becoming scarce, an increase in the convicted criminal population made available a larger body of potential penal laborers. Coincidentally, an extension of the projects undertaken by the state—for example, the construction of military fortifications, roads, canals, and municipal improvements—heightened the demand for unskilled labor. Despite the growth of population in the second half of the eighteenth century, this need could not be met by free labor because of a (claimed) financial inability to pay wages that would attract workers from the free market. Even when slightly higher wages were paid, as occurred during the early years of construction at El Ferrol, free laborers still were reluctant to work on these projects because of poor working conditions. On the other hand, experience had shown that convicts were ideally suited to such labor. From the government's perspective, they were inexpensive to maintain and thoroughly expendable.

Penal policy thus expressed in practice state employment of the last resort, which exploited the large marginal sector. Moreover, the eighteenth-century reforms were instituted just when such a policy became economically disadvantageous and a new ideology could gain acceptance, one that was more suited to the new social needs that began to gain attention. Penal policy was now ready to adapt the enlightened ideas of rehabilitation through a regimen of social discipline and compulsory learning of skills. With the adoption of punitive imprisonment in the nineteenth century, the retributive hard labor of the galleys and presidios was transformed into a system of rehabilitative forced labor that became part of the modern prison system.

# Notes
# Bibliography
# Index

# Notes

### Preface

1   J. Thorsten Sellin, *Penal Servitude: Origin and Survival,* Proceedings
    of the American Philosophical Society, Vol. 109 (Philadelphia, 1965);
    and *Slavery and the Penal System* (New York: Elsevier, 1976).

2   Rafael Salillas, *Evolución penitenciaria en España,* 2 vols, (Madrid:
    Imprenta de la Revista de Legislación, 1918); Fernando Cadalso,
    *Instituciones penitenciarias y similares en España* (Madrid: José Gón-
    gora, 1922).


### Chapter 1

1   Carl Ludwig von Bar, *A History of Continental Criminal Law,* trans.
    Thomas S. Bell (Boston: Little Brown, 1916), p. 36.

2   *Códigos y leyes de España,* ed. A. Aguilera y Velasco (Madrid: F.
    Roig, 1866), vol. 3, pt. 7, title 21, law 4, p. 325. There are several
    general works on the history of the Spanish penal system that contain
    valuable information on penal servitude. The most useful are: Rafael
    Salillas, *Evolución penitenciaria en España,* 2 vols. (Madrid: Imprenta
    Clásica Española, 1918); and Fernando Cadalso, *Instituciones peni-
    tenciarias y similares en España* (Madrid: José Góngora, 1922).

3   For methods of punishment in early modern Europe, see von Bar,
    *Continental Criminal Law,* chs. 7-11; and Georg Rusche and Otto
    Kirchheimer, *Punishment and Social Structure* (New York: Columbia
    University Press, 1939).

4   NR, book 8, title 24, law 2, Nov. 28, 1510; Francisco Felipe Olesa
    Muñido, *La organización naval de los estados mediterráneos y en
    especial de España durante los siglos XVI y XVII* (Madrid: Editorial
    Naval, 1968), 2:749-50.

5   Olesa Muñido, *La organización naval,* 2:757-60; John Guilmartin,
    *Gunpowder and Galleys* (London and New York: Cambridge Univer-
    sity Press, 1975), p. 111.

6 Cristóbal Pérez de Herrera, *Amparo de pobres,* ed. Michel Cavillac (Madrid: Espasa-Calpe, 1975), Introducción, p. 155. For the penalties usually assigned to women, see Francisco Tomás y Valiente, *El derecho penal de la monarquía absoluta (siglos XVI–XVIII)* (Madrid: Editorial Tecnos, 1969), p. 392.

7 In 1580, Fray Juan de San Jerónimo noted in his *Memorias de El Escorial* that despite repeated application of flogging, public shame, and banishment, the number of female delinquents did not decline. Fray Juan de San Jerónimo, *Memorias de El Escorial,* as quoted in Félix Sevilla y Solanas, *Historia penitenciaria española (la galera), apuntes de archivo* (Segovia: Tipográfico de "El Adelantado de Segovia," 1917), p. 233.

8 Pérez de Herrera, *Amparo de pobres,* pp. 119–20. The same opinion was held in regard to male offenders. See *Cortes de León y Castilla* (Madrid: Sucesores de Rivadeneyra, 1882–1903), 5:312, 402; Tomás y Valiente, *El derecho penal,* pp. 343–44, 361; and in the picaresque literature of the period, Mateo Alemán, *Guzmán de Alfarache,* in *La novela picaresca española,* ed. Angel Valbuena Prat (Madrid: Aguilar, 1956), pt. 2, book 1, ch. 8, p. 431.

9 The exact date of the establishment of the *galera* in Madrid is not known. Pérez de Herrera mentions it by name in his *Relación de sus muchos y particulares servicios* (1618), but there are no references to it in extant official sources until 1622. See Pérez de Herrera, *Amparo de pobres,* Introducción, p. 156; and Antonio Domínguez Ortiz, "La galera o cárcel de mujeres de Madrid a comienzos del siglo XVIII," *Anales del Instituto de Estudios Madrileños* 9 (1973): 280.

10 Madre Magdalena de San Jerónimo, *Razón y forma de la galera y casa real que el rey N.S. manda hacer en estos reinos para castigo de las mujeres vagantes, ladronas, alcahuetas y otras semejantes,* as quoted in Sevilla y Solanas, *Historia penitenciaria,* p. 236.

11 Ibid. See appendix for the rules of the *galera.*

12 Leonardo Galdiano y Croy, *Breve tratado de los hospitales y casas de recogimiento* (Madrid: La Imprenta Real, 1677), p. 41.

13 Domínguez Ortiz, "La galera," pp. 284–85. For the number of inmates in 1676 see Galdiano y Croy, *Breve tratado de los hospitales,* p. 41.

14 These documents can be found in the Museo Naval in Madrid. Other assorted papers relating to the galleys also exist in the Archivo General de Simancas, Valladolid. See also I. A. A. Thompson, "A Map of Crime in Sixteenth-Century Spain," *The Economic History Review* 21 (1968): 244–67.

15 Sevilla y Solanas, *Historia penitenciaria,* pp. 30–32, lists this legislation. See also Olesa Muñido, *La organización naval,* 2:762.

16  Tomás y Valiente, *El derecho penal,* pp. 318–19.

17  AGS, Diversos de Castilla, legs. 28, 29; Sevilla y Solanas, *Historia penitenciaria,* pp. 55–56.

18  Sevilla y Solanas, *Historia penitenciaria,* pp. 33, 84–85; For the decree of 1653, see MN, Colección Vargas Ponce, tomo 25, doc. 31, Oct. 26, 1653.

19  *Novísima recopilación de las leyes de España* (Madrid, 1850), book 12, title 14, law 3, Feb. 1734. For the law of 1566, see NR, book 8, title 11, law 9, May 3, 1566.

20  MN, Vargas Ponce, tomo 25, doc. 18, Aug. 6, 1655; Gregorio Lasala Navarro, *Galeotes y presidiarios al servicio de la Marina de Guerra de España* (Madrid: Editorial Naval, 1979), pp. 40–41.

21  Conclusions based on data utilized in this study.

22  The Moriscos were expelled from Spain in 1609–11 and prohibited from returning under penalty of death or perpetual enslavement on the galleys. Many of the Moriscos were renegades as well, since they had renounced Christianity for Islam after leaving Spain for North Africa. In the eighteenth century some renegades were Christians who, after deserting from the Spanish presidios in North Africa where they were serving as soldiers or penal laborers, were recaptured by the Spaniards.

23  MN, Colección Navarrete, tomo 3, doc. 6, f. 14, instrucción 29; MN, Vargas Ponce, tomo 29, doc. 153, Jan. 14, 1683; Olesa Muñido, *La organización naval, 2: 178.*

24  MN, Vargas Ponce, tomo 27B, doc. 66, Oct. 2, 1673; Olesa Muñido, *La organización naval,* 2:781; Sevilla y Solanas, *Historia penitenciaria,* p. 115.

25  MN, Vargas Ponce, tomo 25, doc. 103, Mar. 1, 1657; ibid., tomo 30, doc. 254, Nov. 17, 1691; ibid., doc. 172, Feb. 27, 1690.

26  Ibid., tomo 10, doc. 13, Jan. 27, 1585. For the decree of 1568 see Sevilla y Solanas, *Historia penitenciaria,* p. 109.

27  Antonio Domínguez Ortiz, "La esclavitud en Castilla durante la Edad Moderna," *Estudios de historia social de España* 2 (1952): 399.

28  Adolfo de Castro, "La esclavitud en España," *La España Moderna,* Feb., 1892, p. 137; José de Pellicer, *Avisos históricos,* ed. Enrique Tierno Galván (Madrid: Taurus Ediciones, 1965), p. 56.

29  Slaves serving as *forzados* were specifically excluded from the legislation of 1653 fixing a ten-year limit on life sentences. MN, Vargas Ponce, tomo 25, doc. 207, July 20, 1662.

30  Sevilla y Solanas, *Historia penitenciaria,* pp. 105–7. They could not be auctioned off like the rest of the slaves, because they did not belong to the king.

31   MN, Vargas Ponce, tomo 20, doc. 84, Dec. 8, 1612; ibid., tomo 27, doc. 58, Sept. 21, 1668. There were the squadrons of Spain, Sicily, Sardinia, and Genoa. Also, for a short period of time, there was one for Portugal. See Cesáreo Fernández Duro, *Disquisiciones náuticas* (Madrid: Aribau y Ca, 1877), 2:114.

32   Olesa Muñido, *La organización naval,* 2:754; MN, Vargas Ponce, tomo 20, doc. 126, July 1, 1621.

33   The *buenas boyas forzados* represented an unreliable source of manpower because in theory they could be freed by the king at any time. For an example in 1654, see MN, Vargas Ponce, tomo 25, doc. 37, Jan. 20, 1654; and in 1674, ibid., tomo 27B, doc. 102, July 23, 1674.

34   Sevilla y Solanas, *Historia penitenciaria,* p. 100; Olesa Muñido, *La organización naval,* 2:755.

35   All percentages are based on the corrected figures.

36   Two royal decrees, dated 1653 and 1654, respectively, directed magistrates to send convicted felons to Melilla and Larache. In 1677 all prisoners sentenced to less than three years on the galleys were to be sent instead to La Mamora. AHN, Sala de Alcaldes de Casa y Corte, year 1653, f. 136; year 1654, f. 588; year 1677, f. 557.

37   Pellicer, *Avisos,* p. 56; María Helena Sánchez Ortega, *Documentación selecta sobre la situación de los gitanos españoles en el siglo XVIII* (Madrid: Castellote Editor, 1977), pp. 30–47.

38   Sevilla y Solanas, *Historia penitenciaria,* p. 84; Olesa Muñido, *La organización naval,* 2:754.

39   For a description of this system see Alonso de Castillo Solórzano, *La garduña de Sevilla y anzuelo de las bolsas,* ed. Federico Ruiz Morcuende (Madrid: Clásicos Castellanos, 1942), p. 9.

40   Miguel de Cervantes Saavedra, *La ilustre fregona,* in *Novelas ejemplares,* ed. Fernando Gutiérrez (Barcelona: Editorial Juventud, 1958), 2:63.

41   Luis Vélez de Guevara, *El águila del agua y batalla naval,* in *Revista de archivos, bibliotecas y museos* 10 (1904): 319.

42   Miguel de Cervantes Saavedra, *Don Quijote de la Mancha,* ed. Martín de Riquer (Barcelona: Editorial Juventud, 1966), pt. 1, ch. 22, p. 207.

43   Von Bar, *Continental Criminal Law,* chs. 7–11; *Cortes de León y Castilla,* 5:852.

44   The three principal sources for prison life in sixteenth-century Spain are: Bernardino de Sandoval, *Tractado del cuydado que se debe tener de los presos pobres* (Toledo: En Casa de Miguel Ferrer, 1564); Tomás Cerdán de Tallada, *Visita de la cárcel y de los pobres* (Valencia: Pedro de Huete, 1574); and Cristóbal de Chaves, *La relación de la cárcel de*

*Sevilla* (1591), in *Ensayo de una biblioteca española de libros raros y curiosos,* ed. Bartolomé José Gallardo (Madrid: Rivadeneyra, 1863).

45  Fernand Braudel, *The Mediterranean and the Mediterranean World in the Age of Philip II* (New York: Harper & Row, 1975), 1:460.

46  AGS, Diversos de Castilla, leg. 29, La Coruña.

47  Alemán, *Guzmán de Alfarache*, pt. 2, book 3, ch. 8, p. 568.

48  Cervantes Saavedra, *Don Quijote*, pt. 1, ch. 22, p. 209.

49  Jerónimo de Alcalá Yáñez y Rivera, *El donado hablador,* in *La novela picaresca española*, ed. Angel Valbuena Prat (Madrid: Aguilar, 1956), pt. 1, ch. 6, p. 1239; pt. 2, ch. 13, p. 1335.

50  Conditions at Almadén are discussed in pt. 1, ch. 2, below.

51  Alcalá Yáñez, *El donado hablador,* pt. 2, ch. 13, p. 1336.

52  Royal Pragmatic of May 3, 1566, as quoted in Tomás y Valiente, *El derecho penal,* pp. 455–63.

53  Sevilla y Solanas, *Historia penitenciaria,* pp. 46–50; AGS, Consejo y Juntas de Hacienda, leg. 113 Antigua, no. 16, Apr. 5, 1571; Licenciado J. Castillo de Bovadilla, *Política para corregidores* (Madrid: Luis Sánchez, 1597), vol. 2, book 5, ch. 6, p. 1094.

54  Lasala Navarro, *Galeotes y presidiarios,* pp. 47–58.

55  AHN, Alcaldes de Casa y Corte, year 1642, ff. 490–491v, 488–489v; ibid., year 1654, ff. 439–41; Lasala Navarro, *Galeotes y presidiarios,* pp. 57–58.

56  Sevilla y Solanas, *Historia penitenciaria,* pp. 47–59.

57  AGS, Diversos de Castilla, leg. 29, report of the *Corregidor* of Trujillo, Dec. 22, 1572. See also Cristóbal de Chaves, *La relación de la cárcel de Sevilla,* p. 1370.

58  Sevilla y Solanas, *Historia penitenciaria,* pp. 58–59, 65–67; Lasala Navarro, *Galeotes y presidiarios,* pp. 61–65.

59  For the galley ordinances of 1607–76 see MN, Vargas Ponce, tomo 25B, doc. 218; for the year 1682, ibid., tomo 29, doc. 45, Jan. 2, 1682. See also Lasala Navarro, *Galeotes y presidiarios,* pp. 71–73.

60  MN, Vargas Ponce, tomo 29, doc. 120, Nov. 25, 1684; Fernández Duro, *Disquisiciones,* p. 134; Sevilla y Solanas, *Historia penitenciaria,* pp. 160–66.

61  Guilmartin, *Gunpowder and Galleys,* pp. 269–70.

62  Fernández Duro, *Disquisiciones,* pp. 134–38; MN, Vargas Ponce, tomo 27B, doc. 107, Sept. 14, 1674; ibid., tomo 30, doc. 251, Oct. 13, 1691.

63  MN, Vargas Ponce, tomo 27, doc. 107, Jan. 6, 1670; Gregorio Marañón, "La vida en las galeras en tiempo de Felipe II," in his *Vida e Historia* (Madrid: Colección Austral, 1968), pp. 99–103.

64   MN, Vargas Ponce, tomo 27, doc. 246, Nov. 18, 1680; ibid., tomo 29, doc. 32, Nov. 1, 1681.

65   MN, Vargas Ponce, tomo 27B, doc. 126, July 22, 1675.

66   Sevilla y Solanas, *Historia penitenciaria*, pp. 194–95, 186.

67   Sevilla y Solanas, *Historia penitenciaria*, pp. 178–80; Olesa Muñido, *La organización naval*, pp. 730–38; MN, Vargas Ponce, tomo 27B, doc. 75, Dec. 25, 1673; ibid., doc. 115, Feb. 1676; ibid., tomo 30, doc. 20, Mar. 31, 1687; ibid., tomo 29, doc. 23, Dec. 20, 1683.

68   MN, Vargas Ponce, tomo 29, doc. 135, Feb. 26, 1685; Lasala Navarro, *Galeotes y presidiarios*, p. 76.

69   MN, Vargas Ponce, tomo 31, doc. 218, Oct. 25, 1703; ibid., doc. 218, Nov. 5, 1703; Sevilla y Solanas, *Historia penitenciaria*, p. 80.

70   MN, Vargas Ponce, tomo 22, doc. 100, Dec. 9, 1689; ibid., tomo 24, doc. 42, Feb. 28, 1655; Sevilla y Solanas, *Historia penitenciaria*, pp. 116–20.

71   Olesa Muñido, *La organización naval*, pp. 782–88. Clothing inspections were held weekly on Sundays, and men whose garments were found missing were punished.

72   Biblioteca Nacional de Madrid, MS. 8850, June 4, 1607, f. 51; Sevilla y Solanas, *Historia penitenciaria*, pp. 78–81.

73   MN, Vargas Ponce, tomo 30, doc. 222, June 4, 1691; doc. 231, July 14, 1691; tomo 25, doc. 41, Feb. 25, 1651; doc. 178, June 10, 1686.

74   Fernández Duro, *Disquisiciones*, p. 108; Lasala Navarro, *Galeotes y presidiarios*, p. 70.

75   MN, Vargas Ponce, tomo 32, doc. 190, Dec. 1, 1730; tomo 31, doc. 289, Oct. 20, 1716.

## Chapter 2

1   The mercury mines of Almadén are located near the town of Almadén some sixty-seven miles from the city of Ciudad Real. The town was recaptured from the Moslems by Alfonso VII of Castile in 1151 and was given to the Order of Calatrava, which exploited the mines. In 1512 the territories belonging to the military orders were incorporated into the royal domain; with them came the mercury mines of Almadén.

2   A. Matilla Tascón, *Historia de las minas de Almadén* (Madrid: Gráficas Osca, 1958), p. 94; AHN, Ordenes Militares, Archivo de Toledo, expediente 37.887. ff. 14–36.

3   AHN, Ordenes Militares, Archivo de Toledo, exps. 37.887, 37.888; Matilla Tascón, *Historia de las minas*, p. 95.

AHN, Ordenes Militares, Archivo de Toledo, exps. 37.887, ff. 29–29v.

Antonio Domínguez Ortiz, "La esclavitud en Castilla," pp. 398–402; Matilla Tascón, *Historia de las minas,* pp. 202–6.

AHN, Ordenes Militares, Archivo de Toledo, exps. 37.887, 37.888, 37.889. Germán Bleiberg has studied the "Información secreta" in relation to Alemán's literary formation. See Gormán Bleiberg, "Mateo Alemán y los galeotes," *Revista de Occidente* 39 (1966): 330–63.

The conclusions in this paragraph are drawn from AHN, Ordenes Militares, Archivo de Toledo, exps. 37.887, 37.888.

Ibid., exps. 37.887, 37.888, 37.889.

Ibid.

Ibid., exp. 37.887, f. 149v; exp. 37.889; exp. 37.887, f. 152.

For a description of this jailbreak: ibid., exp. 37.887, último cuaderno.

Ibid.

Ibid., exp. 37.889. See also ibid., exp. 37.887, f. 152; exp. 37.887, f. 147v; exp. 37.888; exp. 37.889, f. 148v.

Ibid., exp. 37.887, f. 148v.

Ibid., exp. 37.888.

For the relationship between vagabondage and thievery, see the petitions of the Castilian Cortes for the sixteenth century in *Cortes de León y Castilla,* vols. 4, 5; and Pérez de Herrera, *Amparo de pobres.*

AHN, Ordenes Militares, Archivo de Toledo, exps. 37.887, f. 150; exp. 37.889.

For a description of sixteenth-century ruffians, see Ruth Pike, *Aristocrats and Traders: Sevillian Society in the Sixteenth Century* (Ithaca: Cornell University Press, 1972), pp. 195–96.

AHN, Ordenes Militares, Archivo de Toledo, exps. 37.887 f. 149; exp. 37.889; Francisco de Lugo y Dávila, *De la hermanía,* in *Teatro popular,* ed. Emilio Cotarelo y Mori (Madrid: Librería de la Viuda de Rico, 1906), p. 133.

AHN, Ordenes Militares, Archivo de Toledo, exps. 37.887, f. 150; exp. 37.889.

Ibid., exp. 37.887, f. 137; exp. 37.888.

Ibid., exp. 37.887, f. 194v.

Matilla Tascón, *Historia de las minas,* pp. 116–17.

Ibid., pp. 96, 117, 125, 166.

AHN, Ordenes Militares, Archivo de Toledo, "Información secreta," exp. 37.888.

Almadén was located in an important pastoral zone. This probably accounts for the presence of meat in the diet of the prisoners. For the economy of this region see Carla R. Phillips, *Ciudad Real, 1500–1750. Growth, Crisis and Readjustment in the Spanish Economy* (Cambridge: Harvard University Press, 1979), pp. 44–48.

27 This prisoner was a Catalan bandit serving an eight-year sentence. His statements and those of his fellow prisoners regarding the food, clothing, and medical services available at Almadén can be found in the "Información secreta." See also Matilla Tascón, *Historia de las minas,* pp. 166–67.

28 AHN, Ordenes Militares, Archivo de Toledo, "Información secreta," exp. 37.888.

29 Ibid.

30 Ibid. Figures for the increase in mercury production during these years are from Matilla Tascón, *Historia de las minas,* p. 111.

31 Information on the Confraternity of San Miguel is taken from a description of the mines in 1613 published by Matilla Tascón, in *Historia de las minas,* pp. 166–68. The mines of Almadén were known officially as the mines of San Miguel; thus, the designation of the Confraternity.

32 This point of view was originally stated in the first *asiento* of 1566. AHN, Ordenes Militares, Archivo de Toledo, exp. 37.887, f. 29.

33 Ibid., "Información secreta," exp. 37.888.

34 Matilla Tascón, *Historia de las minas,* p. 111. The annual consumption of mercury in the Mexican mines grew from 263 quintals in 1559 to 1,387 in 1569, and varied between 3,000 and 3,700 quintals in the period 1597–1606. For additional figures on mercury consumption in the American mines see Pierre and Huguette Chaunu, *Séville et l'Atlantique (1504–1650),* vol. 8 (Paris: S.E.V.P.E.N., 1959), pt. 2, pp. 1958–80.

35 M. F. Lang, "Las minas de Almadén bajo la superintendencia de Miguel de Unda y Garivay," *Hispania: Revista española de historia* 120 (1972): 263.

36 Matilla Tascón, *Historia de las minas,* p. 165.

37 Cadalso, *Instituciones penitenciaria,* p. 103.

38 AGS, Marina, leg. 699, Nov. 16, 1748–Oct. 11, 1749.

39 AHN, Alcaldes de Casa y Corte, year 1787, f. 305, June 2, 1749.

40 Ibid., year 1775, f. 671; year 1787, f. 681.

41 Cadalso, *Instituciones penitenciarias,* p. 113; for improvements in technology at Almadén, see AGS, Guerra Moderna, leg. 4958, year 1781.

42 Salillas, *Evolución penitenciaria,* p. 3; Cadalso, *Instituciones penitenciarias,* p. 115.

43   Cadalso, *Instituciones penitenciarias*, p. 114. The term jail (*cárcel*) is used here in its original meaning of a depository for keeping prisoners.
44   Ibid., p. 115.
45   See Charles Gibson, *The Aztecs under Spanish Rule* (Stanford: Stanford University Press, 1964), pp. 244–46.

## Chapter 3

1   Fernando Cadalso, *Principio de la colonización y colonias penales* (Madrid: J. Góngora y Alvarez, 1896), p. 52; Cerdán de Tallada, *Visita de la cárcel*, p. 44; *Códigos y leyes de España*, pt. 7, title 21, law 4, p. 325.
2   Cadalso, *Instituciones penitenciarias*, p. 301.
3   For Spain's North African policy in the sixteenth century see Braudel, *The Mediterranean*, 2:854–65; and Andrew Hess, *The Forgotten Frontier: A History of the Sixteenth-Century Ibero-African Frontier* (Chicago: University of Chicago Press, 1978).
4   Hess, *The Forgotten Frontier*, pp. 39-43 and chs. 4-5.
5   Diego Suárez, *Historia del maestre último que fué de Montesa y su hermano Don Felipe de Borja* (Madrid: M. Tello, 1889), p. 27. In the eighteenth century the term *gastador* was used to describe convicts sentenced to hard labor on the fortifications. The new meaning was indicative of the change from a free to a penal labor force.
6   Henri-Léon Fey, *Histoire d'Oran avant, pendant et après la domination espagnole* (Oran: A. Perrier, 1858), p. 109.
7   Suárez, *Historia del Maestre*, pp. 107, 147, 161. For others, both nobles and wealthy commoners, see AHN, Consejos, Expedientes de Indultos, legs. 5575, 5576.
8   At the end of the fifteenth century there was some thought of using the newly discovered islands of the Caribbean for transportation purposes, but the idea was quickly abandoned in favor of a restrictive emigration policy. Transportation overseas to Spanish America was unnecessary for penal purposes until the galleys were abolished. For a description of an attempt to settle former *presidiarios* on the island of Puerto Rico in the last quarter of the eighteenth century, see pt. 2, ch. 4, below.
9   Cerdán de Tallada, *Visita de la cárcel*, p. 44.
10   For an elaboration of this point, see pt. 2, ch. 4, below.
11   Information can be found in AGS, Guerra Moderna, legs. 4696-98; and AGS, Secretaría de Tierra, Miscelánea, legs. 3132-42.
12   The Peñón de Alhucemas was added in 1673.

13   AHN, Alcaldes de Casa y Corte, year 1653, f. 136; year 1654, f. 588. As early as 1642 the king ordered all soldiers absent without leave to return to their units within twenty days or face condemnation for life to El Peñón and Larache, where they would serve without pay.

14   León Galindo y de Vera, *Historia, vicisitudes y política tradicional de España en las costas de África* (Madrid: M. Tello, 1884), p. 275. For the decree of 1677, see AHN, Alcaldes de Casa y Corte, year 1677, ff. 557–75; for the decree of 1658, ibid., year 1658, ff. 29–30.

## Chapter 4

1   Sánchez Ortega, *Los gitanos españoles*, pp. 107–8.

2   For an excellent analysis of the view of the eighteenth-century religious and secular thinkers on this problem, see William Callahan, *Honor, Commerce and Industry in Eighteenth-Century Spain* (Boston: Baker Library, Harvard University School of Business Administration, 1972); and, by the same author, "The Problem of Confinement: An Aspect of Poor Relief in Eighteenth-Century Spain," *Hispanic American Historical Review* 51 (1971): 2–24.

3   Benito Jerónimo Feijóo, *Theatro crítico universal,* as quoted in Callahan, "The Problem of Confinement," p. 8.

4   Lorenzo de Normante y Carcavilla, *Espíritu del Señor Melón* as quoted in Callahan, *Honor,* p. 58.

5   Nicolás de Arriquíbar, *Recreación política* (Vitoria: Tomás de Robles y Navarro, 1779), 1:49; Pedro Rodríguez de Campomanes, *Apéndice a la educación popular,* 4 vols. (Madrid: Imprenta de d. A. de Sancha, 1775–76), 3:233.

6   Arriquíbar, *Recreación política,* p. 48; Antonio Javier Pérez y López, *Discurso sobre la honra y deshonra legal,* 2nd ed. (Madrid: La Imprenta Real, 1786), p. 18.

7   Pérez y López, *Discurso,* p. 20; Rodríguez de Campomanes, *Apéndice,* 2:183.

8   The best work on vagrancy in eighteenth-century Spain is María Rosa Pérez Estévez, *El problema de los vagos en la España del siglo XVIII* (Madrid: Confederación Española de Cajas de Ahorros, 1976). See pp. 55–64 for a discussion of the term *vagrant* in the eighteenth century.

9   Ibid., pp. 65–81. For the legislation against vagrancy, see pp. 165–94.

10   Ibid., pp. 232–37. For vagrants in active service in the army and navy, see pp. 236–68.

11   Documents relating to the Peninsular military presidios can be found scattered through AGS, Guerra Moderna, legs. 4793–4988. See other references in AHN, Alcaldes de Casa y Corte, year 1742, ff. 300–302; year 1743, f. 149; year 1749, ff. 334–36, 374–78; year 1750, f. 466; year 1751, f. 17; year 1753, f. 9; year 1762, f. 281.

12   Pérez Estévez, *El problema de los vagos*, pp. 248–86; AHN, year 1775, ff. 669–76, Apr. 30, 1750.

13   Pérez Estévez, *El problema de los vagos*, p. 249, AGS, Guerra Moderna, leg. 4988, Sept. 12, 1788.

14   AGS, Guerra Moderna, leg. 4940, Oct. 31, 1777.

15   Ibid., leg. 4950, Feb. 26–Mar., 1786.

16   The results of this investigation can be found in AGS, Guerra Moderna, leg. 4988, Sept. 12, 1788.

17   Ibid.; and leg. 4962, Jan. 13, 1783, for La Coruña.

18   Callahan, "The Problem of Confinement," pp. 4–5. For the writings of other sixteenth- and seventeenth-century authors on this topic, see Antonio Rumeu de Armas, *Historia de la previsión social en España* (Madrid: Editorial Revista de Derecho Privado, 1944), ch. 10; and Pérez Estévez, *El problema de los vagos*, pp. 296–98.

19   Callahan, *Honor*, p. 60. Ward's views can be found in his *Obra pía: medio de remediar la miseria de la gente pobre de España*, published as an appendix to his *Proyecto económico* (Madrid: J. Ibarra, 1782).

20   Rusche and Kirchheimer, *Punishment and Social Structure*, p. 42; Callahan, "The Problem of Confinement," pp. 1–12. For the early history of the houses of correction in Europe, see J. Thorsten Sellin, *Pioneering in Penology: The Amsterdam Houses of Correction in the Sixteenth and Seventeenth Centuries* (Philadelphia: University of Pennsylvania Press, 1944).

21   Jacques Soubeyroux, *Pauperisme et rapports sociaux à Madrid au XVIII ème siècle* (Lille: Université de Lille III, 1978), 2:635–44. There was another workhouse in Madrid known as the *Hospicio* which was a refuge for paupers and the destitute (mainly the aged and youths) and did not normally receive delinquents. For a description of both workhouses, see John Howard, *The State of Prisons in England and Wales* (Warrington, England: W. Eyres, 1784), sec. 4 (Foreign Prisons), pp. 156–58.

22   AGS, Gracia y Justicia, leg. 807.

23   Conclusions in the following paragraphs are based on an analysis of data in AGS, Gracia y Justicia, leg. 807.

24   Salillas, *Evolución penitenciaria*, 1:74–86.

25   Domínguez Ortiz, "La galera," pp. 277–85; Howard, *The State of Prisons*, p. 156; Salillas, *Evolución penitenciaria*, 1:66, 74.

26 Soubeyroux, *Pauperisme,* 2:641. After 1782, women prisoners from other parts of the country (for example, tobacco defrauders) began to be sent to San Fernando as well.

27 Sellin, *Slavery and the Penal System,* p. 81; Salillas, *Evolución penitenciaria,* 1:66, 86. For the transformation of the houses of correction in the rest of Europe in the eighteenth century, see Max Grünhut, *Penal Reform: A Comparative Study* (Oxford, Clarendon Press, 1948), pp. 25–27.

28 Howard, *The State of Prisons,* p. 153; Cadalso, *Instituciones penitenciarias,* p. 157.

29 Francois A. F. La Rochefoucauld-Liancourt, *Noticia de las cárceles de Filadelfia,* trans. Ventura de Arquellada (Madrid: Imprenta Real, 1801), pp. 85–86. Information on the Madrid jails is found in Arquellada's notes to this edition.

30 Francisco Lastres, *La cárcel de Madrid, 1572–1877* (Madrid: La Revista Contemporánea, 1877), p. 9; Rochefoucauld-Liancourt, *Noticia,* p. 91.

31 Cadalso, *Instituciones penitenciarias,* pp. 194, 159.

32 Ibid., p. 194. For the table of fees, years 1736, 1741, and 1781, see AVM, Secretaría, sec. 1, leg. 101, no. 20, year 1736; sec. 2, leg. 236, no. 4, year 1781.

33 Cadalso, *Instituciones penitenciarias,* p. 201; Rochefoucauld-Liancourt, *Noticia,* p. 81; Francisco de Quevedo Villegas, *El buscón,* ed. Américo Castro (Madrid: Clásicos Castellanos, 1960), pp. 187–89.

34 Howard, *The State of Prisons,* pp. 155–56; AVM, Secretaría, sec. 2, leg. 236, no. 4, year 1781.

35 Howard, *The State of Prisons,* pp. 155–61.

36 AHN, Sala de Alcaldes, year 1786, ff. 238–73. For an account of the use of torture in Spain, see F. Tomás y Valiente, *La tortura en España* (Madrid: Editorial Ariel, 1973).

37 The principal collection of documents relating to the Madrid jails can be found in the Archivo de Villa, but most of it concerns the nineteenth century. The material for the eighteenth century is fragmentary and limited.

38 Lastres, *Le cárcel de Madrid,* pp. 11–14; AVM, Secretaría, sec. 3, leg. 103, no. 6, sec. 1, leg. 233, year 1831, no. 45; sec. 3, leg. 102, no. 13, year 1787.

39 Lastres, *La cárcel de Madrid,* p. 12; for Howard's description, see *The State of Prisons,* p. 156.

40 Gonzalo Anes, *El Antiguo Régimen: Los Borbones* (Madrid: Alianza Editorial, 1976), p. 323.

41   Howard, *The State of Prisons*, pp. 155–56; Lastres, *La cárcel de Madrid*, p. 14.

42   For example, in 1793, a total of 1,526 reales was collected and distributed among the prisoners of both Madrid jails during Easter week. AHN, Alcaldes de Casa y Corte, year 1793, ff. 183–87; year 1792, ff. 1041–45; Howard, *The State of Prisons*, p. 160. The accounts of the *procuradores de pobres* of the Cárcel de Villa for a few years in the eighteenth century still exist in the Archivo de Villa.

43   Charitable organizations in the sixteenth and seventeenth centuries are described in Salillas, *Evolución penitenciaria*, 1:163–73. For private donations for poor prisoners, see AVM, Secretaría, sec. 2, leg. 239, no. 2, year 1765, and other examples scattered throughout the collection.

44   The best discussion of the Madrid associations and others can be found in Salillas, *Evolución penitenciaria*, 1:163–229, 239–404. For the work of the Countess of Montijo, one of the founders of the Asociación de Señoras, see Paula de Demerson, *María Francisca de Salas Portocarrero, Condesa de Montijo: Una figura de la Ilustración* (Madrid: Editora National, 1975), ch. 5.

45   Manuel de Lardizábal, "Discurso sobre las penas," in José Antón Oneca, "Estudio preliminar: El derecho penal de la Ilustración," *Revista de la Escuela de Estudios Penitenciarios* (1966): 591–746; Israel Drapkin, "Manuel Montesinos y Molina—An Almost Forgotten Precursor of Penal Reform in Spain," ed. Marvin Wolfgang in *Crime and Culture*, (New York: John Wiley and Sons, 1968), pp. 321–22. For the ideas of Beccaria, see Marcello Maestro, *Cesare Beccaria and the Origins of Penal Reform* (Philadelphia: Temple University Press, 1973).

46   Grünhut, *Penal Reform*, ch. 3.

47   Salillas, *Evolución penitenciaria*, 1:192–96; AHN, Sala de Alcaldes, year 1794, ff. 183–94; year 1788, vol. 2, ff. 555–94.

48   Salillas, *Evolución penitenciaria*, 1:255–67, 191–216. The Asociación de Señoras also introduced a work program into the *galera*. In fact this was its original project and its most successful one.

49   Ibid., pp. 215–16; AHN, Alcaldes de Casa y Corte, year 1792, ff. 1011–40; year 1796, ff. 283–89.

50   Salillas, *Evolución penitenciaria*, 1:242–44.

## Chapter 5

1   AGS, Marina, leg. 699, Oct. 11, 1749; Sevilla y Solanas, *Historia penitenciaria*, p. 35.

2   AGS, Marina, leg. 699, Oct. 11, 1748–Nov. 16, 1749; Sevilla y Solanas, *Historia penitenciaria,* p. 35.

3   AHN, Alcaldes de Casa y Corte, year 1787, vol. 2, ff. 681–82, June 5, 1751.

4   For a discussion of Bourbon policies toward the gypsies, see Sánchez Ortega, *Los gitanos españoles.* According to the author, their real objective was to exterminate the gypsies.

5   AGS, Marina, leg. 700, Jan. 9, 1769; leg. 695, July 13, 1766, and Oct. 12, 1765; Pérez Estévez, *El problema de los vagos,* pp. 248–88.

6   Pérez Estévez, *El problema de los vagos,* p. 249. The experiment with the gypsies was an acknowledged failure by 1760. A decree in 1763 ordered their release from the arsenals, with the exception of those sentenced for crimes.

7   Sevilla y Solanas, *Historia penitenciaria,* p. 204; Antonio Domínguez Ortiz, *La sociedad española en el siglo XVIII* (Madrid: C.S.I.C., 1955), pp. 227–28. It is not clear how many actually served at Cádiz and El Ferrol in the 1750s and 1760s, but Cartagena was always their principal center.

8   AHN, Alcaldes de Casa y Corte, year 1765, f. 671, Feb. 25, 1765.

9   *Novísima Recopilación,* book 12, title 100, law 7, Mar. 12, 1771.

10  The chain pumps, worked by the prisoners and slaves twenty-four hours a day, were used to remove water from the drydocks where ships were being constructed or repaired. AGS, Marina, leg. 699, Dec. 17, 1765; Feb. 1, 1769.

11  *Novísima Recopilación,* book 12, title 100, law 7, Mar. 12, 1771; Lardizábal, *Discurso de las penas,* pp. 603–6, 710.

12  AGS, Marina, leg. 708, Oct. 10, 1773.

13  Ibid., leg. 700, year 1772; leg. 694, July 13, 1762.

14  Lasala Navarro, *Galeotes y presidiarios,* p. 115. In 1802 and 1804 the courts were prohibited from sentencing prisoners to Cartagena, but this legislation proved ineffective. Salillas, *Evolución penitenciaria,* 2:14.

15  In 1771 there were 721 *presidiarios* at La Carraca and 588 at El Ferrol. In 1808 there were approximately 1,000 prisoners at each of the three arsenals. AGS, Marina, leg. 700, Dec. 30, 1771; Lasala Navarro, *Galeotes y presidiarios,* p. 114.

16  Salillas, *Evolución penitenciaria,* 2:118.

17  Sevilla y Solanas, *Historia penitenciaria española,* pp. 224–27; MN, Vargas Ponce, tomo 35, doc. 61, Mar. 12, 1754.

18  Pérez Estévez, *El problema de los vagos,* pp. 263–66; AGS, Marina, leg. 693, Oct. 10, 1773; leg. 699, June 3, 1761.

19  AGS, Marina, leg. 706, Aug. 22, 1761; leg. 708, Sept. 30, 1767.

20  Ibid., leg. 708, July 12, 1774; Apr. 5, 1770; July 6, 1757.

21  AGS, Secretaría de Hacienda, leg. 978, years 1792–97.

22  AGS, Guerra Moderna, leg. 4975, Feb. 4, 1785; leg. 4923, Mar. 9, 1775; AHN, Alcaldes de Casa y Corte, year 1788, f. 877; year 1797, f. 757.

23  AGS, Secretaría de Hacienda, leg. 978, Oct. 9, 1797.

24  Ibid., leg. 978, July 26, 1793.

25  AGS, Guerra Moderna, leg. 4885, Sept. 21, 1764.

26  Ibid., leg. 4950, Feb. 8, 1779.

27  Salillas, *Evolución penitenciaria*, 2:126. This building became known as the "Cuartel de Presidiarios." AGS, Marina, leg. 700, Jan. 8, 1772.

28  The date of its construction is not clear. Salillas believed that it probably was built in the 1760s. See Salillas, *La vida penal en España* (Madrid: Imprenta de la Revista de Legislación, 1888), p. 238.

29  AGS, Marina, leg. 700, Sept. 18, 1778; Nov. 6, 1773.

30  Bread prices oscillated between eight and sixteen reales a pound (excluding years of severe scarcity), while wine prices remained fixed around three reales per *azumbre* (equivalent to four pints). Domínguez Ortiz, *La sociedad española en el siglo XVIII*, p 212.

31  AGS, Marina, leg. 699, Feb. 19, 1765; leg. 700, 1774.

32  Ibid., leg. 697, Sept. 20, 1777.

33  Pérez Estévez, *El problema de los vagos*, p. 256. The vegetable stew in this one meal contained salt pork, however. The northern region of Spain had a higher consumption of meat than any other area. For example, individual consumption of meat in the city of Bilbao in the mid-eighteenth century was four times that of the average for the rest of the country. Vicente Palacio Atard, "Notas acerca de la historia de la alimentación," in his *Los españoles de la Ilustración* (Madrid: Ediciones Guadarrama, 1964), p. 298.

34  Vicente Vizcaíno Pérez, *Discursos políticos sobre los estragos que causan los censos, felicidades y medios de su extinción, comercio fomentado y general abundancia de comestibles en España* (Madrid, 1766), as quoted in Palacio Atard, "Notes," p. 295. For the diet of the poor of Madrid, see Soubeyroux, *Pauperisme*, 1:148–61.

35  AHN, Consejos, leg. 6774, as quoted in Palacio Atard, "Notas acerca de la alimentación," pp. 301–6.

36  AGS, Marina, leg. 696, May 1772. For the petition of 1752, see ibid., leg. 694, Aug. 2, 1752.

37  Salillas, *Evolución penitenciaria*, 2:160. For the petition of 1783, see AGS, Marina, leg. 698, Aug. 8, 1783.

38  AGS, Marina, leg. 698, Aug. 8, 1783.

39  Ibid., leg. 700, Jan. 8, 1772.

40  Ibid., leg. 699, Feb. 2, 1765. For the change in their ration, see ibid., Feb. 19, 1765.

41  Ibid., leg. 699, Feb. 19, 1765.

42  Ibid., leg. 694, May 16, 1772; leg. 696, Oct. 10, 1773.

43  Henry Swinburne, *Travels through Spain in the Years 1775 and 1776* (London: P. Elmsly, 1779), p. 124.

44  AGS, Guerra Moderna, leg. 4962, July 26, 1787.

45  AGS, Marina, leg. 700, Jan. 8, 1772.

46  Ibid., leg. 708, Oct. 12, 1763; leg. 700, Jan. 8, 1772; Antonio Meijide Pardo, *Contribución a la historia de la industria naval de Galicia: Los arsenales del Ferrol en el siglo XVIII* (Lisbon: Congreso Internacional de historia dos descubrimientos, 1961), p. 26.

47  Sevilla y Solanas, *Historia penitenciaria,* p. 230; Swinburne, *Travels,* p. 125. For the price rise in the second half of the eighteenth century, see Jaime Vicens Vives, ed., *Historia social y económica de España y América* (Madrid: Editorial Vicens-Vives, 1972), 4:183–85.

48  Salillas, *Evolución penitenciaria,* 2:14.

49  This new system was created in the *Ordenanza de los Presidios Arsenales* in 1804, and its text has been published in Lasala Navarro, *Galeotes y presidiarios,* ch. 16.

50  Rafael Salillas, *La vida penal en España,* (Madrid: Imprenta de la Revista de Legislación, 1888), p. 238.

51  Lasala Navarro, *Galeotes y presidiarios,* pp. 114–15.

## Chapter 6

1  David Ringrose, *Transportation and Economic Stagnation in Spain, 1750–1800* (Durham, N.C.: Duke University Press, 1970), p. 14; Richard Ford, *A Handbook for Travellers in Spain* (Carbondale, Ill.: Southern Illinois University Press, 1966), 1:21.

2  Gonzalo Menéndez Pidal, *Los caminos en la historia de España* (Madrid: Cultura Hispánica, 1951), p. 123; Ringrose, *Transportation,* pp. 14–15.

3  Menéndez Pidal, *Los caminos,* pp. 128–33.

4  Joseph Townsend, *A Journey through Spain in the Years 1786 and 1787* (London: C. Dilly, 1791), 1:210–15; Ringrose, *Transportation,* p. 16.

5  Townsend, *A Journey,* 1:366–69; Ringrose, *Transportation,* p. 16.

6  Townsend, *A Journey,* p. 206; AGS, Marina, leg. 705, Oct. 1, 1763; Nov. 7, 1763.

7   AGS, Marina, leg. 705, Mar. 2, 1764; Mar. 10, 1764.

8   Ibid., leg. 706, Mar. 11, 1767; Sánchez Ortega, *Los gitanos españoles,* p. 232.

9   Domínguez Ortiz, *La sociedad española en el siglo XVIII,* p. 228.

10  AGS, Marina, leg. 706, Feb. 8–14, 1767.

11  Pérez Estévez, *El problema de los vagos,* pp. 234–36. For the brigades of vagrants, see ibid., p. 270.

12  Ibid., p. 227. In 1766, as a result of the popular riots of that year, the government decreed the expulsion of all vagrants from the city. They were given the choice of either entering an *hospicio* or voluntarily joining the road workers. All those still around four days after the publication of this decree were to be arrested and sent to the army.

13  This was in accord with a practice introduced throughout Spain in the late 1760s. See Pérez Estévez, *El problema de los vagos,* p. 222; Salillas, *Evolución penitenciaria,* 2:17–18.

14  AHN, Alcaldes de Casa y Corte, year 1775, f. 867. Documents for the initial years of the Prado presidio have disappeared from the collection in the Archivo de Villa of Madrid (section: Secretaría). The earliest *legajos* date from 1784.

15  AGS, Gracia y Justicia, leg. 807.

16  AHN, Alcaldes de Casa y Corte, year 1776, f. 129.

17  Ibid., ff. 124–42. See also Tomás y Valiente, *El derecho penal,* pp. 366–67.

18  AVM, Secretaría, sec. 2, leg. 324, no. 13, year 1805.

19  AGS, Gracia y Justicia, leg. 807.

20  Carlos Cambronero, "El Prado de Madrid," *Revista Contemporánea* 129 (1904): 9–21.

21  AVM, Secretaría, sec. 2, leg. 234, no. 16, year 1806; sec. 2, leg. 323, no. 13, year 1784.

22  Ibid., sec. 3, leg. 324, no. 16, year 1784; AHN, Alcaldes de Casa y Corte, year 1776, f. 129.

23  AHN, Alcaldes de Casa y Corte, year 1775, f. 868.

24  Howard, *The State of Prisons,* p. 156.

25  AHN, Alcaldes de Casa y Corte, year 1777, ff. 399–407.

26  Ibid., f. 407.

27  Salillas, *Evolución penitenciaria,* 2:23; AHN, Alcaldes de Casa y Corte, year 1784, no folio, Sept. 28, 1784.

28  AHN, Alcaldes de Casa y Corte, year 1788, vol. 2, no folio, May 3, 1788.

29  AVM, Secretaría, sec. 2, leg. 322, no. 13, year 1784.

30  Ibid., year 1785.

31  Ibid., sec. 2, leg. 234, no. 16, year 1806; Salillas, *Evolución peniten-ciaria*, 2:28–30.
32  AVM, Secretaría, sec. 2, leg. 324, no. 16, year 1784; year 1806.
33  Ibid., sec. 2, leg. 324, no. 8, year 1803.
34  AGS, Guerra Moderna, leg. 4958, Jan. 31, 1781; Oct. 29, 1781.
35  Salillas, *Evolución penitenciaria*, 2:80–84; Tomás y Valiente, *El dere-cho penal*, pp. 366–68.
36  AGS, Guerra Moderna, leg. 4962, Jan. 7, 1783; leg. 4954, July 24, 1780.
37  Ibid., leg. 4971, Feb. 15, 1784; Salillas, *Evolución penitenciaria*, 2:30.
38  AGS, Guerra Moderna, leg. 4984, Jan. 30, 1787. For the Guadalme-dina River project, see ibid., leg. 4980, June 27, 1786.
39  *Novísima Recopilación,* book 12, title 40, law 12, Jan. 27, 1787; AGS, Guerra Moderna, leg. 4984, Jan. 30, 1787; leg. 4980, Mar. 7, 1786.
40  AGS, Guerra Moderna, leg. 4975, Nov. 4, 1785; leg. 4980, Oct. 11, 1788; leg. 4958, Oct.–Mar. 1781.
41  AHN, Alcaldes de Casa y Corte, year 1795, ff. 552–56; *Novísima Recopilación,* book 12, title 40, law 21.
42  AHN, Alcaldes de Casa y Corte, year 1795, ff. 552–56; Salillas, *Evolución penitenciaria,* 2:83–84.
43  Salillas, *Evolución penitenciaria,* 2:94; AGS, Secretaría de Hacienda, leg. 719, Oct. 30, 1788, and Apr. 20, 1789; AGS, Guerra Moderna, leg. 4971, Dec. 24, 1784.
44  AHN, Alcaldes de Casa y Corte, year 1788, vol. 1, ff. 862–862v, 842–47; Townsend, *A Journey,* 2:206.
45  AHN, Alcaldes de Casa y Corte, year 1788, vol. 1, f. 847.
46  AVM, Secretaría, sec. 2, leg. 322, no. 17, year 1789.
47  Ibid., sec. 2, leg. 323, no. 19, year 1796; year 1797; year 1799.
48  Ibid., sec. 2, leg. 324, nos. 1, 2, 4, 5, 6, years 1801–4.
49  Ibid., sec. 2, leg. 323, nos. 15, 19.
50  Ibid., sec. 2, leg. 323, nos. 9–11, 19.
51  The transients were *rematados* destined for the overseas presidios who were serving temporarily while awaiting the departure of the chain. Others included black slaves whose owners had placed them in the presidio for insubordination or other misdemeanors. They served at the pleasure of their owners and were released whenever their masters wanted them.
52  Conclusions based on official reports of escapes in the presidio collec-tion of the AVM (Secretaría) for these years.

53   Data in this paragraph and the following pages derived from the collection of the transcripts of sentences of the years 1796–1800 in the AVM (Secretaría). For *presidiarios* who spent their terms in the hospital, see AHN, Alcaldes de Casa y Corte, year 1776, ff. 124–42.

54   Massimo Livi Bacci, "Fertility and Nuptiality Changes in Spain from the Late 18th to the Early 20th century," *Population Studies* 22:2 (July 1968): 216–24; Soubeyroux, *Pauperisme,* 1:24–29.

55   AVM, Secretaría, sec. 3, leg. 324, no. 8, year 1803; Sept. 3, 1803; sec. 1, leg. 88, no. 67, year 1801; Salillas, *Evolución penitenciaria,* 2:46–51.

56   Statistics derived from AHN, Consejos, year 1804, leg. 9475.

57   Ibid.; AVM, Secretaría, sec. 2, leg. 324, no. 7, year 1803.

58   Ibid., sec. 2, leg. 324, no. 8, year 1803.

59   Ibid., sec. 2, leg. 324, no. 16, year 1806.

60   The discussion of the *Reglamento* of 1807 in the following pages is based on AHN, Alcaldes de Casa y Corte, year 1807, ff. 1205–12; AVM, Secretaría, sec. 2, leg. 324, no. 16, year 1806 (includes two copies of the *Reglamento*—the original one, dated Dec. 13, 1805, and the amended document, dated May 26, 1807.

61   AHN, Alcaldes de Casa y Corte, year 1788, f. 842.

62   See note 60, above.

63   Salillas, *Evolución penitenciaria,* 2:43, 392–93.

### Chapter 7

1   AHN, Alcaldes de Casa y Corte, year 1687, f. 205; year 1658, f. 29.

2   Ibid., year 1677, f. 146.

3   AGS, Guerra Moderna, leg. 4699, Mar. 28, 1706. See also ibid., Apr. 22, 1701; leg. 4698, Oct. 10, 1692.

4   Ibid., leg. 4698, Mar. 3, 1699; leg. 4699, Dec. 21, 1701; Mar. 28, 1706.

5   Salillas, *Evolución penitenciaria,* 2:5.

6   Cadalso, *Instituciones penitenciarias,* p. 304.

7   For decrees against freeing prisoners before the termination of their sentences, illegal transfers, and other such practices, see AGS, Guerra Moderna, legs. 4698, 4699.

8   AHN, Alcaldes de Casa y Corte, year 1717, ff. 270–73; AGS, Guerra Moderna, leg. 4700, July 21, 1701.

9   Cadalso, *Instituciones penitenciarias,* p. 305.

10  *Reglamento para el gobierno de desterrados en la Plaza de Ceuta,*
    Oct. 15, 1743. AGS, Guerra Moderna, leg. 3660. See also Cadalso,
    *Instituciones penitenciarias,* p. 305.
11  AGS, Guerra Moderna, leg. 3660, Oct. 15, 1743, *Reglamento,* provi-
    sions 1–8.
12  Ibid., leg. 4698, Aug. 2, 1692; leg. 4700, Apr. 24, 1701.
13  Ibid., leg. 3660, June 16, 1749; Cadalso, *Instituciones penitenciarias,*
    p. 305.
14  AGS, Guerra Moderna, leg. 3660, Oct. 15, 1743, provisions 11–16.
15  Ibid., provision 4.
16  Ibid., provision 7. For complaints about the quality and quantity of the
    food, see ibid., leg. 4919, Jan. 16, 1773.
17  Ibid., leg. 3660, Apr. 11, 1749; leg. 4977, Feb. 8, 1786.
18  Ibid., leg. 3660, Aug. 8, 1749; leg. 4898, year 1768.
19  For the *Reglamento* of 1791, see Cadalso, *Instituciones penitenciarias,*
    pp. 307–8.
20  AGS, Guerra Moderna, leg. 4919, Jan. 16, 1773; leg. 4945, Jan. 23,
    1778 (Alhucemas).
21  AGS, Marina, leg. 699, Mar. 30, 1767.
22  AGS, Guerra Moderna, leg. 3660, July 27, 1749; Aug. 1, 1749; Aug.
    12, 1749.
23  AHN, Alcaldes de Casa y Corte, year 1765, f. 671.
24  AGI, Santo Domingo, leg. 2503, Feb. 25, 1769; AGS, Guerra Mod-
    erna, leg. 4893, year 1766.
25  AGS, Marina, leg. 699, Mar. 30, 1767. Of this number, 923 were
    serving in the arsenal, and 291 were in the *depósito* awaiting transpor-
    tation to the overseas presidios.
26  A continuous series of monthly reports with figures for the number of
    *presidiarios* in each presidio is no longer in existence. Only a few
    reports for scattered years can be found. After 1776, the practice of
    sending yearly reports was introduced, but almost all of them have
    disappeared. Those that are still extant can be found in AGS, Guerra
    Moderna, legs. 4934 and 4935. Conclusions in this paragraph are
    based on this surviving material.
27  Salillas, *Evolución penitenciaria,* 2:8.
28  AGS, Guerra Moderna, leg. 4959, May 1, 1782; Gabriel de Morales,
    *Datos para la historia de Melilla* (Melilla: "El Telegrama del Rif,"
    1909), p. 595.
29  AGS, Guerra Moderna, leg. 4981, Mar. 25, 1787.
30  For example, the wife of a *presidiario* who was working as a baker in
    the presidio, and another, whose husband was a master dyer, in the

town. AGS, Guerra Moderna, leg. 4972, May 5, 1785; May 10, 1785. For *presidiarios* in the fixed regiments, see ibid., leg. 4981, Mar. 25, 1787.

31 Morales, *Datos para la historia de Melilla,* pp. 595–96. Documents in the AGS contain numerous petitions by former *presidiarios* asking to remain in the presidios, with both negative and positive replies.

32 AGS, Estado, leg. 495, Mar. 10, 1620; AGS, Guerra Moderna, leg. 4976, Aug. 10, 1786.

33 AGS, Guerra Moderna, leg. 4976, Aug. 10, 1786; leg. 4930, June 27, 1776.

34 Ibid. See also leg. 4918, Mar. 22, 1772.

35 Ibid., leg. 4930, June 27, 1776.

36 Ibid., leg. 4912, May 17, 1788.

37 Ibid., leg. 4898, May 14, 1768.

38 *Novísima Recopilación,* book 12, title 40, law 8, Nov. 24, 1782. For the legislation of 1765 and 1769, see AGS, Guerra Moderna, leg. 4893, Feb, 27, 1765, and leg. 4906, Nov. 5, 1767, and Nov. 11, 1767.

39 Conclusions based on a study of cases in AGS, Guerra Moderna, Colección: Presidios y Presidiarios.

40 AGS, Guerra Moderna, leg. 4981, July 13, 1787. Some returned mutilated—for example, a renegade who had been away for twenty-two years and had lost both hands. Ibid., leg. 4971, 1784.

41 AGS, Gracia y Justicia, leg. 1049; AHN, Alcaldes de Casa y Corte, f. 443, year 1772; AGS, Guerra Moderna, leg. 4898, May 14, 1768.

42 AHN, Alcaldes de Casa y Corte, year 1772, f. 443; ibid., Consejos, leg. 5993, f. 118, Sept. 25, 1770.

43 *Novísima Recopilación,* book 12, title 40, law 7, Mar. 12, 1771.

44 AGS, Guerra Moderna, leg. 4951, May 12, 1780; leg. 4976, Aug. 10, 1786. In 1780 there was a new agreement with Morocco.

45 The extant sources can be found in AGS, Guerra Moderna, legs. 4934, 4935.

46 AGS, Guerra Moderna, leg. 4985. Conclusions in the following paragraphs are based on a statistical analysis of this material and in leg. 4934.

47 AGI, Arribadas, legs. 287, 548.

48 Conclusions based on data from the inventory of criminal cases of the *Sala de Alcaldes de Casa y Corte,* years 1780–89. AHN, Consejos, leg. 2793. For banditry in the 1780s, see Tomás y Valiente, *El derecho penal,* pp. 268–71.

49 *Novísima Recopilación,* book 12, title 40, law 7, Mar. 12, 1771.

50   For tobacco smuggling in Spain, see José Pérez Vidal, *España en la historia del tabaco* (Madrid: Consejo Superior de Etnología Peninsular, 1959).

51   Francisco Aguilar Piñal, *La Sevilla de Olavide, 1767-1778* (Seville: Ayuntamiento, 1966), p. 131.

52   Pérez Vidal, *La historia del tabaco,* pp. 355-58.

53   Ibid., pp. 358-60.

54   Francisco Rodríguez Marín, *Cantos populares españoles,* (Seville: F. Alvarez y Compañía, 1883), 4:404-8; Pérez Vidal, *La historia del tabaco,* p. 352.

55   AHN, Consejos, leg. 5993, Sept. 25, 1770.

56   *Novísima Recopilación,* book 12, title 40, law 10, Dec. 31, 1784; Sevilla y Solanas, *Historia penitenciaria española,* p. 206.

57   Lasala Navarro, *Galeotes y presidiarios,* pp. 98-100.

58   Ibid.

59   Gonzalo Anes, *El Antiguo Régimen: Los Borbones* (Madrid: Alianza Editorial, 1976), pp. 93-94.

60   For changes in the countryside in the eighteenth century, see Antonio Domínguez Ortiz, *Sociedad y estado en el siglo XVIII español* (Barcelona: Ariel, 1976), ch. 22.

61   P. Molas Ribalta, *Los gremios barceloneses en el siglo XVIII. La estructura corporativa ante el comercio de la revolución industrial* (Madrid: Confederación Española de Cajas de Ahorros, 1970), p. 62.

62   Ibid.

63   AGS, Guerra Moderna, leg. 4975, Apr. 19, 1786.

64   "Running the gauntlet" is a punishment in which a double file of men face each other and, armed with clubs or other weapons, strike at an individual who is made to run between them. The usual sentence was eight to ten runs.

65   This provision applied to deserters who were serving sentences for other offenses in the presidios at the time of their desertion.

66   *Novísima Recopilación,* book 12, title 40, law 8, Nov. 24, 1782. AGS, Guerra Moderna, leg. 4936, June 2, 1777 (Havana to Oran); leg. 4923, June 4, 1773 (New Orleans to Ceuta). In the other direction, AGI, Santo Domingo, leg. 2139, Sept. 8, 1786 (Ceuta to Havana); AGI, Arribadas, f. 548, Nov. 20, 1788 (Ceuta to Manila).

## Chapter 8

1   On the obrajes, see Richard Greenleaf, "The Obraje in the Late Mexican Colony," *The Americas* 23 (1967): 227-50; John Super,

"Querétaro Obrajes: Industry and Society in Provincial Mexico, 1600–1812," *Hispanic American Historical Review* 56 (1976): 197–216; and Samuel Kagan, "Penal Servitude in New Spain: The Colonial Textile Industry" (Ph.D. diss., City University of New York, 1977).

2   Charles Verlinden, *The Beginnings of Modern Colonization* (Ithaca: Cornell University Press, 1970).

3   Greenleaf, "The Obraje," pp. 242–43; Charles Gibson, *The Aztecs under Spanish Rule* (Stanford: Stanford University Press, 1964), pp. 244–46.

4   Bernard Bobb, *The Viceregency of Antonio María Bucareli in New Spain, 1771–1779* (Austin: University of Texas Press, 1962), p. 85.

5   AGI, Santo Domingo, leg. 2501, July 15, 1765; leg. 2129, Nov. 31, 1772.

6   Prisoners from local jails worked on fortifications in Caribbean ports from the end of the sixteenth century. Bibiano Torres Ramírez, "Alejandro O'Reilly en Cuba," *Anuario de estudios americanos* 24 (1967): 1357.

7   AGI, Santo Domingo, leg. 2129, Nov. 31, 1772.

8   Ibid.; and monthly reports for the years 1768 and 1769 in leg. 2122. The rest of the work force consisted of free laborers—overseers and specialized workers.

9   Ibid., leg. 2129, May 28, 1769; Aug. 13, 1769.

10  Ibid., leg. 2501, May 20, 1765; Nicolás Cabrillana, "Las fortificaciones militares en Puerto Rico," *Revista de Indias* 107 (1967): 172.

11  Although 445 prisoners were authorized in the decree of 1765, this number was reduced almost immediately to 350. AGI, Santo Domingo, leg. 2503, Feb. 25, 1769. The period of Governor Miguel de Muesas, 1769–76, has been studied by Altagracia Ortiz-Squillace in "Eighteenth-Century Reforms in the Caribbean: The Governorship of Miguel de Muesas, 1769–1776" (Ph.D. diss., City University of New York, 1977). I am grateful to her for information on the progress of the fortifications during those years.

12  These figures seem modest when compared with those for Havana, where monthly rates in 1768 and 1769, for example, were never lower than 13 percent, and the average for both years was 16 percent. AGI, Santo Domingo, leg. 2122.

13  AGI, Santo Domingo, leg. 2366, June 30, 1786; leg. 2502, July 15, 1768; leg. 2506B, Nov. 17, 1775.

14  Ibid., leg. 2504, Nov. 20, 1771; Mar. 20, 1772.

15  Ibid., leg. 2505, May 27, 1773; Sept. 30, 1773.

16  Ibid., leg. 2503, Nov. 30, 1769; Dec. 29, 1769; May 30, 1770.

17   Ibid., leg. 2505, May 27, 1773.
18   AGS, leg. 695, May 24, 1765; AHN, Alcaldes de Casa y Corte, year 1779, f. 516v; Sevilla y Solanas, *Historia penitenciaria*, p. 213.
19   AGI, Santo Domingo, leg. 2505, July 28, 1774; Oct. 25, 1774; leg. 2503, Oct. 25, 1774; AGS, Guerra Moderna, leg. 4950, Mar. 25, 1779. As early as 1769, O'Reilly had suggested resettling *presidiarios* on the island of Puerto Rico so as to increase its population. AGI, Santo Domingo, leg. 2503, Feb. 25, 1769.
20   For additional comments on transportation, see chs. 3 and 7, above.
21   Biblioteca Nacional, Madrid, Sala de Manuscritos, Raros, 14.090, year 1566; *Novísima Recopilación,* book 8, title 24, law 13, Mar. 12, 1771; AHN, Alcaldes de Casa y Corte, year 1787, ff. 898–95; AGS, Secretaría de Hacienda, leg. 978; AGS, Guerra Moderna, leg. 4962.
22   AGI, Santo Domingo, leg. 2127, Feb. 8, 1771.
23   Ibid., leg. 2929, Nov. 9, 1773.
24   Ibid., leg. 2505, May 18, 1773.
25   AGS, Marina, leg. 696, Aug. 22, 1777; leg. 697, May 17, 1779.
26   AHN, Alcaldes de Casa y Corte, year 1776, ff. 124–42; year 1795, ff. 552–56; *Novísima Recopilación,* book 12, title 40, law 12, Jan. 27, 1787. For Havana and Veracruz, see AGN (Mexico), Ramo de Presidios y Cárceles, vol. 24, ff. 336–336v, Mar. 14, 1786; f. 287, Dec. 31, 1791. Documents from the AGN (Mexico) facilitated by Dr. Samuel Kagan.
27   AGI, Santo Domingo, leg. 2132, June 14, 1773; leg. 2127, Feb. 27, 1771.
28   Ibid., leg. 2509, Nov. 19, 1784; leg. 2128, July 7, 1771.
29   Ibid., leg. 2509, July 26, 1785.
30   AGS, Marina, leg. 697, Aug. 5, 1777; AGI, Santo Domingo, leg. 2505, May 23, 1773.
31   *Novísima Recopilación,* book 12, title 40, law 7, Mar. 12, 1771; law 15, Mar. 28, 1772; AGI, Santo Domingo, leg. 2128, Aug. 24, 1772.
32   AGI, Santo Domingo, leg. 2132.
33   Colin MacLachlan, *Criminal Justice in Eighteenth Century Mexico. A Study of the Acordada* (Berkeley: University of California Press, 1974), p. 81.
34   AGI, Santo Domingo, leg. 2132, June 14, 1773.
35   MacLachlan, *Criminal Justice,* pp. 80–81, 115–16; AGN (Mexico), Cárceles, vol. 1, ff. 13–16v, 20–25; vol. 13, ff. 180–84, 206–207v, 208–212v, 214–216v; vol. 24, ff. 6–7, 8–13. See also Christon I. Archer, "The Deportation of Barbarian Indians from the Internal Provinces of New Spain, 1789–1810," *The Americas* 29 (1973): 376–85.

36  MacLachlan, *Criminal Justice,* p. 42. For the data of 1773, see AGI, Santo Domingo, leg. 2132, June 14, 1773. I am indebted to Dr. G. Douglas Inglis for a copy of this list.

37  AGN (Mexico), Cárceles, vol. 24, ff. 294–95.

38  Ibid., ff. 314–17.

39  Ibid., ff. 260–89, 336.

40  AGI, Santo Domingo, leg. 2509, Apr. 3, 1789. For complaints by the Havana officials about desertions and releases, see, for example, AGN (Mexico), Cárceles, vol. 24, ff. 321–22.

41  MacLachlan, *Criminal Justice,* pp. 78–80, 115–16; and Alicia Bazán Alarcón, "El Real Tribunal de la Acordada y la delincuencia en la Nueva España," *Historia Mexicana* 13 (1964): 317–46.

# Bibliography

## Primary Sources

*Manuscript Collections*

Madrid. Archivo de Villa. Secciones: Secretaría; Cárcel de Corte; Cárcel de Villa; General; Presidio Correccional.

Madrid. Archivo Histórico Nacional. Secciones: Consejos; Ordenes Militares, Archivo de Toledo; Sala de Alcaldes de Casa y Corte.

Madrid. Biblioteca Nacional. Secciones: Ms. 8850; Raros 14.090.

Madrid. Museo Naval. Secciones: Colección Navarrete; Colección Vargas Ponce.

Mexico City. Archivo General de la Nación. Sección: Presidios y Cárceles.

Seville. Archivo General de Indias. Secciones: Arribadas; Audiencia de Santo Domingo.

Valladolid. Archivo General de Simancas. Secciones: Consejo y Juntas de Hacienda; Diversos de Castilla; Gracia y Justicia; Guerra Moderna; Secretaría de Hacienda; Secretaría de Marina; Secretaría de Tierra.

*Published Documents and Contemporary Works*

Alcalá Yáñez y Rivera, Jerónimo. *El donado hablador.* In Angel Valbuena Prat, *La novela picaresca española.* Madrid: Aguilar, 1966.

Alemán, Mateo. *Guzmán de Alfarache.* In *La novela picaresca española*, edited by Angel Valbuena Prat. Madrid: Aguilar, 1956.

Arriquíbar, Nicolás de. *Recreación política.* Vitoria: Tomás de Robles y Navarro, 1779.

Barrionuevo, Jerónimo. *Avisos.* In *Colección de escritores castellanos.* 4 vols. Madrid: M. Tello, 1892–94.

Beleña, Eusebio. *Recopilación sumaria de todos los autos acordados de la real audiencia y sala de crimen de Nueva España.* Mexico: F. de Zuñiga y Ontiveros, 1787.

Calderón de la Barca, Pedro. *Dramas de honor.* 2 vols. Edited by Angel Valbuena Briones. Madrid: Clásicos Castellanos, Madrid: 1956.

Castillo de Bovadilla, J. *Política para corregidores.* 2 vols. Madrid: Luis

Sánchez, 1597.

Castillo Solórzano, Alonso de. *La garduña de Sevilla y anzuelo de las bolsas.* Edited by Federico Ruiz Morcuende. Madrid: Clásicos Castellanos, 1942.

Cerdán de Tallada, Tomás. *Visita de la cárcel y de los pobres.* Valencia: Pedro de Huete, 1574.

Cervantes Saavedra, Miguel de. *Don Quijote de la Mancha.* Ed. Martín de Riquer. Barcelona: Editorial Juventud, 1966.

Cervantes Saavedra, Miguel de. *La ilustre fregona.* In *Novelas ejumplares,* edited by Fernando Gutiérrez. Barcelona: Editorial Juventud, 1958.

Chaves, Cristóbal de. *La relación de la cárcel de Sevilla.* In *Ensayo de una biblioteca española de libros raros y curiosos,* edited by Bartolomé José Gallardo, Vol. 1. Madrid: Rivadeneyra, 1863.

*Los códigos españoles concordados y anotados.* 12 vols. Madrid: Imprenta de la Publicidad, a cargo de M. Rivadeneyra, 1847–51.

*Códigos y leyes de España.* Edited by A. Aguilera y Velasco. Vol. 3. Madrid: F. Roig, 1866.

*Cortes de los antiguos reinos de León y Castilla.* Vol. 5. Madrid: Sucesores de Rivadeneyra, 1903.

Ford, Richard. *A Handbook for Travellers in Spain.* Carbondale: Southern Illinois University Press, 1966.

Galdiano y Croy, Leonardo. *Breve tratado de los hospitales y casas de recogimiento.* Madrid: Imprenta Real, 1677.

García, Carlos. *La desordenada codicia de los bienes ajenos.* In *La novela picaresca española,* edited by Angel Valbuena Prat, Madrid: Aguilar, 1956.

Hermosilla, Diego de. *Diálogo de los pajes.* Madrid: Imprenta de la Revista Española, 1901.

Howard, John. *The State of Prisons in England and Wales.* Warrington, England: W. Eyres, 1784.

Lardizábal, Manuel de. *"Discurso sobre las penas."* In José Antón Oneca, "Estudio preliminar: El derecho penal de la Ilustración." *Revista de la Escuela de Estudios Penitenciarios* 10 (1966): 591–746.

Lugo y Dávila, Francisco de. *De la hermanía.* In *Teatro popular,* edited by Emilio Cotarelo y Mori. Madrid: Librería de la Viuda de Rico, 1906.

*Nueva Recopilación de las leyes de España.* 3 vols. Madrid: La Imprenta Real de la Gazeta, 1721.

Pellicer, José de. *Avisos históricos.* Edited by Enrique Tierno Galván. Madrid: Taurus Ediciones, 1965.

Pérez de Herrera, Cristóbal. *Amparo de pobres.* Edited by Michel Cavillac. Madrid: Espasa-Calpe, 1975.

Pérez y López, Antonio Javier. *Discurso sobre la honra y deshonra legal.* 2nd ed. Madrid: La Imprenta Real, 1786.

Quevedo Villegas, Francisco de. *El buscón.* Edited by Américo Castro. Madrid: Clásicos Castellanos, 1960.

Rochefoucauld-Liancourt, François A. F. La. *Noticia del estado de las cárceles de Filadelfia.* Translated by Ventura de Arquellada. Madrid: Imprenta Real, 1801.

Rodríguez de Campomanes, Pedro. *Apéndice a la educación popular. 4 vols. Madrid: Imprenta de A. de Sancha,* 1775-76.

Sánchez Ortega, María Helena. *Documentación selecta sobre la situación de los gitanos españoles en el siglo XVII.* Madrid: Editora Nacional, 1977.

Sandoval, Bernardino de. *Tractado del cuydado que se debe tener de los presos pobres.* Toledo: En Casa de Miguel Ferrer, 1564.

Suárez, Diego. *Historia del maestre último que fué de Montesa y su hermano don Felipe de Borja.* Madrid: M. Tello, 1889.

Swinburne, Henry. *Travels through Spain in the Years 1775 and 1776.* London: P. Elmsly, 1779.

Townsend, Joseph. *A Journey through Spain in the Years 1786 and 1787.* London: C. Dilly, 1791.

Vélez de Guevara, Luis. *El águila del agua y batalla naval.* In *Revista de archivos, bibliotecas y museos* 10 (1904).

**Secondary Sources**

*Books*

Aguilar Piñal, Francisco. *La Sevilla de Olavide, 1767-1778.* Seville: Ayuntamiento, 1966.

Anes, Gonzalo. *El Antiguo Régimen: Los Borbones.* Madrid: Alianza Editorial, 1976.

Bamford, Paul *Fighting Ships and Prisons: The Mediterranean Galleys of France in the Age of Louis XIV.* Minneapolis: University of Minnesota Press, 1973.

Billaçois, F. *Crimes et Criminalité en France sous l'Ancien Régime.* Paris: École Pratique des Hautes Études, 1971.

Bobb, Bernard. *The Viceregency of Antonio María Bucareli in New Spain, 1771-1779.* Austin: University of Texas Press, 1962.

Bonger, Willem. *Criminality and Economic Conditions.* Edited by A. J. Turk. Bloomington: Indiana University Press, 1969.

Braudel, Fernand. *The Mediterranean and the Mediterranean World in the Age of Philip II.* 2 vols. New York: Harper & Row, 1975.

Cadalso, Fernando. *Instituciones penitenciarias y similares en España.* Madrid: José Góngora, 1922.

Cadalso, Fernando. *Principio de la colonización y colonias penales.* Madrid: J. Góngora y Alvarez, 1896.

Callahan, William. *Honor, Commerce and Industry in Eighteenth-Century Spain.* Boston: Baker Library, Harvard University School of Business Administration, 1972.

Callahan, William. *La Santa y Real Hermandad del Refugio y Piedad de Madrid, 1618–1832.* Madrid: Instituto de Estudios Madrileños, 1980.

Castan, Nicole. *Justice et répression en Languedoc à l'époque des Lumières.* Paris: Flammarion, 1980.

Chaunu, Pierre and Huguette. *Séville et l'Atlantique (1504–1650).* Vol. 8. Paris. S.E.V.P.E.N., 1959.

Cockburn, J. S., editor. *Crime in England, 1500–1800.* London: Methuen, 1977.

Demerson, Paula de. *María Francisca de Salas Portocarrero, Condesa de Montijo: Una figura de la Ilustración.* Madrid: Editora Nacional, 1975.

Domínguez Ortiz, Antonio. *Alteraciones andaluzas.* Madrid: Narcea S.A. de Ediciones, 1973.

Domínguez Ortiz, Antonio. *El Antiguo Régimen: Los Reyes Católicos y los Austrias.* Madrid: Alianza Editorial, 1973.

Domínguez Ortiz, Antonio. *Delitos y suplicios en la Sevilla imperial (La crónica negra de un misionero jesuita)* In his *Crisis y decadencia de la España de los Austrias.* Barcelona: Ediciones Ariel, 1969.

Domínguez Ortiz, Antonio. *La sociedad española en el siglo XVII.* 2 vols. Madrid: C.S.I.C., 1963–70.

Domínguez Ortiz, Antonio. *La sociedad española en el siglo XVIII.* Madrid: C.S.I.C., 1955.

Domínguez Ortiz, Antonio. *Sociedad y estado en el siglo XVIII español.* Barcelona: Ariel, 1976.

Drapkin, Isreal. "Manuel Montesinos y Molina—An Almost Forgotten Precursor of Penal Reform in Spain." In *Crime and Culture,* edited by Marvin Wolfgang. New York: John Wiley and Sons, 1968.

Elliott, John. *Imperial Spain, 1469–1716.* New York: New American Library, 1963.

Fernández Duro, Cesáreo. *Disquisiciones náuticas.* Vol. 2. Madrid: Aribau y Ca, 1877.

Fey, Henri-Léon. *Histoire d'Oran avant, pendant et après la domination espagnole.* Oran: A. Perrier, 1858.

Forster, Robert, and Orest Ranum, eds. *Deviants and the Abandoned in French Society*. Baltimore: The Johns Hopkins University Press, 1978.

Foucault, Michel. *Discipline and Punish: The Birth of the Prison*, New York: Vintage Books, 1979.

Galindo y de Vera, León. *Historia, vicisitudes y política tradicional de España en las costas de Africa*. Madrid: M. Tello, 1884.

Gibson, Charles. *The Aztecs under Spanish Rule*. Stanford: Stanford University Press, 1964.

Grünhut, Max. *Penal Reform: A Comparative Study*. Oxford: Clarendon Press, 1948.

Guilmartin, John. *Gunpowder and Galleys*. London and New York: Cambridge University Press, 1975.

Hamilton, Earl J. *American Treasure and the Price Revolution in Spain, 1501-1650*. Cambridge: Harvard University Press, 1934.

Hamilton, Earl J. *War and Prices in Spain, 1651-1800*. Cambridge: Harvard University Press, 1947.

Hess, Andrew. *The Forgotten Frontier: A History of the Sixteenth-Century Ibero-African Frontier*. Chicago: University of Chicago Press, 1978.

Hufton, Olwen. *The Poor of Eighteenth-Century France, 1750-1789*. Oxford: Clarendon Press, 1974.

Ignatieff, Michael. *A Just Measure of Pain: The Penitentiary in the Industrial Revolution, 1750-1850*. New York: Columbia University Press, 1978.

Kamen, Henry. *Spain in the Later Seventeenth Century, 1665-1700*. London and New York: Longman, 1980.

Lasala Navarro, Gregorio. *Galeotes y presidiarios al servicio de la Marina de Guerra de España*. Madrid: Editorial Naval, 1979.

Lastres, Francisco. *La cárcel de Madrid, 1572-1877*. Madrid: La Revista Contemporánea, 1877.

Lea, Henry Charles. *A History of the Spanish Inquisition*. 4 vols. New York: American Scholar Publications, 1966.

Lynch, John. *Spain under the Habsburgs*. 2 vols. New York: Oxford University Press, 1964-69.

MacLachlan, Colin. *Criminal Justice in Eighteenth Century Mexico. A Study of the Acordada*. Berkeley: University of California Press, 1974.

Maestro, Marcello. *Cesare Beccaria and the Origins of Penal Reform*. Philadelphia: Temple University Press, 1973.

Marañón, Gregorio. "La vida en las galeras en tiempo de Felipe II." In his *Vida e Historia*. Madrid: Colección Austral, 1968.

Martines, Lauro, editor. *Violence and Civil Disorder in Italian Cities, 1200-1500*. Berkeley: University of California Press, 1972.

Matilla Tascón, A. *Historia de las minas de Almadén*. Madrid: Gráficas Osca, 1958.

Meijide Pardo, Antonio. *Contribución a la historia de la industria naval de Galicia: los arsenales del Ferrol en el siglo XVIII*. Lisbon: Congreso Internacional de historia dos descubrimientos, 1961.

Menéndez Pidal, Gonzalo. *Los caminos en la historia de España*. Madrid: Cultura Hispánica, 1951.

Molas Ribalta, P. *Los gremios barceloneses en el siglo XVIII. La estructura corporativa ante el comercio de la revolución industrial*. Madrid: Confederación Española de Cajas y Ahorros, 1970.

Morales, Gabriel de. *Datos para la historia de Melilla*. Melilla: "El Telegrama del Rif," 1909.

Nadal, Jordi. *La población española (siglos XVI a XX)*. Barcelona: Editorial Ariel, 1973.

Nagy, Edward. *Villanos, hampones y soldados en tres comedias de Luis Vélez de Guevara*. Valladolid: Sever-Cuesta, 1979.

Olesa Muñido, Francisco Felipe. *La organización naval de los estados mediterráneos y en especial de España durante los siglos XVI y XVII*. 2 vols. Madrid: Editorial Naval, 1968.

Pérez Estévez, María Rosa. *El problema de los vagos en la España del siglo XVIII*. Madrid: Confederación Española de Cajas de Ahorros, 1976.

Pérez Moreda, Vicente. *Las crisis de mortalidad en la España interior, Siglos XVI-XIX*. Madrid: Siglo Veintiuno Editores, 1980.

Pérez Vidal, José. *España en la historia del tabaco*. Madrid: Consejo Superior de Etnología Peninsular, 1959.

Phillips, Carla Rahn. *Ciudad Real, 1500-1750. Growth, Crisis and Readjustment in the Spanish Economy*. Cambridge: Harvard University Press, 1979.

Pike, Ruth. *Aristocrats and Traders: Sevillian Society in the Sixteenth Century*. Ithaca: Cornell University Press, 1972.

Ringrose, David. *Transportation and Economic Stagnation in Spain, 1750-1800*. Durham, N.C.: Duke University Press, 1970.

Rodríguez Marín, Francisco. *Cantos populares españoles*. Vol. 4. Seville: F. Alvarez y Compañía, 1883.

Rumeu de Armas, Antonio. *Historia de la previsión social en España*. Madrid: Editorial Revista de Derecho Privado, 1944.

Rusche, Georg, and Otto Kirchheimer. *Punishment and Social Structure*. New York: Columbia University Press, 1939.

Salillas, Rafael. *Evolución penitenciaria en España*. 2 vols. Madrid: Imprenta Clásica Española, 1918.

Salillas, Rafael. *La vida penal en España*. Madrid: Imprenta de la Revista de Legislación, 1888.

Samaha, Joel. *Law and Order in Historical Perspective. The Case of Elizabethan Essex.* New York: Academic Press, 1974.

Sánchez Ortega, María Helena. *Documentación selecta sobre la situación de los gitanos españoles en el siglo XVIII.* Madrid: Castellote Editor, 1977.

Sellin, J. Thorsten. *Penal Servitude: Origin and Survival.* Proceedings of the American Philosophical Society, vol. 109. Philadelphia, 1965.

Sellin, J. Thorsten. *Pioneering in Penology: The Amsterdam Houses of Correction in the Sixteenth and Seventeenth Centuries.* Philadelphia: University of Pennsylvania Press, 1944.

Sellin, J. Thorsten. *Slavery and the Penal System.* New York: Elsevier, 1976.

Sevilla y Solanas, Félix. *Historia penitenciaria española (la galera), apuntes de archivo.* Segovia: Tipográfico de "El Adelantado de Segovia," 1917.

Soubeyroux, Jacques. *Pauperisme et rapports sociaux à Madrid au XVIIIème siècle.* 2 vols. Lille: Université de Lille III, 1978.

Thompson, I. A. A. *War and Government in Habsburg Spain, 1560–1620.* London: Athlone Press, 1976.

Tomás y Valiente, Francisco. *El derecho penal de la monarquía absoluta (siglos XVI–XVIII).* Madrid: Editorial Tecnos, 1969.

Tomás y Valiente, Francisco. *La tortura en España.* Madrid: Editorial Ariel, 1973.

Verlinden, Charles. *The Beginnings of Modern Colonization.* Ithaca, N.Y.: Cornell University Press, 1970.

Vicens Vives, Jaime, ed. *Historia social y económica de España y América,* Vols. 3, 4. Madrid: Editorial Vicens-Vives, 1972.

Von Bar, Carl Ludwig. *A History of Continental Criminal Law.* Translated by Thomas S. Bell. Boston: Little Brown, 1916.

Weisser, Michael. *Crime and Punishment in Early Modern Europe.* New Jersey: Humanities Press, 1979.

Wolf, John B. *The Barbary Coast. Algiers under the Turks, 1500 to 1830.* New York, Norton, 1979.

*Articles*

Archer, Christon I. "The Deportation of Barbarian Indians from the Internal Provinces of New Spain, 1789-1810." *The Americas* 29 (1973):376–85.

Bazán Alarcón, Alicia. "El Real Tribunal de la Acordada y la delincuencia en la Nueva España." *Historia Mexicana* 13 (1964):317–46.

Bleiberg, Germán. "Mateo Alemán y los galeotes." *Revista de Occidente* 39 (1966):330–63.

Cabrillana, Nicolás. "Las fortificaciones militares en Puerto Rico." *Revista de Indias* 107 (1967):157–88.

Callahan, William. "The Problem of Confinement: An Aspect of Poor Relief in Eighteenth-Century Spain." *The Hispanic American Historical Review.* 51 (1971):1–24.

Cambronero, Carlos. "El Prado de Madrid." *Revista Contemporánea* 129 (1904):9–21.

Castro, Adolfo de. "La esclavitud en España." *La España Moderna,* Feb., 1892, pp. 128–49.

Domínguez Ortiz, Antonio. "La esclavitud en Castilla durante la Edad Moderna." *Estudios de historia social de España* 2 (1952):369–428.

Domínguez Ortiz, Antonio. "La galera o cárcel de mujeres de Madrid a comienzos del siglo XVIII." *Anales del Instituto de Estudios Madrileños* 9 (1973):277–85.

Greenleaf, Richard. "The Obraje in the Late Mexican Colony." *The Americas* 23 (1967):227–50.

Henriques, U. R. Q. "The Rise and Decline of the Separate System of Prison Discipline." *Past and Present* 54 (1972):61–93.

Lang, M. F. "Las minas de Almadén bajo la superintendencia de Miguel de Unda y Garivay." *Hispania: Revista española de historia* 120 (1972):261–76.

Livi Bacci, Massimo. "Fertility and Nuptiality Changes in Spain from the Late 18th to the Early 20th Century." *Population Studies* 22:1 (Mar. 1968):82–102; 22:2 (July 1968):211–34.

Masson, Paul. "Les galères de France, 1481–1781: Marseilles, port de guerre." *Annales de la Faculté de Lettres d'Aix* 20 (1937–38):1–4, 7–479.

Mendizábal, Francisco. "Investigaciones acerca del origen, historia y organización de la Real Chancillería de Valladolid." *Revista de archivos, bibliotecas y museos* 20 (1914):61–73, 243–64, 437–52.

Palacio Atard, Vicente, "Notas acerca de la historia de la alimentación." In his *Los españoles de la Ilustración.* Madrid: Ediciones Guadarrama, 1964, pp. 287–306.

Pike, Ruth. "Crime and Punishment in Sixteenth-Century Spain." *The Journal of European Economic History* 5 (1976):689–704.

Pike, Ruth. "Penal Labor in Sixteenth-Century Spain: The Mines of Almadén." *Societas—A Review of Social History* 3 (1973):193–205.

Pike, Ruth. "Penal Servitude in the Spanish Empire: Presidio Labor in the Eighteenth Century." *Hispanic American Historical Review* 58 (1978):21–40.

Ringrose, David. "The Impact of a New Capital City: Madrid, Toledo, and New Castile, 1560–1660." *Journal of Economic History* 33 (1973):761–91.

Super, John. "Querétaro Obrajes: Industry and Society in Provincial Mexico, 1600–1812." *Hispanic American Historical Review* 56 (1976):197–216.

Thompson, I. A. A. "A Map of Crime in Sixteenth-Century Spain." *Economic History Review* 21 (1968):244–67.

Torres Ramírez, Bibiano. "Alejandro O'Reilly en Cuba." *Anuario de estudios americanos* 24 (1967):1357–88.

Weisser, Michael. "Crime and Punishment in Early Modern Spain." In *Crime and the Law. The Social History of Crime in Western Europe Since 1500,* edited by V. A. C. Gatrell, Bruce Lenman, and Geoffrey Parker. Atlantic Highlands, N.J.: Humanities Press, 1980.

Zysberg, André. "La société des galériens au milieu du XVIIIème siècle." *Annales, Economies, Sociétés, Civilisations* 30 (1975):43–65.

*Unpublished Material*

Kagan, Samuel. "Penal Servitude in New Spain: The Colonial Textile Industry." Ph.D. Dissertation, City University of New York, 1977.

Ortiz-Squillace, Altagracia. "Eighteenth-Century Reforms in the Caribbean: The Governorship of Miguel de Muesas, 1769–1776." Ph.D. dissertation, City University of New York, 1977.

# Index

Abril, Pascual, 32
Acapulco, Mexico: presidio of, 145
*Acordada*, tribunal of, 144, 145, 147
Agudo, town of, 32
Albacete, city of, 78
Alcalá Yáñez y Rivera, Jerónimo de, 17
Alcoholics: 51, 52; in presidio of Madrid, 102, 105, 107
Aldea, Miguel de, 35, 166n27
Alemán, Mateo, 6, 16–17, 29, 33, 35, 36, 165n6
*Alguaciles*, 74. *See also* Guards
Alhucemas, presidio of: 42, 111; administration of, 115–16; total population in, 119
Alicante, presidio of: 53–54; castle of, 67
Almadén, mines of: 27–40 *passim;* production levels at, 27, 37–38; as terrestrial galleys, 28, 39–40; sources for a study of, 29; mercury poisoning at, 35, 37, 38, 39, 149; labor shortages at, 38; abolition of penal contingent at, 39; free workers at, 39; significance in penal history, 39–40, 150; location of, 164n1. *See also Forzados,* at Almadén
Almadén, town of, 34, 36 164n1, 165n26
Almagro, town of, 30
Andalusia, 71, 89, 128
Antequera, city of, 96
Aragon, kingdom of: 71, 127; canal of, 89
Aranda, count of, 93
Arquellada, Ventura de, 59

*Arraeces,* 9, 24
Arriquíbar, Nicolás de, 50
Artisans: crime rates among, 131
Asociación de la Caridad, Madrid, 63, 64, 153
Asociación de Señoras, Madrid, 63–65, 153, 171n48
Asturias: audiencia of, 71; region, 78, 143
Atarés, Cuba, fort of: 136
*Auditor de las Galeras,* 8

Badajoz: presidio of, 52, 54; jail in, 60; city of, 88
Baena, Francisco de, 32
Bakers: 30, 131; in Madrid, 82
Bamford, Paul, xi
Banditry, 125
Bandits: 31, 97; Morisco, 31, 34; Mexican, 145; Catalan, 166n27
Banishment, as punishment, 3, 5, 7, 20, 32, 49
*Barberotes,* 24
Barbers, 30
Barber-surgeons, 24, 149
Barcelona: presidio, 52; city of, 88, 90, 98; *depósito* in, 98
Basque Provinces, 89, 143
Beans, as a ration: on galleys, 21–22, 149; in naval arsenals, 81, 82; in Caribbean presidios, 140
Beccaria, Cesare, 57, 64, 147, 153
Beggars, 56, 57
Beriberi, 22
Bigamists: galley penalty for, 7; at Almadén, 31

*Presidiarios*, Public Works Presidio, Madrid *(continued)*
among, 176*n51*. *See also* Madrid, Public Works Presidio
—Public Works Presidio, Málaga: labor of, 96, 97; number and kinds of, 96, 97; *reglamento* for, 96, 98; escapes, 97; treatment of and conditions among, 97–98. *See also* Málaga, Public Works Presidio
—San Juan: employed on fortifications, 137; numbers of, 137–38, 181*n11*; diseases among, 138, 139, 140–41; rations of, 139–40; absenteeism among, 140–41; unsericeables among, 141, 142; permanent settlement of, 141–42, 184*n19*; demand for, 142; contingents from Spain, 143, 144; contingents from Mexico, 143–44; offenses among, 145; deaths and releases, 146–47. *See also* San Juan, Puerto Rico, presidio of
Presidio: definition of term, 41
*Presidio del Camino Imperial,* Madrid, 95, 96. *See also Presidio del Puente de Toledo,* Madrid
*Presidio del Prado*, Madrid: creation of, 91; penal population in, 91–92, 106–7; administration and financing of, 93, 95, 106; as a *depósito*, 93–94; moved to new location, 94–95; abolition of, 95; re-establishment of, 106; sources for, 175*n14*. *See also Presidiarios, Presidio del Prado*
*Presidio del Puente de Toledo*, Madrid: 95, 99, 106, 107; creation and administration of, 95, 106; location of, 95, 106; penal population in, 99, 106–7. *See also Presidio del Camino Imperial,* Madrid; *Presidiarios, Presidio del Puente de Toledo*
*Presidio Nuevo*, 95. *See also Presidio del Prado,* Madrid
Presidio sentence: xii, 129, 150; origins of, 41–42, 45, 112

Presidios, Caribbean, 152. *See also* Havana, Cuba, presidio of; San Juan, Puerto Rico, presidio of
*Presidios de corrección. See* Correctional presidios
Presidios, North Africa: establishment of, 42–43; as places of banishment, 43, 44; as a form of criminal transportation, 43–44; penal population in, 44, 116–17, 118–19; conversion into general penal institutions, 44–45, 150, 151; manpower shortages in, 111, 116; vagrants in, 111–12; administration of, 112–16, 151; problem of desertion in, 114, 118–24, 151; as penal colonies, 117–18, 133, 151; exchange of prisoners among, 132–33. *See also Presidiarios,* North African presidios
Presidios, Peninsular: creation of penal contingents in, 52; numbers and kinds of prisoners, 52–53; conditions in, 53, 54; conversion into *depósitos*, 54
Price Revolution, 4
Prisoners, transfer of: among North African presidios, 132, 152; between North African and Caribbean presidios, 132–33, 135; 152
*Procurador de pobres*, 63, 171*n42*
Procurers, male: galley penalty for, 7
Professional classes: crime rates among, 131
Prohibited arms, use of, 126
Prostitutes: 33; in San Fernando, 56–57, 153
Public shame, as punishment, 3, 5
Public Works Presidios: 39, 89, 116; *depósitos* converted into, 93, 98; as *presidios de corrección*, 109, 151–52
Puerto de Santa María, city of: 18, galley chapel in, 23; galley hospital in, 23

Quevedo y Villegas, Francisco de, 59

*Rapé. See* Snuff

JACKET DESIGNED BY MIKE JAYNES
COMPOSED BY LANDMANN ASSOCIATES, INC., MADISON, WISCONSIN
MANUFACTURED BY MALLOY LITHOGRAPHING, INC.
ANN ARBOR, MICHIGAN
TEXT AND DISPLAY LINES ARE SET IN TIMES ROMAN

ധ

Library of Congress Cataloging in Publication Data
Pike, Ruth
Penal servitude in early modern Spain.
Bibliography: pp. 185–193.
Includes index.
1. Convict labor — Spain — History. I. Title.
HV8931.S7P54 1982     365'.65'0946     82-70551
ISBN 0-299-09260-7